外国语言文学与文化研究文库
WAIGUO YUYAN WENXUE YU
WENHUA YANJIU WENKU

WAIYU WANGLUO JIAOXUE
YANJIU YU SHIJIAN

外语网络教学研究与实践

主　编 ◎ 刘重霄

副主编 ◎ 栾　婷　刘　欣

首都经济贸易大学出版社

Capital University of Economics and Business Press

·北京·

图书在版编目(CIP)数据

外语网络教学研究与实践/刘重霄主编. ——北京:首都经济贸易大学出版社,2020.10
ISBN 978-7-5638-3151-7

Ⅰ.①外… Ⅱ.①刘… Ⅲ.①计算机网络—应用—外语教学—研究 Ⅳ.①H09-39

中国版本图书馆 CIP 数据核字(2020)第 209082 号

外语网络教学研究与实践
刘重霄　主　编
栾　婷　刘　欣　副主编

责任编辑	佟周红　彭　芳
封面设计	小　尘
出版发行	首都经济贸易大学出版社
地　　址	北京市朝阳区红庙(邮编100026)
电　　话	(010)65976483　65065761　65071505(传真)
网　　址	http://www.sjmcb.com
E - mail	publish@cueb.edu.cn
经　　销	全国新华书店
照　　排	北京砚祥志远激光照排技术有限公司
印　　刷	北京建宏印刷有限公司
成品尺寸	170 毫米×240 毫米　1/16
字　　数	218 千字
印　　张	12.75
版　　次	2020 年 10 月第 1 版　2020 年 10 月第 1 次印刷
书　　号	ISBN 978-7-5638-3151-7
定　　价	49.00 元

图书印装若有质量问题,本社负责调换
版权所有　侵权必究

前　言

　　一场突如其来的新型冠状病毒肺炎（COVID-19）疫情，打破了人们的正常生活、工作和学习秩序。为保障师生个人生命安全及解决学校授课问题，教育部办公厅先后发出"延期开学""停课不停学"等通知，北京教委也号召进行"线上指导性教学"。各大高校积极响应政策，结合各校实际情况，有效运用先进的互联网技术，以其作为课程和知识的载体，制订"停课不停教，停课不停学"的教学计划。

　　首都经济贸易大学结合自身情况，按照学校疫情防控的总体部署，实施以网络教学为主、以多样化学习方式为辅的"停课不停教，停课不停学"举措，保证学校教学的有序开展。外国语学院按照学校关于疫情期间网络授课的部署安排，于2月初成立了网络授课领导小组，着手讨论并制订网络授课方案。鉴于学院教学任务繁重、教学对象层次广、课程类型多等情况，学院建立了专门讨论网络授课的微信群，随时交流培训、建课、授课过程中出现的问题。本学期，外国语学院开设本科课程50门，48门（96%）采取网络教学；开设研究生课程20门，18门（90%）采取网络教学。

　　疫情期间，外国语学院的教师在积极进行疫情防护的同时，开展网络授课，参加学校组织的课程培训，完成了大学英语（二）、大学英语综合（二）、研究生公共英语等课程的统一网络课程建设，为实施大规模线上线下教学模式改革奠定了基础；其他公共课程和专业课程也采用微信实时在线指导、直播、慕课等多种授课形式，设置了相应的网络课程。

　　特殊的时代背景对传统教学提出了挑战，也为改革原有教学方式、探索新的教学模式、提升整体教学质量创造了契机。正如外国语学院院长吴瑾瑾老师所言，"一场突如其来的新冠肺炎疫情将外国语学院老师们推向教学改革前沿，把学校的英语教学直接引入网络教学新时代。在认真做好学院防疫工作的同时，外国语学院老师们以饱满的热情、高度负责的态度积极投入网课建设，他们以教研室为单位，主动探讨各种形式的教改新途径，设计新型网络教学方案，努力为学生提供高水平的英语课程，积极应对疫情，保障学生学习质量"。

　　本论文集以此为背景，汇集广大教师在教学模式改革、教学内容建设、教学评价方式、课堂教学管理、学生就业等方面的研究成果,为深化教学改革和人才培养提供借鉴和参考。

刘重霄

目 录

新冠疫情期间大学英语线上教学的调查
  ——以首都经济贸易大学大学英语课程为例 …………………………… 1
商务英语线上线下混合教学模式研究 ……………………………………………… 9
疫情期间大学英语在线教育的机遇与挑战 ………………………………………… 16
基于产出导向法理论的大学英语教学模式探究 …………………………………… 21
新冠疫情下开展线上英语教学模式的尝试与思考 ………………………………… 27
"互联网+"下的大学英语教学思考与对策 ………………………………………… 32
疫情防控下高校线上教学实践与探索
  ——以基于超星泛雅平台和腾讯会议的中级法语课程为例 ………… 38
建构性作答方式英语听力课堂测评任务设计原则及方法初探
  ——以研究生公共英语听力网络录播课为例 ………………………… 45
思政元素融入大学英语课堂之我见 ………………………………………………… 58
论生生互动在高级英语课程中的作用 ……………………………………………… 64
非英语专业大学生写作错误引发的思考以及问题解决方法探析 ………………… 70
高校英语专业教学中的体验式学习模式探析 ……………………………………… 76
浅析机考对大学英语教学的反拨作用 ……………………………………………… 83
疫情期间高校线上教学的几点心得 ………………………………………………… 87
商务英语线上线下混合课建设与实践 ……………………………………………… 92
Promoting Autonomy and Learning Effect of EFL Learners via Online Learning …… 100

The Strategies of Improving College Students' intercultural communicative
　　Competence ………………………………………………………… 109
对[自然]与 NATURE 的认知语言学探析 ……………………………… 119
Ways to Cultivate Cultural Awareness in Intercultural Communication …… 134
A Comparative Study of Diet Cultures between China and English-Speaking Countries:
　　Taking Britain, the United States, Canada and Australia as Examples ………… 149
浅谈中英颜色词的文化差异 ……………………………………………… 168
读书会驱动的翻译专业硕士自主学习模式探索 ………………………… 172
译者——翻译行为主体研究简述 ………………………………………… 182
对外法语教学中的熟语教学探究 ………………………………………… 190

新冠疫情期间大学英语线上教学的调查
——以首都经济贸易大学大学英语课程为例*

赵海燕**

(首都经济贸易大学 北京 100070)

摘 要: 为获得疫情期间线上教学的及时反馈,以指导下一步的外语教学,我们对大学英语线上教学进行了调研,包括政策层面的支持、线上学习平台的情况、线上学习影响因素等,并结合外语学科学习的特点,对暴露出的问题进行了分析并提出改进意见,对未来的线上教学进行了前瞻性探讨。

关键词: 大学英语;线上教学;影响因素及问题;改进;前瞻

引言

新冠肺炎疫情暴发,在教育部"停课不停教,停课不停学"的号召下,利用互联网和信息化教育技术进行在线教学,成为各大高校开展教学工作的主旋律。特殊时期的防控要求对传统教学提出了挑战,也为我们探索新的教学模式创造了契机。大学英语课程作为一门重要的公共基础课程,经过一个学期的在线教学,学生学习效果如何?教学面临哪些问题?今后将如何应对?教育部已做出"下学期要做好线上和线下教学两手准备"的指示,因此,我们迫切需要了解本学期的在线教学情况,以指导未来的外语教学。

基于以上背景,学期之末,我们首都经济贸易大学外国语学院对大学一年级的103名同学进行了英语课程问卷调查,并对其中的10名同学进行了深度访谈,获得

---

* [基金项目]2017首都经济贸易大学发展规划处项目"'一带一路'与首都经济贸易大学英语师资队伍建设"阶段性研究成果。

** [作者简介]赵海燕(1972—),女,山东人,首都经济贸易大学外国语学院教授、博士、硕士生导师,研究方向为中华文化与英美文化的接触与变容、中国英语教育文化维度的多元化、大学英语教育。

了本学期线上教学的及时反馈,以期为将来推进信息化建设和教学改革提供借鉴和参考。

一、大学英语线上学习的教学安排

大学英语一年级有普通班38个,学生约1 000人,任课教师15人;此外还有国际班和特色班,学生约1 000人。本研究所探讨的教学效果仅局限于普通班教学。普通班教研组采取了统一的教学计划、教学内容、教学进度:①精读课堂利用超星"学习通"网络平台开展教学。"学习通"是基于教学服务打造的课程学习、知识传播与分享平台,适合用于大学英语精读综合课堂的学习。教学内容在依托《大学英语综合教程(全新版)》的基础上,附加同专题的音视频、阅读、写作等板块。课件由教研组分工创作、集体统筹后上传平台,以周为单位发布学习任务。②视听说课堂利用"U校园"平台开展教学。"U校园"是外研社开发的在线学习平台,能为高校听力课堂教学、评、测、研提供一站式教学方案。教材为《新视野大学英语视听说教程》,以周为单位发布学习任务。③写作课利用外研社"批改网"平台开展教学。"批改网"是一款英语作文智能批改服务系统,能够基于语料库和云计算技术提供英语写作自动在线批改服务。教学内容和教学任务由教师自定。④师生还各有班级微信群,主要用于发布教学信息、沟通学习计划、答疑等。教师也可根据本班学生个体需要,自主使用其他平台。

除了年级共同的"学习通""U校园""批改网"平台,笔者还尝试采用微信群录播、"腾讯会议"直播的授课形式,进行调整和补充。就大学英语这门课程而言,被调研学生群体共使用了5个线上教学平台,即:"学习通",用于"精读课堂"授课;"U校园",用于"视听说课堂"授课;"微信群",用于课后答疑辅导;"腾讯会议",用于写作专题讲评;"批改网",用于写作专题操练。

以上为本学期大学英语课程的基本教学情况和线上平台的使用情况,是本研究线上教学调研的基本信息来源。此次调研采取了"调查问卷+深度访谈"的方式,以下将综合两种调查方式对结果予以说明、分析。

二、大学英语线上学习平台调查

针对线上学习平台的调查内容主要包括:学生对于教育管理方支持线上学习的政策是否有所了解?各网络教学平台是否支持了线上教学活动?学生对线上学习平台总体效果的评价如何?

(一)学生对线上教学相关支持政策的了解

本部分调查主要设计了这几个问题:①是否了解或听说过学校支持线上学习

的政策;②是否接触过教学平台使用培训或线上学习方法培训;③是否知道有关网上学习的电子图书资源。

问卷和访谈结果显示,差不多上90%的同学都选了否定选项,多数学生在疫情之前未接受过线上学习培训,不了解在线学习的电子图书资源,不清楚支持线上学习的政策等。进一步的数据表明,68%的学生认为,教学平台使用培训和线上学习方法培训很有必要。而43%的学生表达了对网上学习的电子资源的需求,希望学校能提供更为便捷地获得电子资源的途径,从而进一步改善教学空间环境。学生诉求主要体现为希望进一步加强校园网建设,扩大校园网和教学平台的资源优化共享。二者应相辅相成,发挥双方的最大效用。

(二)学生对线上学习平台技术服务的反馈

学生对线上学习平台技术服务的反馈主要从以下4个参照因素进行考量:①画面音频的清晰度;②工具使用的便捷度;③平台运行的稳定度;④网络速度的流畅度。

调查结果及进一步的访谈表明:学生对网课持开放态度,包容性较强。

一是学生对"学习通""U校园""批改网""腾讯会议"这几种教学平台的技术支持总体比较满意,认为设计比较成熟,使用比较方便。90%的同学认为画面音频、工具使用和平台运行都"不存在问题"。

二是73%的同学认为平台技术的一些不足影响并不严重,可以接受。对于"网络速度的流畅度",学生认为,这是线上教学相较线下不可控的原因之一,不稳定因素可能来自平台和使用者双方,如用户家里wifi信号不稳定、腾讯视频会议在会员开视频的情况下会出现卡顿、声音或画面延迟等现象。

(三)学生对线上学习平台总体效果的评价

考量纬度有:①课程教学资源匹配;②教学内容设计合理;③难度系数适度;④教学内容体量适中;⑤人际交流互动便捷;⑥课程考核评估合理;⑦教师反馈作业和答疑及时;⑧课堂学习效率;⑨线上学习监测到位;⑩线上教学平台总体满意度。

问卷调查和访谈的结果显示:①对"课程教学资源匹配""教师反馈作业和答疑及时""难度系数适度"等均认可度很高(9分);②对"课程考核评估合理"认可度一般(7分);③除对"腾讯会议"直播互动满意外,对其他几个平台的"人际交流互动便捷"认可度较低(5分),认为非常不方便;④对"线上学习监测到位"认可度相对较低(6分),认为存在管理和监测漏洞;⑤对"线上教学平台总体满意度"的均值为8分,满意度较高,但对总体"课堂学习效率"的评价是差强人意,比线下低。

调查发现,75%的学生比较关注平台的便捷性和互动功能体验,认为互动功能普遍较差是目前几个线上平台的短板。目前的问题主要集中在"人际交流互动便捷""课程考核评估合理""线上学习监测到位"等几个方面。对几个平台的具体认可度为:批改网9分＞U校园8.5分＞学习通8分＞腾讯会议7分＞微信群录播6分。

总体而言,"学习通"和"U校园"以设计比较人性化,操作简便快捷胜出;"腾讯会议"以直播时共享屏幕及师生互动便捷见长;"批改网"以批改作文效率高而被青睐;微信群以师生沟通反馈及时而被认可。

三、线上学习影响因素及问题分析

对学生而言,线上教学的优缺点是什么？存在的问题与挑战又有哪些？线上与线下学习效果有何不同？针对这些问题,我们开展了调查,获得了相应的反馈。

(一)对线上教学优缺点的反馈

线上教学的优点,按照从高到低排序主要有这几点:①突破时空限制,可以随时随地学习;②可以反复回放,便于知识复习巩固;③可以按需选择学习内容,针对性更强;④有更多自由支配时间,有助于自主学习能力的培养。

线上教学的缺点,按照从高到低排序主要有这几点:①学生自制力差、管理能力差,学习效率低下;②教师无法即时了解学生的学习状态;③师生之间、学生之间交流与协作不畅,不利于互动;④网课太多不利于身体健康,尤其会对视力造成损伤;⑤教学平台设计普遍不利于互动。

总体而言,学生对于线上教学的正面积极评价多于负面消极评价。其中,"突破时空限制,可以随时随地学习"和"可以反复回放,便于知识复习巩固"这两个优点得到了近70%的学生的认可。从缺点评价来看,"学生自制力差、管理能力差,学习效率低下"以及"教师无法即时了解学生的学习状态"两项相对比较突出,近60%的学生表示认可,是线上教学最受关注的话题。而"教学平台设计普遍不利于互动""网课太多不利于身体健康"等也是相对突出的缺点。调研进一步揭示了线上学习存在的问题及影响因素。

(二)线上学习存在的主要问题

根据学生反馈,将线上学习存在的问题按照影响范围由大到小依次排列:①自律性差,未能养成良好的线上学习习惯;②没有老师的引领,自主学习能力弱;③课堂听课效率低,无效时间多;④对线上教学策略及教学方法不适应;⑤部分教学内容设计不合理,不适合线上教学;⑥教学平台功能不完善,影响了学习效果;⑦对教学平台和工具使用不熟悉;⑧课程配套电子教学资源不足;⑨学习任务量、挑战度增加;⑩网络速度及稳定性问题;⑪掌控和维持好课堂教学秩序的问题。

调查发现,在线上学习这种"人—机"交互的学习模式中,相比较而言,"机器"方面的问题小于"人"方面的问题。线上教学对学生最大的挑战主要体现在学生"自律性"、"自主学习能力"以及"听课效率"三个方面。有超过67%的学生认为"自主学习能力""自律性"这两个方面是个人网上学习面临的最大挑战。41%的学生认为"对线上教学策略及教学方法不适应"和"教学平台功能不完善"也是影响学习效果的原因;由于外语学科独具语言习得特点,38%的同学反映课程的"部分教学内容设计不合理,不适合线上教学";还有32%的同学认为"教学平台和学习工具"没有很好发挥其功能;仅有约13%的同学认为"课程配套电子教学资源不足";8%的同学认为"学习任务量、挑战度增加"。

"学生自制力、管理时间的能力及执行力差"被列为影响学习效果的首要因素。大部分学生反馈,这是他们网上学习最大的挑战和障碍。没有了老师的引领和实时监管,自我管理能力差的学生缺乏时间概念,学习倦怠,参与性差。网课期间的考勤表明,学生出勤人数和作业上交人数相比线下减少了约一半。一些学生不能按时上课、不及时提交作业,同时又容易被互联网上的各种信息分散注意力,从而不能养成良好的线上学习习惯,课堂效率低下。

(三)线上与线下学习效果的比较

与传统线下学习相比,线上学习效果如何?对此,我们设计了这几个选项:①网课比传统线下学习效果差;②网课比传统线下学习效果好;③学习效果没有太大区别。

调查结果显示:有63%的学生更倾向于线下教学,认为"网课比传统线下学习效果差";25%的学生倾向于上网课,认为"网课比传统线下学习效果好";有约12%的学生认为都可以接受,"学习效果没有太大区别"。100%的学生表示本学期网上教学的推行改变了之前他们对线上学习的认知,并有68%的学生表示将来他们也会使用"线下+线上"相结合的方式学习。

由此说明,从习惯于线下教学到忽然全面"切入"线上教学,学生经过了一段时间的适应,对线上教学的优缺点有了进一步的认知。68%的学生对于线上学习方式持肯定、接受的态度,但91%的学生更倾向于在线人—人交互的学习方式,而非人机交互的学习方式。

四、对线上教学的改进意见

针对以上调研暴露的问题,特提出以下对策:

(一)线上平台技术层面:克服技术短板

总体而言,我校大学英语课程使用的外语教学平台如"学习通""U校园""批改网"等经过新冠肺炎疫情期间线上教学的全方位检验,证明其总体效果是好的,教学平台技术的开发基本可以满足线上学习的需求。但是外语课堂语言学习的规律性也对平台功能提出更大挑战。在线上平台技术层面,存在的具体问题如下:

1. 互动系统有较大差距。师生互动不畅,口语讨论、即时辩论等环节运作不理想,凸显线上学习的弊端,而语言习得的特点和规律性要求外语课堂具有较高的互动性和即时性。由此看出,如何更顺畅、更高效地实现网上人际互动是当下教学平台面临的瓶颈问题。

2. 设计科学合理的测评体系,既要考虑到其有效性,又要考虑到其人性化,还要考虑到其可操作性。当下,落实过程性考核,实施发展性评价,是公共基础课程教学改革和评估的重点及难点。发展性评价,是基于对学生学习过程的观察与测试而做出的,要求在教学过程中及时向教学双方反馈相关测试的结果与效果。线上教学发展性评价的关键在于平台的试题库及在线考试系统建设。能否提供高分辨率和辨识度的考评系统尤其是口语测评系统,应当是判断外语教学平台是否优秀的重要指标。

当前在攻克技术关的同时,要立足实际,争取多平台互补,弥补互动和测评短板。如"腾讯会议"直播以人际沟通方便、即时交流见长,可以作为其他几个平台的补充,一定程度上弥补了其他平台互动性较差的不足,从而扬长补短,充分体现了外语教学"互动合作式课堂"的特点。

(二)政策落实层面:加强线上教学策略培训

当前,从教育部到各高校对线上学习均给予充分重视,虽有政策层面的宣传和号召,但具体落实起来还需做更多工作。同时,线上学习同传统学习方式差别很大,有自己的特点和规律,线上学习策略培训亟须展开,相关课题亟须研究。在政策落实层面,面临的具体问题如下:

一是"学生自制力、管理时间的能力及执行力差"被列为影响学习效果的首要因素,是线上学习最大的挑战和障碍。学生学习倦怠,参与性差,课堂效率低下,不能养成良好的线上学习习惯。其后果集中体现为"对线上教学策略及教学方法不适应"。而引人注意的是,78%的学生认可这一点:线上学习问题的关键是自制力和执行力问题,如果学生能自律,养成良好的自主学习习惯,线上和线下区别并不大。所以,线上学习策略相关研究亟须开展,如何帮助学生养成良好的线上学习习惯?如何提高在线学习效率?如何克服学习倦怠心理?如何增强时间管理能力?等等。线上学习策略培训旨在帮助学生创建线上学习的积极心态,获得高效的学习策略和技巧,提高科学管理时间的能力。

二是就教学平台技术层面的操作而言,存在"对教学平台和工具使用不熟悉"的问题。一般而言,学生群体接受新事物能力强,技术适应性上问题不大,但"适应"并不意味着"熟练掌握操作"。对教师群体而言,该问题更为突出。随着平台功能的逐步完善,操作会进一步复杂化。同时"熟练操作"不等同于掌握线上学习策略。线上平台功能效用发挥的最大化,是以师生熟练掌握操作为前提的,同时也和网课学习策略密切相关,这是目前普遍被忽略的课题。

三是线上教学存在不确定性,要求教学双方准备应急预案。相对线下面对面教学,线上教学具有较大的不可确定性。例如,突然掉线、死机、成员忘关音频导致课堂杂音严重等,都会影响课堂教学质量和效果。如何应对这些突发状况也是线上教学学习策略培训应当涵盖的内容。

(三)对未来大学英语线上教学模式的展望

1. 对线上精读课堂的考量:"学习通"和"腾讯会议"相结合的教学模式,即学生自学为主,教师掌控进度和规划,密切跟踪、答疑、督促并监控。因为"学习通"课堂即时互动性较差,所以应和"腾讯会议"直播相结合。目前需要加强的环节有:①弥补线上互动学习的不足;②引导和检验学生对文化层面的理解和深化。可考虑将线下实施的"以学生为中心"的项目驱动式或任务探究式教学模式搬至线上。针对教材以不同专题为单元的编撰特点,把每单元专题作为项目或任务,指导学生予以完成,实现生生合作和师生互动。其基本流程如下:课前布置专题任务—学生团队协作调研—课堂活动("腾讯会议"成果呈现)—教师点评、深化、拓展—课后反思总结。同时教师通过直播补充对文化背景的挖掘和中西文化对比拓展,引导语篇层面的美文赏鉴和写作技巧分析。这种课堂形式还需进一步实践检验,但至少可以相当程度上弥补"学习通"精读课堂的不足。

2. 对线上听力课堂的考量:"U校园"和"腾讯会议"相结合的教学模式,即自主线上完成,学生为主,教师掌握进度为辅,监控、答疑。同时,辅助以"腾讯会议"直播方式,解决互动问题。"U校园"平台需要改进的三个环节有:①平台的测评体系,尤其是口语测评体系辨识度不高;②需要精心设计组织教学资源,目前主题不够鲜明,练习体系性差;③课堂即时互动性较差。

3. 对线上写作课堂的考量:"批改网"和"腾讯会议"相结合的教学模式,即沿用"批改网"+"腾讯会议"直播平台相结合的英文写作教学模式,遵循"作文练习—直播点评讲解—反思再练习—再点评讲解"的基本流程,分专题规划进行,循环往复。该部分是笔者考量年级组共同设定的平台及学生需求后,尝试的多平台上课方式。批改网的缺点是:①评价体系主要注重词、句微观层面,而对篇章主题宏观层面考量不足;②师生互动性差。"腾讯会议"直播的突出优点是:屏幕能共享,适合点评、分析作文,老师上课可掌控互动,课堂效率高。因此,"腾讯会议"直播点评重点针对语篇层面,同时加强师生互动,弥补"批改网"的短板。实践证明,该模式作为多平台互补的一个范例,获得学生93%的认可度,学生反馈其有规划性、针对性强,因而学习收获大。在使用"批改网"之前,教师对学生进行了平台使用详细讲解,学生反馈使用讲解帮助大,从而也证明教学平台使用培训和线上学习方法培训具有必要性。

结语

本次疫情期间大学英语课程线上教学调研的范围主要局限于笔者所任教班级,覆盖了一定数量的学生群体,问题的设计侧重从线上学习活动主体的视角考察平台,充分地考虑到了技术因素和人的因素,能够详细、全面地探知学生对相关问题的反应和建议,其获得的大学英语线上教学数据具有代表性。本研究调查到疫情期间大学英语线上教学的概貌和暴露的问题,并结合外语学科学习的特点进行分析并提出改进意见,对未来的线上教学进行了预测。本次线上教学的宝贵经验对未来的线上教学具有重要意义。同时,在下一步的研究中,笔者希望能够综合校方、教师方、平台出品方等的反馈资料,进行更精细、全面的考量。

商务英语线上线下混合教学模式研究

张春玲*

(首都经济贸易大学 北京 100070)

摘 要：现代信息技术的快速发展为商务英语教学带来了无限资源。网络技术与课堂教学深度融合，不仅可以优化教学结构、提高教学效率，还能促进学生创新能力的发展和综合素质的提高。本研究根据商务英语教育特点，综合教学目标和教学对象，通过教学设计，探索分析线上线下混合式教学在商务英语课程教学中的应用模式，力图寻求商务英语教学的理论支持，解决网络化教学实践中遇到的难题，从而满足学生的个性化学习需求，切实提升商务英语教学的丰富性、互动性与实效性，提高学生英语综合能力和终身学习能力。

关键词：线上线下；混合教学模式；商务英语；课堂教学；网络教学

引言

随着互联网、信息技术的快速发展，网络教学突破了时间、空间的限制，具有便捷、高效的优势，成为现代教学的重要组成部分。尤其是在2020年，受疫情影响，国家赋予教育新使命，技术与教育加速融合，使教育迈向"互联网+教育"新常态，推动"学习革命"向"质量革命"转变。网络教学在全国开展，慕课(MOOC)、腾讯会议、微信、学习通等平台的广泛应用，为商务英语教学改革带来了契机。

经济全球化使国际商贸活动日益频繁。商务英语能力成为国家经济发展中不可或缺的核心竞争力之一。商务英语教学与互联网、多媒体技术和网络技术相结合，可以达到资源利用的最大化以及效率的最优化，是商务英语教学改革的重要基础和重要途径，也是商务英语教学发展的必然趋势。然而，传统的线下教学难以满

---

* [作者简介]张春玲(1964—)，女，首都经济贸易大学外国语学院副教授，博士，研究方向为应用语言学。

足学生日益增长的知识需求，而流行的线上教学缺乏人与人之间真实的情感交流和互动。在网络教学不能完全取代传统教学的今天，如何有效地将两者结合起来，形成线下课堂与互联网、移动终端相结合的立体教学服务模式，成为一个新研究课题。

一、商务英语线上线下混合教学模式的内涵

何克抗提出，"混合式学习，即 blending learning，就是要把传统学习方式的优势和 E-learning 数字化或网络化学习优势结合起来，既要发挥教师引导、启发、监控教学过程的主导作用，又要充分体现学生作为学习过程主体的主动性、积极性和创造性。只有将二者结合，使二者优势互补，才能获得最佳的学习效果"。

有别于传统的一般信息化教学与网络教学，线上线下混合教学模式是依托现代信息科学与技术，对教育系统从宏观教育规划、战略管理到微观学习环境、学习模式、课程体系、教学方法、质量评价模式进行全面改革，把互联网创新成果与个性化教学资源进行深度融合，对教学环境进行有效的设计，通过课前导学、线上自主学习、讨论、课堂重点难点讲解、课后反馈与评价等为商务英语学习带来全新的体验。混合式教学既要求学生课前利用网络进行个性化自主学习，更强调学生回到课堂开展问题探究和讨论交流。在教学中线上教学和课堂讲解相得益彰，使抽象的知识具体化、直观化、简单化，有利于激发学生的学习兴趣，提高教学效果。在互联网技术支持下，混合式教学已经发展成为一种有效的教学手段。

将线上线下混合教学模式应用于商务英语教学，是根据商务英语的特点、教学目标和教学对象，依照商务活动开展的流程及所需商务技能设计的教学任务与练习，其利用丰富的网络资源，通过学生与计算机之间的交互操作，把感知、理解、巩固和运用融合为一体，打破线性化教学模式的传统，使学生可以多层次、多角度地获得知识信息，完成学习任务。线上线下教学交替使用，可以提升商务英语教学效率，达到优化教学效果的目的。

二、商务英语线上线下教学模式的设计

商务英语学科知识具有开放性，教学内容涉及与国际商务有关的各个环节。商务英语是一种专业的语体，强调在国际商务活动中，用特定的词汇和表达方式来满足行业的交际需求，其使用有明确的目的性和实践性，应用于特定的商业领域。混合式教学设计应遵循能力导向、自我发展、合作建构、知行并进的商务英语教育原则。

(一)加强理论与实践教学的深度融合,提高大学生的创新能力

具有深度的课堂教学强调帮助学生挖掘并深度反思事物背后更为深刻的要素,使学生充分认识自我,加强对所学知识、方法和能力的自我省察。在混合式教学中,教师通过网络创设情境,布置教学任务,让学生根据情境自我设计,相互探究,积极实践,完成相应的学习任务,实现学习迁移,提高创新能力。教师利用微信、QQ群、腾讯会议等平台进行网络互动教学,教学中体现基于项目的自主学习教学理念。每个模块的学习目标为完成一个工作项目,而此项目来源于真正职场,是包含多种能力的综合性任务。学生完成项目所需要的沟通技能、交际技巧和语言能力,可以通过完成不同部分的任务,自主地进行建构。教师通过超星、泛雅学习平台对课程内容、学习要求、互动讨论、作业提交及互评、课程测试、考核和成绩获取方式等进行系统的介绍与讲解,实现"课前导学""课堂教学""课后应用""综合评估",达到教学效果最优化。

(二)科学规划教学内容,促进学生自我发展

在互联网技术平台下为学生提供多种学习方式及渠道。教师精心选取教学内容,实现网络课程教学、课堂讨论教学、实践教学的有机融合。通过思考调查、讨论辩论等交流合作方式学习,使学生能更好地适应个性化需求,强化语言实践,最终提高综合语言能力。教师利用网络收集和整理相关主题的资料,根据商务项目实际需求开发学习情境,启迪学生思考,积极投入认知学习。教师依托教材、移动学习平台、网络数字课程,使用通行的商务语言、实用的商务知识、多维的商务文化、鲜活多样的商务案例,将英语学习与商务知识有机融合,使教学内容更为丰富,更具实用性和针对性。

根据学生的反馈和需求,教师利用互联网平台通对学生学习过程的动态采集和分析等功能,灵活、科学地设计教学任务和设置课前课后练习,开拓学生的商务视野,提升他们的跨文化能力和交际能力,为步入职场打下良好的文化基础。可规划的教学内容包括:①选取内容真实、题材丰富的音频资源,设计题型多样的听力练习,挖掘语言精华,循序渐进地提升学生的听力技能;②结合实际商务场景,模拟商务写作,利用句酷批改网、微信群上传输出任务,展示真实范文,帮助学生熟悉和掌握常用商务写作规范和技巧;③设计多样的阅读活动,以篇章内容为导向,传授国际商务知识与语言知识;④设计开放式主观任务,如撰写调查报告,开展公司SWOT分析,进行课堂展示等;⑤讲练结合,以练促学,提升职业素养,展示真实的商务案例,对比不同国家职场文化差异,培养跨文化意识,激发学生思考和解决实际问题的能力。

对于难懂的商务知识和商务理论，教师可以利用多媒体视频等补充材料，突出要点。直观的多媒体课件有助于概念的理解和方法的掌握，图文声像并茂，多角度调动学生的情绪、注意力和兴趣；既能扩充学生的课外知识，开阔他们的眼界，又能有效地弥补学生对商务外语实践认识的不足，使学生掌握教学内容，提高认知速度及效果。

（三）以"任务驱动"为理念，项目为导向，加强合作意识

教学任务与未来需求和就业相关。依据课程总体目标，通过任务教学法，以"创新""个性化""多样化"为基本原则，实践基于项目的自主学习理念。课前教师梳理内容、制作知识点清单，安排学生收看在线课程和视频资料，研读教材和文献资料，了解知识点之间的联系以及各项技能在工作中的应用。任务教学法主要目的是启发学生关于沟通技能的已有认知，引导其产生对将要学习内容的兴趣，并且留给学生思考和发挥的空间。

教学内容通过线上传授给学生后，课堂内更需要高质量的学习活动巩固，线下将课堂变成互动场所，让学生有机会在具体环境中创建内容，独立解决问题，开展探究式活动，培养学生的学习能力、思维能力和创造力，更是教学质量的检验手段。教师为学生提供与交际项目相关的语言练习，涉及词汇、句型、对话等内容，主要训练学生在巩固英语语言知识的基础上进行更加有效的交流。教师布置交际任务，以小组讨论、角色表演，课堂展示的形式，引导学生综合运用所学内容，通过师生合作、小组协商完成任务。此外，教师还可采用答疑和检查的方式了解学生的学习状况。

（四）创设仿真情境，知行并进

传统教学中对商务知识的讲解使学生始终有游离于商务环境之外的感觉。现代信息教育技术以其特有的科学性、多样性、灵活性、仿真性、形象性，为商务英语教学提供了强大的平台和技术支持，提供给学生更多的交互场所和交互学习内容。学生通过亲身实践、分析案例、模拟商务交际，感知国际商务文化。以商务英语作为语言交流工具的商务流程贯穿于教学活动的始终，能够营造教学互动的局面，活跃学习气氛，提高教学效率。

教师创新教学理念，利用情境模拟教学法，在线创设逼真的交际场景。例如，学生可以在互联网上与教师或其他同学进行商务谈判、进出口贸易等情境模拟。利用视频化手段呈现职场情境，使学生转换人物角色，置身于当堂所学内容相关的商务环境中，进行大量的仿真交际练习，强化商务英语听、说、读、写、译的交际能力。这种身临其境的场景体验，可以增强语言的真实感，激发学生参与交际活动的兴趣,并能督促学生在一个完整模块的学习之后巩固相关语言点,应用所学的交际技巧,并在特定商业情境中完成学习任务。情境教学克服了单纯书本学习的枯燥与乏味的弊端,使学生因为学习内容更贴近交际需要而大大提高学习积极性,从被动练习者变成主动参与者,提高了学生的学习兴趣和教学参与度。情境教学解决了传统教学中学生积累了大量知识而在真正交际中却手足无措的问题,加深了对商务文化差异的认知和理解,提高了语言交际的效果,是真正践行"做中学"。

三、多元动态评价体系的建构

(一)形成性评价与终结性评价相结合的多维、动态、全过程评价

商务英语是英语语言技能与国际商务知识相结合的课程。它以服务国际商务活动为教学目标,其目的是培养以英语为工具,独立熟练、直接有效地进行国际商务活动的人才;其教学内容具有较强的实用性和实践性。传统的评价手段很难有效地对其进行测量。创新的评价体系强调以考促学,以评促学,提升课程学习广度、深度、挑战度,构建形成性评价与终结性评价相结合的多维度、动态、全过程评价体系。教师利用课堂讨论、小组协作展示、调查问卷、访谈和电子邮件的方式对学生运用商务知识和解决问题的能力进行有效观察,做出形成性评价;针对线上考试特点,教师紧紧围绕教学目标,对商务英语的听、说、读、写、译基本技能的实践内容以及商务技能内容,利用教学网测验工具或其他线上考试平台进行测验及终结性评估;充分利用大数据技术分析学生的在线学习行为,对学生的自主学习进行实时监督。

(二)自我评价、小组评价和教师评价相结合

自我评价是学生基于自我认识,依据自身认可的评价指标,对自身素质的发展做出的判断。它可以使学生充分体验成长的喜悦,促进学生自我调整、改善学习效果。小组评价中学生不仅可以反思自己在小组协作中的表现,也可以评价小组其他同学的行为表现,使学生更明确评价标准。构建自我评价、小组评价和教师评价等多方评价体系,改变传统评价中教师为唯一评价主体、学生处于被动地位的情况,营造更为和谐、客观的评价环境,从而有利于激发学生的学习动机,提高他们的学习主动性和自主性。

四、加强学生自主学习能力培养

建构主义理论强调学生是认知主体,知识与能力的习得是学生在主动建构认知框架的过程中完成的。混合式学习模式可提供丰富的学习资源、真实的语料,有

利于学习情景的创设,无疑为学习者提供了自主学习的机会和条件。学生根据学习目标与任务,利用互联网优质的教育资源,通过网络学习平台、专题学习网站等丰富多彩的学习形式,激发自主学习的兴趣,开展个性化学习,自主确定学习进程,自主选择课程资源,自主诊断学习效果。

建立网络互动、创新等自主学习模式,坚持"线上自主探索 + 线下协作研讨"有效融合。学生充分利用 QQ 群和微信群进行信息交流,互通有无。混合模式下的自主学习有利于学生完成和深化对所学知识的建构,激发学生的创新能力。同时,教师可利用教学网络平台对学生的自主学习进行监督和指导,对学生在自学过程中遇到的问题和困难进行在线答疑,并重点对在线学习方法给予针对性的指导,以提高学生自学的质量和效率。

结语

线上线下相结合的教学模式颠覆了传统的教学模式,为商务英语教学提供了广阔的空间。以学习者为中心、以强化个体实践为中心、以信息交流为中心的混合教学模式是现代信息技术与传统教学深度融合的课堂革命,给学生带来了全新的体验,促进了高校教育的可持续发展。混合式教学理念不仅在于学习方式的混合,它还包含了不同教学模式的混合、教学资源的混合和教学环境的混合。它将教学从室内扩展到课堂外,利用在线平台将丰富的教学资源与互联网结合起来进行教学,实现了教学的个性化、教学资源的多样化、教学环境的智能化,优化了教学结构,促进了学生创新能力的发展和综合素质的提高。在互联网的支持下,混合式教学已经发展成为一种有效的教学手段,也是推动教学方式转变、提高人才培养质量的重要发展趋势。

参考文献

[1]鲍文. 商务英语教育论[M]. 上海:上海交通大学出版社,2017.

[2]何克抗. 从 Blending Learning 看教育技术理论的新发展[J]. 国家教育行政学院学报,2005(9).

[3]杜娟. 混合式学习模式下中学生自主学习能力培养的策略研究[J]. 课程教育研究,2019(4).

[4]李春景. 建构主义视角下虚拟仿真场景辅助大学《商务英语》教学研究[J]. 商务英语探索,2017(7).

[5]肖伟跃,车晓毅,蔡悦华,等. 创新训练与实践教学深度融合的模式与体

系构建[J].科技创新导报,2015(21).

[6]王立非.新标准商务英语综合教程[M].北京:外语教学与研究出版社,2018.

[7]吴沈娟.信息技术支持下高职混合式教学模式研究与实践[J].时代金融,2020(8).

[8]朱雪梅.混合式教学:未来学校教学组织的新模式[N].中国教育报,2019-06-06.

[9]袁红,向毅.基于线上与线下相结合混合教学模式的探讨[J].新教育时代(教师版),2016(5).

[10]余胜泉,路秋丽,陈声健.网络环境下的混合式教学:一种新的教学模式[J].中国大学教学,2005(10).

疫情期间大学英语在线教育的机遇与挑战

张东芹[*]

(首都经济贸易大学 北京 100070)

摘 要:2020年初新型冠状病毒肺炎疫情袭来,高校积极响应教育部发出的"停课不停教,停课不停学"号召,开启远程教学模式。科技的发展,给师生们搭建了丰富的在线教学平台,远程教学也给大学教师带来新的机遇与挑战,这既是时代赋予教师的新使命,也是教师专业发展的新要求。

关键词:疫情期;大学英语;在线教育;机遇与挑战

引言

新型冠状病毒肺炎疫情肆虐袭来,让所有人始料未及,它打破了一切正常的生活与学习秩序,全国人民经历着一场没有硝烟的阻击战,学生和教师莫能置身事外。"停课不停教,停课不停学"成为新学期的特殊开启方式,为抗击疫情进行线上教学也给高校教师带来前所未有的机遇和挑战。

一、远程教学机遇

一场突如其来的新型冠状病毒肺炎疫情改变了全国人民的生活方式,也改变了全国大中小学校的教学方式,学生的课堂由线下转移到了线上。外国语学院按照学校关于疫情期间网络授课的部署,于2月初成立了网络授课领导小组,着手讨论并制订网络授课方案。疫情期间,学院教师在积极备战疫情防护的同时,抓紧时间做好网络授课准备,参加学校组织的课程培训,完成了大学英语(二)、研究生公共英语等课程的统一网络课程建设,为实施大规模线上线下教学模式改革奠定了

---

[*] [作者简介] 张东芹(1985—),女,首都经济贸易大学外国语学院讲师,博士,研究方向为英美文学。

基础。其他公共课程和专业课程教师也借助网络课程平台，建立了相应的网络课程，采用微信、实时在线指导、直播、慕课等多种授课模式，按照原定教学计划，进入了正常的网络授课程序。2020年春季学期开学前，外国语学院推荐了在线教学的平台和通信工具，如超星学习通、钉钉、雨课堂、腾讯会议、腾讯课堂、微信或QQ群等，以及其他在线资源供教师们选择，强调教师可以选择适合自己的教学手段，给予教师极大的自由度和自主权。

在教育部"停课不停学"的统一部署下，不少网络教育平台开放在线课程及数据资料，为辅助网络授课、指导课后自学提供了优质资源。教师在设计练习、布置作业等环节，充分利用网络资源，在巩固线上教学的同时，能够有效激发学生对英语学习的兴趣。疫情期间，大学英语课程教学利用外研社U校园和超星学习通在线学习平台发布课程内容和作业，进行签到、讨论和测试，穿插中国大学慕课和网络公开课等学习视频，并辅之以微信群答疑，可以达到课程教学要求和目标。其实，每一个教学平台都有其独特优势以及无法避免的缺点，因此，教师不必在选择教学平台上花费太多的时间和精力。选择一个平台，把它的功能充分发挥，使它真正地实现服务于课堂就足够了；同时选择使用多个教学平台，也会给学生造成负担，能满足学生真实需求的就是最好的。

网络环境下大学英语教学以其开放性、个性化、丰富性超越了传统大学英语课堂教学。大学英语网课形式类似翻转课堂，即教师将录制的讲课视频和课件等学习材料传至网上，让学生远程学习，固定课堂学习时间集中由教师解难答疑，基本实现了知识传递与知识内化。翻转课堂尽管存在着局限性，如教师在课前需要花大量的时间制作学习视频，同时还要考虑知识点的覆盖是否全面，重点和难点的讲解是否清晰和突出等，但在大学英语远程教学中的应用是可行的。这种教学模式颠覆了传统的讲授式课堂模式，教学结构、教师以及学生的课堂角色都发生了转变。在线教学更要发挥学生的主观能动性，考察重点不在于教师讲了多少，而在于学生学了多少。

先学后教的远程教学形式，让学生成为学习的主体，使学生的自我监控、自我指导和自我强化等能力得到提高。按照现代教育标准，学校教学重在培养学习能力而非机械地接收学习内容。而能力的获得和发展不是别人可以代劳的。教师应摒弃陈旧的"灌输式"教学模式，给学生以自主学习、合作学习、交际学习的机会，创造自主学习的条件。

教师可以利用闲暇时间浏览学生喜欢观看的一些网络直播，了解学生课余生活的内容，了解流行的话题和学生的思维方式，适当学习网络直播平台的交流方式,这样有助于拉近教师和学生之间的距离,活跃课堂气氛,提高课堂效率。通过线上教学体验,笔者发现学生对于网络教学这一新鲜形式充满了好奇。教师如果利用好这一形式,再和学生多开展互动,就基本能够取得和线下课堂一样的教学效果。

二、远程教学对教师的挑战

疫情期间的远程教学使原来封闭局限的大学课堂走向开放多元,也对教学理念、教学方法、教学模式等造成一定的冲击,传统大学课堂的生态平衡被打破,大学课堂和大学教师都面临着"重塑"的挑战。

在线下课堂教学中,如果教师风趣幽默,就能够较容易地打动学生,而在线上教学中,教师首先要面对的一个问题就是,如何与手机争夺学生的注意力,让假装听课而偷着刷微博、看微信、聊QQ的学生把注意力集中到课堂上来,从而提高学生的自律性。在线上课堂中,教师和学生之间隔着屏幕交流,教师不太容易判断学生的学习状态和学习效果。这就对教师的教学设计和授课技巧提出了更高的要求。远程教学的课堂设计更需要考虑线上授课的局限性和学生的特点,适当增强授课的趣味性,这样才能充分调动学生互动的积极性,以保障在线课堂的学习效果。同时,远程教学更深层次的挑战则在于:网络上有海量的信息和知识,有微课件、有慕课(MOOC)、翻转课堂、移动公开课等网络课程,学生可以各取所需,比线下课堂所得可能更新、更丰富、更完善;同样一门课程,学生可以看名校的网络视频公开课,聆听本学科最知名教授的讲解,这让大规模的个性化学习成为可能,学生可以随时随地享受优质教育资源,来自世界一流大学的知名教授也给普通高校教师带来巨大压力。

移动互联网时代不仅带来教学模式与学习方式的转变,教师的教学策略、教学内容设计、在教学中所担当的角色也需要进行相应的调整,从更新教学观念到重新构建教学能力,从改革课堂教学模式到刷新师生交往方式,都要突破传统的教学理念。学生自主使用移动设备登录网络平台学习,要求教师能够掌握信息技术,实现技术与课程的整合,利用教学过程中的动态数据分析,实现教学优化。

以笔者教授的大学英语为例,笔者采用微课教学模式,具体操作为:学生在线学习重点教学知识,并用超星学习通和U校园全程记录学习的过程数据;教师在后台收集学生的学习数据,之后根据学生学习情况进行答疑和指导,同时进行教学优化。微课作为一种新的学习方式,具有应用、分析、评价的功能,能够增进学生与教师之间的互动,使课堂成为应用互动、体验和探究学习方式,促进知识理解和应用的场所。

随着技术和教育的深入结合,当代教师正面临教学模式的转型,要认清教育变革的方向,接受时代的挑战,勇于改变,善于利用信息技术,优化课堂教学,为学生创设一种自知、自由、自主的学习氛围,最终达到提高教学质量的目的。教育工作者是需要终身学习的,因此,教师要不断加强自身的理论学习,顺应教学环境的改变,转变自身的教学理念,将学生视为课堂主体,确保自身的教学理念符合教学改革的要求,从而提高大学英语教学效果。

三、教学启示

(一)人文和科学素养教育并重

在大学英语教学中增加科普文章的阅读和学习,如与科学发现、科技发展、医学突破、跨学科教育等相关的文章。疫情期间,国际期刊论文和评论不断更新,教师可以鼓励学生结合时事新闻阅读英语文献,着力培养大学生用外语搜集和获取国际信息的能力。

(二)强化学生自主学习和合作学习的能力

与传统的课堂教学模式相比较,在线学习模式需要学生有更强的自主学习能力和自律性。教师应帮助学生了解线上学习的特点和自主学习的重要性,并进一步引导学生制订符合自己学习情况的计划和目标,或者鼓励学生自主组成学习小组。学习小组可以为学生创造表达自己观点和合作学习的机会,同时成员之间也可以互相监督学习进度共同进步。教师指导学生进行自我评价和自我反思,根据出现的问题更改学习策略或调整学习方案。

(三)明确教师的定位

首先,教师的指导作用依然重要。教师要时刻关注学生线上学习状态,积极调动学生远程自主学习的积极性,使其明确学习方案和目标,据此选择适合自己的线上学习策略和方法。其次,加强教师团队协作建设,教师之间互帮互助,实现专业发展。以笔者所在的教研室为例,疫情期间的大学英语线上授课任务是教研室教师们一起分工合作完成的,资料共享在一定程度上减少了单个教师的工作量,有利于教师对某一章节的教学内容精耕细作,在教学设计上投入更多时间。同时,各个教师在交流过程中相互学习和借鉴教学经验,能够更加有效地提高业务水平,实现整体发展。大学英语教学体系中团队合作完成的课程资源丰富多样,各位教师最擅长的教学内容也都淋漓尽致地展现出来,学生涉猎的知识面也会更广。

结语

新型冠状病毒肺炎疫情是一场灾难,但它促使人们进行思考。疫情期间,大学英语远程教学是教师非常宝贵的人生经历。作为高校教师,我们必须依靠业务水平的提高,坚守好教学阵地,保障线上教学质量。特殊的时代背景对传统教学提出了挑战,也为探索新的教学模式、改革原有教学方式、提升整体教学质量创造了契机,为日后的大学英语教学提供了启示与经验。

参考文献

[1]蔡基刚.疫情之下,反思高校英语教学的科学素养缺失[J].当代外语研究,2020(2):39-47.

[2]刘莉."新冠疫情"背景下大学英语课程线上教学学习策略调查[J].通化师范学院学报(自然科学),2020(4):93-99.

[3]刘璐.从疫情期大学英语视听说网络授课看在线教学[J].教研资讯,2020(2):69-71.

[4]江慧.浅析新冠肺炎疫情期间大学生在线英语教育[J].英语广场,2020(5):62-64.

[5]王华珍.翻转课堂理念下应用型本科高校大学英语教改中的突出问题与对策[J].吉林工程技术师范学院学报,2018(4):66-68.

[6]夏纪梅.大学英语教学改革对教师的挑战:教师发展问题与对策[J].中国外语,2007.

基于产出导向法理论的大学英语教学模式探究*

王 鹏**

（首都经济贸易大学 北京 100070）

摘 要：全球化、信息化背景下的高等教育，亟须对英语课程进行创新性的改革。本研究在产出导向法理论指导下，通过借鉴并吸收翻转课堂和基于问题式学习这两大国内外热点教学模式革新的一些思想，提出大学英语 PBL 翻转教学模式。该模式包括课前知识传递、课中知识内化和课后知识固化三个阶段，对于提高学习者语言综合应用能力，培养学习者自主学习、创新思维、协作探究等能力素养提供了探索性新路径，值得在大学英语教学中进一步推广。

关键词：产出导向法；PBL；翻转课堂

引言

随着全球化进程不断推进、互联网技术的不断提高，中国高校迈进高等教育的国际化、信息化阶段，大学英语课程在教学环境、教学模式等诸多方面进入加快变革时期。《国家中长期教育改革与发展规划纲要（2010—2020）》明确提出推进高等教育国际化发展、培养国际化人才的战略目标。面对新目标、新挑战，大学英语课程建设正经历着一个教学理念不断更新，教学内容日益丰富，教学方法和手段逐渐完善，教学条件和环境更加优化的过程。与此同时，大学英语课程的现行改革虽然在一定程度上改善了学习者的语言表达能力，然而教学实践却依然遵循以教师为主体、主导地位，以语言技能操练为主要学习内容和培养目标的传统教学模式，忽视了对学习者的创新思维、创新精神、互联网技术的培养，难以从语言教学过程

---

* [基金项目]本研究为 2019 年首都经济贸易大学校级教改项目"基于产出导向法理论的大学英语教学模式"的阶段性成果。

** [作者简介]王鹏(1974 -)，女，首都经济贸易大学讲师，研究方向为应用语言学和高等教育学。

中培养学生分析问题、解决问题的能力。而基于问题式学习和翻转课堂教学模式，突出学习者在课程学习中的主体地位，借力慕课平台整合课外线上资源，设计自主学习、课堂自主、协作探究等教学环节，使学习者在使用语言分析、解决问题的过程中实现语言表达、合作探究等能力的提升。

一、概念的界定

(一)基于问题式学习

基于问题式学习(Problem - Based Learning，PBL)教学模式起源于20世纪50年代美国西余大学医学院的综合课程教学。作为一种新型教学模式，PBL是随着建构主义思潮兴起而发展起来的，最早应用于医学领域。60年代，美国神经病学教授巴罗斯(Barrows)进一步发展了这一模式，提倡将学习置于有意义的复杂问题情境之中，通过协作学习、分组讨论等多种方法来解决具体问题，从而培养解决复杂问题和自主学习的能力[1]。PBL教学模式是以问题为导向的教学模式，学生所有的学习都围绕设计的问题而展开。将PBL教学模式应用到大学英语教学中，就是将英语中的基础知识和英语课文中的知识点寓于设计的问题之中，让学生在解决问题的过程中掌握知识，提高英语应用能力。它基本的教学形式是"以学生为主体、以问题为中心"，学生在教师的指导下主动参与到教学活动中去[2]。

20世纪90年代，PBL教学模式在西方教育界迅速发展，成为西方教育改革的新模式。90年代末，我国国内学者开始关注并引进PBL教学理论，并尝试将其运用到教学实践之中。例如，《远程教育中以问题为本的学习方式》[3]和《问题式学习——一条集中体现建构主义思想的教学改革思路》[4]等文章相继发表，把PBL教学模式引向国内教育学领域，之后由教育学逐步向管理学、医学、工学等领域延伸。南京师范大学支永碧副教授发表了《PBL在中国外语教学中的应用》，开始关注"问题为本的学习"理论，讨论了问题为本的学习在中国外语教学中的价值、所面临的问题，以及今后的发展方向[5]；之后，丁后银副教授发表文章，指出"问题为本的学习"的教学模式是当前我国英语教师课堂教学改革的新方向[6]。

---

[1] 丁远坤.建构主义的教学理论及其启示[J].高教论坛，2003(3).
[2] 陈战.PBL教学模式对大学英语的影响.[J].吉林省教育学院学报，2013(8).
[3] 赵莉.远程教育中以问题为本的学习方式[J].天津电大学报，2000(3).
[4] 刘儒德.问题式学习:一条集中体现建构主义思想的教学改革思路.[J].教育理论与实践，2001(5).
[5] 支永碧.PBL在中国外语教育中的应用:意义、困境与出路[J].外语与外语教学，2009(7).
[6] 丁后银."问题为本的学习"与"行动研究"的整合[J].外语与外语教学，2009(3).

（二）翻转课堂

翻转课堂作为一种新型教学模式，近年来成为全球教育界关注的热点。翻转课堂最初的构想来源于美国林地公园（Wood land Park）学校的乔纳森·伯尔曼（Jonathan Bergman）和亚伦·萨姆斯（Aaron Sams）这两位化学教师的教学实践[①]。2011年，可汗学院里程碑式地推动了翻转课堂，使其演变为全球教育界备受瞩目的新型教学模式。

所谓翻转课堂，就是在信息化环境下，教师提供以教学视频为主要形式的学习资源，学习者在课前完成对教学视频等学习资源的观看和学习，师生在课堂上一起完成作业答疑、协作探究和互动交流等教学活动的教学模式[②]。作为一种新型教学模式，翻转课堂即"课前视频授课，课上学生习作"，与传统教学模式的"课上教师授课，课后学生习作"有如下差异：首先，它颠覆了传统的教学理念，通过课前学习者观看微视频，实现知识的传递，使"以学生为中心""因材施教""非指导性教学"等教学理念得以践行。其次，该模式以微视频为主要载体，对基础知识加以提炼、传递，促进知识的内化。再次，翻转课堂转换了教师和学生在教学过程中固有的角色：一方面，在以"掌握学习法"为理论基础的翻转课堂模式下，学生对学习活动自我监管、自负其责，成为主动内化知识的自主学习者。另一方面，它遵循"最近发展区"理念，由教师充当矛盾调节者、资源提供者、活动组织者，为学生提供个性化学习咨询服务，促进学生知识的固化，提升解决实际问题的能力。

二、基于问题式学习和翻转课堂在大学英语教学中的互融性分析

基于问题式学习在鼓励学生独立探究、协作探究，培养学生的自主学习、互动交流等能力上发挥了重要作用，但在大学英语的具体教学实践应用中也遇到了一些困难和挑战。首先，由于提出问题、呈现问题的开放性特点，教师在设计主题、呈现问题时通常要花费很长时间，这无疑给大学英语教师带来更大压力，不利于工作热情和工作效能的激发。其次，大学英语的教学目标是"培养学生的英语综合应用能力，特别是听说能力，使他们在今后学习、工作和社会交往中能用英语进行有效交际，同时增强其自主学习能力，提高综合文化素养，以适应我国社会发展和国际交流的需要"[③]。其中，交际能力的提高和综合文化素养的养成，在很大程度上取决于教师在课堂上给予学生更多交流互动的机会，以及在课上、课下提供针对性的

---

① 张跃国,渝江. 透视"翻转课堂"[J]. 中小学信息技术教育,2012(3).
② 钟晓流,述强,丽珍. 信息化环境中基于翻转课堂理念的教学设计研究[J]. 开放教育研究,2013(1).
③ 教育部高等教育司. 大学英语课程教学要求[M]. 北京:外语教学与研究出版社,2007.

引导和帮助。然而,近年来压缩课时量的英语学分制改革,导致教师在课堂上更为密集地进行知识传授,学生在课上交流互动的机会更难获得①。再次,依据认知负荷原理,问题的发散性和复杂性加大了认知负荷,不利于语言较薄弱的学习者发挥主观能动性,实现知识的主动建构和内化。

针对上述问题,翻转课堂为基于问题式学习提供了有益补充和修正。其一,翻转课堂中的微课,即微型教学视频,针对知识要点和难点,为问题的确立、呈现提供了大量优质在线视频资源,既减少了教师的备课量,又在一定程度上弥补了他们在教育技术应用能力(如微视频制作能力)上的欠缺,更以其情境性和新颖性为教学注入了生命活力。其二,经过课前微课学习,课堂上教师稍加引导和评价,即可组织学生在真实情境中互动交流和应用言语,为满足教学目标中对交际能力和自主能力的培养提供技术支持。其三,学生依照自身语言水平和认知能力,可反复观看微视频,掌握知识,增强信心,为课上的合作学习和互动交流提供信息及心理支持,促进了分层教育和个性化学习的落实。

同样,基于问题式学习对于翻转课堂的有益补充也不可忽视。翻转课堂若能和基于问题式学习模式中诸如自主探究和协作探究等解决问题的具体策略、实施过程相结合,将有益于学生创新能力的培养。具体到"大学英语"这门课程,基于问题式学习的策略、步骤在翻转课堂上的应用,能在最大程度上促进师生的交流,充分发挥教师的激励、咨询等作用,有效调动学生在教学过程中的主观能动性;有助于学生的自主学习、沟通合作、探究创新等综合素质的培养;增强英语交际和综合运用能力,满足社会发展和国际交流需要。

综上所述,基于问题式学习与翻转课堂在大学英语教学中的有机融合,能够满足我国教育信息现代化的发展要求,适应高等教育对国际化人才培养的战略目标,值得进行全面深入地探索和实践。

三、PBL 翻转教学模式在教学中的实际应用

2020年上半年由于疫情原因,学校采用了网课的形式完成教学任务。笔者在网课教学中使用了 PBL 翻转教学模式,进一步探究新的教学模式以满足学生的学习需求。

网课教学期间,笔者基于翻转课堂教学模式为学生在课前提供了视频、音频、文本等形式的学习资料,并用这些资料设置了不同难度和形式的问题,便于学生通

---

① 杨小彬. 转型期大学英语课程设置中的学生需求分析[J]. 湖北大学学报(哲学社会科学版),2013(4).

过解答这些问题更好地理解课文内容。设置的问题有的学生可以个人解答,有的则需要小组通力合作解答,即分成几个部分,每个学生完成一部分,在上课前进行小组汇总。学生根据自身的语言水平和分析能力,反复学习资料,掌握知识,增强信心,在课前充分理解课文学习要点和重点,自主完成部分知识点的学习,留下未能解决的问题在课堂中共同讨论,从而加快课上的合作学习和互动交流的进度。之后通过直播的形式为学生解答疑难问题,同时检查学生小组任务的完成情况并进行评价。课后再以翻译、写作、讨论等方式安排作业,以此检查学生课堂上的学习效果。

笔者对 PBL 翻转教学模式进行了一学期的使用,发现其能更好地调动学生学习的自主性和积极性,教师由课堂讲授知识点转为进行课堂讨论,知识点的讲解由课上转到课下,给教师和学生留出更多的时间进行实际操练,提高了学生的语言应用能力。

结语

教育信息化、全球化背景下的大学英语改革,需要进一步更新教学理念和教学模式,以实现国家教育改革发展的战略目标,培育出创新型、合作型、反思型国际化人才。基于问题式学习和翻转课堂在理论基础、学习特点等方面的可融性、互补性,为信息环境下的大学英语改革提供了值得全面深入探索的新路径——大学英语 PBL 翻转教学模式。研究中笔者发现,针对大学英语学科具体技能、主题建构的模式探索、实证分析,以及基于微视频设计及效果评价的问卷调查和访谈记录将更具针对性,也更详尽、客观地说明该模式在大学英语教学改革中的可行性和推广价值。课堂教学并非教学过程的全部,随着知识经济化、社会化的进一步深入,课堂外教学活动的开展和针对性的研究将成为大学英语等学科建设探索的趋势。因此,针对该模式下指导学生设置问题情境、展现成果的研究,也将成为今后理论研究和实践探索的重点。在今后的教学实践与理论研究中,笔者希望通过对该模式的持续探索,给大学英语改革带来些许启发。

参考文献

[1]丁远坤.建构主义的教学理论及其启示[J].高教论坛,2003(3).

[2]陈战.PBL 教学模式对大学英语的影响[J].吉林省教育学院学报,2013(8).

[3]赵莉.远程教育中以问题为本的学习方式[J].天津电大学报.2000(3).

[4]刘儒德.问题式学习:一条集中体现建构主义思想的教学改革思路[J].教育理论与实践,2001(5).

[5]支永碧.PBL在中国外语教育中的应用:意义、困境与出路[J].外语与外语教学,2009(7).

[6]丁后银."问题为本的学习"与"行动研究"的整合[J].外语与外语教学,2009(3).

[7]郑光锐.开发学生英语自主学习潜能的PBL教学模式探析[J].教育科学,2011(6).

[8]易祯.基于问题为本的学习(PBL)在大学英语教学中的应用研究[J].海外英语(中旬刊),2010(8).

[9]王志晨,付小达,李娟.网络环境下大学英语PBL教学模式研究[J].中国现代教育装备,2011(21).

[10]张跃国、张渝江.透视"翻转课堂"[J].中小学信息技术教育,2012(3).

[11]钟晓流、宋述强、焦丽珍.信息化环境中基于翻转课堂理念的教学设计研究[J].开放教育研究,2013(1).

[12]杨小彬.转型期大学英语课程设置中的学生需求分析[J].湖北大学学报(哲学社会科学版),2013(4).

新冠疫情下开展线上英语教学模式的尝试与思考

李彬彬*

(首都经济贸易大学 北京 100070)

摘 要:2020年,面对突如其来的新冠疫情,教育部做出"停课不停学"的工作部署。线上教学成为热门话题,也成为大学英语教师必须面对的一个新课题。线上教学使大学英语教师的教学由教室转到网络、由线下转到线上,使学生的学习由集中学习变成自主学习。教与学形式的变化,使得线上英语教学必须根据学科特点不断做出调整,进行有益的尝试。本研究以线上教学以来亲身教学经历为基础,对线上英语教学模式的尝试进行了反思,希望进一步提升线上教学效果。

关键词:线上教学;教学平台

引言

2020年,面对突如其来的新冠疫情,教育部做出"停课不停学"的工作部署,线上教学成为热门话题。事实上,线上教学模式随着近几年的信息化发展,在高校教育中已得到一定程度的应用。线上教学改变了过去传统教学模式下师生面对面的单一化教学方式,促使师生之间打破时空局限,教师可以利用互联网更加有效地进行教学。近日,有"互联网+教育"研究团队进行的调查显示,疫情期间在线教学基本成为常态,79.34%的调研对象所在学校已经开展在线教学,在线教学比例在城市和农村分别为83.41%、77.42%。根据百度搜索大数据,关键词"在线教育"的搜索指数从2020年1月17日的300增长到2月10日的接近5 000,与此同时段教育类行业的百度网盘企业用户数量最多[1]。

---

* [作者简介]李彬彬(1975—),女,黑龙江人,首都经济贸易大学外国语学院讲师,研究方向为英语教学法。

一、线上教学模式应用价值

传统的课堂教学模式具有一定的局限性,学生接收信息的方式较为单一,所学习的知识大部分都是"死知识",其创新精神没有得到全面的培养。传统的课堂教学模式是以教师主动进行知识讲解为主,单一对学生进行知识灌输,这种满堂灌的教育方式严重阻碍了学生学习的主动性[2]。

而线上教学突破了地域限制,教师只需借助一台电脑、一部手机就可以开展教学活动,解决了因疫情防控而不能出行、聚集的问题,教师在家就可以完成教学任务。一方面,对教师而言,线上教学成为大学英语教师必须面对的一个新课题。线上教学使大学英语教师的教学场所由教室转到网络、由线下转到线上,丰富了教师的教学方式,也使得信息技术成为每个教师的必修课。另一方面,对学生而言,学生的学习方式由集中学习变成了自主学习,学生获取知识的途径更广泛,对于一些自律的学生来说,学习效果更好。因此,线上教学对于提高我校学生的英语水平,使之能在未来的工作岗位上有效地运用所学到的知识,具有重要意义。

二、线上教学模式的基本构成

线上教学是以班级为单位组织授课和双向互动,以录播课为主,采取"录播 + 线上答疑"形式的教学模式。有条件的学校可以采用"直播 + 线上答疑"的形式。课后辅导可以采用"点播"或"线上答疑"形式。[3]

线上教学系统主要由三个部分构成:①教师端。教师端由教师与教师可操作的网络设备组成,教师可以利用网络设备来开展教学工作。常见的网络设备包括电脑、pad、手机等。②信息传输层(即教学平台)。信息传输层是整个线上教学的中转层,是教师端与学生端连接学习的平台。选择好的平台十分重要,是保证教学效果的必要条件。③学生端。学生端包括学生和学生可操作的网络设备。学生是线上学习的主体,学生可以通过网络设备在教学平台上学习知识。

以我校选用的学习通平台为例,说明一下大学英语线上教学构成的基本情况。首先,需要教师端和学生端在电脑或手机上下载学习通这个平台。其次,教师通过学习通在线直播,离线传输,收改作业,发起讨论,答疑解惑,统计成绩等;学生在学习通上在线学习,回看教学视频和教学课件,上交作业,参与讨论,向教师提问,等等。学习通这个平台师生操作方便,互动及时快捷,但同时也存在一些问题,例如,一旦教师端或学生端的网络出现异常,知识传递受阻,就会直接影响教学效果。况且师生都是第一次使用此平台,实际操作过程中难免会出现这样或那样的问题,这就需要师生具备良好的信息技术应用能力,线上教与学是对师生信息技术应用水平的检验。师生必须通过不断的学习,熟练掌握此平台各项功能的使用方法,才能取得良好的线上教与学的效果。

三、线上教学模式的初探

艾丽(Alley)明确指出,线上学习不能局限于使用网络获得教材,学生和教师应使用各种工具沟通互动,切磋技能,相互支持鼓励,最终达到个人的领悟与成长[4]。

(一)教师面临的挑战

线上教学改变了教师传统黑板教学的习惯,使得教师由主导者变成引导者,这种角色的转变,促使教学队伍进行不断的学习和提升。另外,线上教学是全体教师共同组织的课堂,不再是单个教师的课堂,大家的教学内容、教学方法都在一定程度上公开,这对教师团队成员之间关系的协调带来很大的挑战。例如,就我们所教授的大学英语Ⅱ这门课程而言,十几名英语教师使用的是同一本教材,教师需要通过集体备课的形式分享教学内容,取长补短,促进教学水平的共同提升。与此同时,教师团队也面临着另外一个更大的挑战,就是学生的反馈。在线下课堂教学中,大多数学生很少会直接对教师提出意见。但是线上教学则不同,在线上教学平台上学生可以各抒己见,对教师的教学提出质疑。因此,教师团队要学会适应这样的特点,调整心态,倾听不同的声音,主动与学生进行沟通,了解学生的需求,并根据学生提出的合理建议进行改进。

(二)学生面临的挑战

线上教学有利于学生共享网络学习资源,开阔学生的眼界。但同时,线上教学也对学生的自主学习提出了较高的要求。线上教学使学生从固定教室的被动学习转变为随时随地的主动学习。在传统的课堂教学模式下,在固定的时间和地点,教师进行讲授,学生被动学习,而线上教学通过运用互联网,以时空的自由性打破了这一传统,这也是在线教学的核心。线上教学很大程度上依赖学生的主动性和自觉性。自控能力较好,学习主动性较强的学生,会取得较好的效果和成绩;而自控能力较差,学习缺乏主动性的学生,缺乏老师的监管,很可能就会偷懒,长此下去就会影响成绩。自控能力差的学生,需要学生家长的监督与配合,家长应与老师及时沟通与交流。

(三)学生对于线上教学的反馈

我校实施英语线上教学已有一学期,教师在期末英语口语考试中针对线上学习的感受对学生进行调查,几乎百分之百的同学都提到了以下几点:①线上教学拉开了学生和教师之间的距离,隔着屏幕进行沟通,难免会产生距离感,线上建立的情感链接比较脆弱,很容易被打破。②学生遇到不会的问题,不能及时向教师提问,一方面阻碍了学生学习的积极性,另一方面也影响了学生的学习效果。③由于长时间进行线上学习,每天面对着电脑屏幕,眼睛超负荷工作,学生视力大幅下降。④同学之间受空间限制,缺乏有效的沟通与交流,关系变得冷淡,有些学生出现了焦虑的情绪,长此下去,将会损害身心健康。

四、线上教学模式的进一步探索

怎样才能进行有效的线上英语教学?萨蒙(Salmon)及贾尔斯(Giles)将线上教学时整门课程的进展流程区分为"鼓励并指导新手上路""成员进行线上社交""信息交流""知识建构""自立发展"五个阶段[5]。在"鼓励并指导新手上路"阶段,线上教师要确保学生有足够的学习动机。"成员进行线上社交"阶段,要让学生能自在地与其他学生进行沟通。"信息交流"阶段,是线上教学中师生开始自由交流信息的时期。"知识建构"阶段,教师会帮助学生构建知识体系。"自立发展"阶段,教师要鼓励学生进行自学。

大学英语有效的线上教学模式,也可以依萨蒙及贾尔斯的五阶段论规划,这与一般教案规划理论将教学流程分为"准备活动""发展活动""综合活动"的顺序是一致的。第一步是"准备活动",在大学英语的线上单元教学中即为导入部分:揭示单元教学目标,让学生了解本单元的学习目标、围绕单元主题的相关背景知识等进行讲解。第二步是"发展活动",教师讲解课文,分析课文结构,突破难句,解释重点词汇,概括写作手法,突出中心思想。第三步是"综合活动",主要是检验学生在发展活动中学习的成果,由教师针对学习主题发起讨论,学生主动参与,教师与学生进行交流互动。学生独立完成课后作业及练习,最后进行单元测验,检验学习效果。

结语

传统的线下课堂教学在一定程度上限制了学生的发展,学生获取知识的渠道和能力的提升都是有限的。线上教学扩大了学生获取知识的渠道,突破了单一的课堂教学模式,大大提高了学生的学习兴趣。在未来的教学实践中,应对线上教学模式进行深入探索和大胆创新,同时,考虑将线上和线下教学有机结合起来,取长补短,对整个教学模式进行合理调整与优化,促进教学效果的大幅提升,为国家培养更多英语水平过硬的应用型人才。

参考文献

[1] ALLY M. Foundations of Educational Theory for Online Learning[C]//ANDERSON T,ELLOUMI,F. Theory and Practice of Online Learning. Athabasca:Athabasca University,2005.

[2] SALMON G,GILES K. Moderating Online[Z]. Presented to the Online Educa. Berlin,1997.

[3] 东方财富网[EB/OL].[2020-03-17] https://baijiahao.baidu.com/s?id=16613713037336966633.

[4] 范瑛. 网络教学模式的创新改革对我国高校线上教育的影响与研究[J]. 教育科学,2016(03):244.

[5] 李丽霞. 浙江中小学将全面实行线上教学[N/OL]. 新京报,2020-02-06 http://www.bjnews.com.cn/edu/2020/02/06/685624.html.

"互联网+"下的大学英语教学思考与对策

方俊青*

(首都经济贸易大学 北京 100026)

摘 要:针对"互联网+"环境下的大学英语教学,本研究从大学生身份转变的角度分析了学生在大学英语学习中存在的问题和困难,依次从学生、教师、教学管理部门三方面论述了"互联网+"环境对学习带来的机遇和挑战,并阐述了应做出的转变和对策,最后结合实践教学案例,分享了笔者教学过程中解决问题的方法,供读者参考。

关键词:"互联网+";大学英语教学;翻转课堂

引言

"互联网+"时代的到来,对社会的方方面面都产生了重大而深刻的影响,尤其是受全球疫情的冲击,线下教学转为线上教学,大学英语教学也从传统的言传身教,面对面的交流和学习,变成隔着屏幕,依靠软件和网络平台开展的线上教学。"互联网+"环境下如何更好地利用线上资源,整合线下资源,优化大学英语教学,如何完成学习方式、教学模式以及考核评判机制的转变,更有效地开展英语学习和教学工作,是学生、教师以及教学管理部门面临的挑战。本研究首先从大学生身份转变角度分析了大学英语学习的特点,存在的困难和问题;其次,结合"互联网+"环境阐述和论证了其对大学英语教学的影响;再次,从师生和教学管理部门的角度出发,提出了各方面应对"互联网+"环境下大学英语教学的对策;最后,通过具体教学案例论证和分析了英语教学的若干举措和方法,供读者借鉴参考。

---

* [作者简介]方俊青(1975—),女,北京人,首都经济贸易大学外国语学院讲师,研究方向为跨文化交际学、应用语言学等。

一、大学英语教学的背景和存在的问题

（一）大学英语学习的背景和特点

大学生们经历了高考的严格筛选，从初高中紧张繁重的任务督导型学习阶段过渡到大学看似轻松的内驱自律型选课上课阶段，学习模式和方法以及授课环境都发生了较大的改变。大学英语是一门强调实践性、注重实用性、突出交流和互动性的实践类课程，不同于以语法和词汇为基础的应试英语。大学英语学习要求学生变被动为主动，从原来听课做笔记转变为当面交流用心记，能够完成从应试教育尤其是笔试类考试到面对面考核测试的转变；在学习态度、学习方式和应试准备等方面都需要积极调整，以适应课程特点。大学英语教学相比较以前的学习更深入和完善：一方面，词汇量扩充拓展，所涵盖的内容更加宽广；另一方面，贯穿英美文化，提供的视野和视角更加开阔，不同于以往英语学习中读和写的规范性和标准化，更加注重语言的交际实用性和灵活性，这是对初入大学的新生转变思路和改变学习方法的重大挑战。从某种意义上讲，大学英语学习更像是一个多人协作、重在参与的锻炼，而不是一个人闭门苦读、潜心钻研的修炼。

（二）大学英语学习存在的问题和困难

部分同学在大学英语初学阶段会感觉不适应：课时从每天最少两节变成一周两次，上课从做题、讲题、总结变成思考、讨论以及各种形式的展示，有的学生在课堂交流中存在听不清、说不出、发不准等困难，甚至产生畏难心态和消极情绪，不知道如何学习大学英语甚至抵触这门课程。大学新生需要消除行为和心理上的惯性，把原来依赖老师教学、被动吸收知识的学习模式，转变为大胆发言、积极交流想法的学习模式；把单纯的书本学习转变为利用"互联网+"下的媒体工具，如各种视听说资料、电脑软件、手机APP、微博、微信等进行学习；授课环境也应该随英语教学的需要而改变，教师和相关教学主管部门可依据英语学习的要求，充分尊重课程特点，大胆创新，构建良好的交流和学习环境，增加所需的软硬件设施等。

二、"互联网+"环境对大学英语教学的影响分析

（一）"互联网+"环境对大学英语教学带来的机遇

"互联网+"已经上升为国家战略，"互联网+"是一种融合了互联网、信息通信技术和传统产业特点的业界新生态，是三者的有机结合和创新，交叉衍生出许多新的技术和经济发展形态，如移动互联网、大数据、云计算、人工智能等。"互联网+"技术的先进性、拓展性和灵活性，使其在教育领域也发挥了巨大的作用，可以

弥补传统教学手段的不足,打造出图文并茂、赏心悦目、细节完整、功能完备的学习环境。

在"互联网+"的技术支持下,学生的学习灵活性大大增强,学生不再囿于相对固定的空间和时间,可以充分利用碎片化时间,做到随时随地,有选择性的学习和课后根据个体需要反复温习重点内容。这样的学习模式的变化无疑是巨大和有效的,比传统课堂上的黑板、粉笔,甚至于大屏幕和PPT更能够吸引学生,提高学生的主动性、趣味性和指向性,取得良好的学习效果。例如,学生可以在线存储自己的口语练习,不断比较分辨需要提高和改进的地方,也可借助在线智能软件进行口语评分,通过增加练习,积累数据,随着训练时间增加,在学习系统中会清晰地看到自己的进步;学生可以筛选自己喜欢的学习内容和形式,而不是受限于教师的知识水平和视野,根据自己的兴趣爱好真正做到以学生为中心的翻转课堂教学,教师只需做适当的引导、点评、审核。上述做法正契合教育部颁布的《大学英语课程教学要求》中所提出的要求:"新的教学模式应以现代信息技术特别是网络技术为支撑,使英语教学朝着个性化学习、不受时间和地点限制的方向发展。"

(二)"互联网+"环境对大学英语教学带来的挑战

"互联网+"环境在给大学英语教学带来机遇的同时,也带来了新的挑战,给学生、教师和教学管理部门带来了不小的冲击。在缺乏线下课堂教学环境,教师无法面对面引导、监督、答疑,缺少同学互助、互动的情况下,学生很容易产生学习任务拖延或者学习效果不佳等情况。有的学生面对手机、电脑、iPad等,自控力不够,沉迷于游戏、娱乐;有的学生不能有效选择自己的学习内容;有的学生对软件系统使用不够熟练。教师作为教学主体,面临教学任务和模式的转变,时间紧任务重,接触新鲜事物有学习过渡的阶段,会遇到很多困难,而且需要自己动手解决遇到的软硬件问题,而传统教学中则有学校提供相关支持,学校可以组织教师进行培训学习,委派技术人员来教室修复硬件问题。疫情期间,全体教师化身网络主播,因为操作不熟练、软硬件故障、直播环境陌生等原因出现了许多问题,甚至是教学事故。教师需要花费大量时间熟悉各种网络平台,制作课件定期投放到学习平台上,进行录播或直播,还需要解决网速和网络稳定性等技术性问题。对英语教师来说,教学互动的效果会直接影响到课堂教学质量和学生的积极性。

教学管理部门需要逐渐熟悉"互联网+"模式下的教学管理工作,尤其是疫情出现以后,不得不依靠"互联网+"模式从事教学工作的管理,如何组织线上教学工作,为师生提供软硬件保障,做好服务工作,以及如何应对"互联网+"模式下的教学和测试,制定相对公平科学的师生考核考评机制,尚需要时间去摸索。英语教学不同于以应试为主的书面教学,更重视学习者的平时积累和临时应变能力,这些都是传统笔试无法考核到的。"互联网+"所构建的网络环境,能够使学校师生在软件平台上通过摄像头进行交流沟通,虽然不如面对面交流互动方便,但摆脱了空间上的局限性。例如,某些软件自带回放和评分评级功能,便于师生和教学管理者通过回放查缺补漏以及评判教学效果等。

三、各方面应对"互联网+"环境下英语教学的对策

(一)学生迎接"互联网+"环境应完成的转变和对策

开展以学生为教学中心的翻转课堂教学和以"互联网+"模式为支撑的线上线下混合教学,是目前教育教学工作所达成的共识,也是未来很长一段时间的发展方向。尤其是对大学英语教学这种偏实践的课程来说,语用能力主要取决于学生能否大胆张开嘴,因此应多找机会锻炼和改进,在实战中提高能力和水平。学生首先要在思想意识上完成转变,充分发挥主观能动性,多寻找和把握实践机会,努力得到锻炼和提高;此外,学生还要有独立思考和选择判断的能力,能够在口语表达、语言反馈、词汇筛选、语气语态等方面符合规范、正确选用。

(二)教师应做的自我转变

教师作为传统教学主体,在"互联网+"的环境下,要完成从线下教学模式到线上线下混合教学模式的转变,完成从以教师教授为主的传统教学方式到教师引导学生为主的翻转课堂教学方式的转变,完成从考试考评的传统考核方式到基于互联网进行综合考评的考核方式转变。为完成上述转变,教师需要不断充电,在提高自身教学水平的同时,掌握多种授课技能,包括对"互联网+"工具的应用,多注重英语教学的鼓励和引导,要让学生能够大胆开口,最大程度灵活运用已有的语法结构和词汇去表达思想,努力做到整句输出,语流顺畅,达到有效交流的目的;根据学生的个体情况有选择性地因材施教,引导和制定学习的方向和提升计划。

(三)教学主管部门的对策

教学主管部门应对"互联网+"环境下英语教学的对策应该是渐进性和系统性的。渐进性主要是指针对不同阶段"互联网+"技术的发展以及师生的参与度,逐渐提供相应的保障和制定相应的管理规定;系统性则体现在教学理念、教学模式、教学条件及保障等全方位的协调并举和创新改革,而不是单一方面的修修补补或者形式上的换汤不换药。总体而言,教学主管部门针对"互联网+"带来的挑战,要围绕学生和教师新的转变和任务,提供软硬件支撑条件和保障措施,在整合利用好现有资源的条件下,搭建适合"互联网+"环境的学习和授课平台,疫情期

间,微博、微信、慕课(MOOC)、腾讯课堂、雨课堂、U校园、学习通等众多互联网平台为保障线上教学提供了强有力的支持,教学管理部门可以根据自身条件,和上述平台开展选择性的交流合作,并根据教学效果和反馈结果,积极调整管理思路和政策,与时俱进,推陈出新,保障教育教学在新环境下的顺利开展和有序发展。

(四)教师英语教学的案例分析

笔者作为一线大学英语教师,教学中积累了许多具体案例。

1. 英语教学中,笔者通过用问卷、访谈、小组讨论等形式了解学生进入大学前学习英语的情况,对学生大学英语学习的诉求和理想中的大学英语课堂模式,以及对班级学生的整体英语程度都进行摸底,了解学生的心理状态。笔者在教学中注重聆听、思考、引导、鼓励和启发,针对学生被动学习,不爱开口,缺乏自信的情况,逐一谈话询问原因和进行分析,以自己的亲身经历引导和说服学生,帮助学生发掘对英语学习的兴趣和内驱力,总结困难,梳理思路,克服心理障碍,从战略上认识到英语交际能力在日后生活和工作中的重要性。大多数学生经过耐心细致地思想教育后,都有了更好的学习状态和方向,取得了英语学习的进步。

2. 针对某些有一定基础但对英语文化缺乏了解的学生,笔者在掌握他们每个人的学习情况之后,选择蕴含英语文化背景的影视作品、音乐作品、书籍资料以及优质微信公众号等进行推荐,鼓励学生之间互相分享和点评,取得了良好的效果,同时也增加了他们对语言学习的信心和兴趣。笔者多次组织与学生生活和学习密切相关的话题进行讨论,教学生用批判式思维(critical thinking)分析问题,使得不少学生进入了积极的学习状态。比如,临近期末,如何地道表达"我太累了",如何表达"点赞、刷屏、有人@我";疫情期间,组织丰富多彩的在线活动,讨论"特殊时期(疫情)如何缓解压力和焦虑?""室内和户外运动的利与弊""在线学习期间,如何保持自律,克服拖延症?""是否适应在线学习?有哪些利与弊?如何克服困难?如何评价和提出改进建议?""在线学习期间,如何灵活高效的安排作息时间,劳逸结合,解锁新技能?"等。

3. 在线考核的难度较大,口试题目相对宽泛和抽象,学生在整学期缺乏面对面交流的情况下增加了心理交流障碍。笔者深度思考后进行了考试时间和形式的调整:把两人一组每组5分钟的期末口试时间延长为20分钟,增加了热身、引导和总结环节,给学生充分思考的时间,消除心理障碍,激发学生的热情。这种调整效果显著。面对"Online books will mean the end of bookstores. Do you agree or disagree? Give your reasons."这样的问题时,学生往往无从下手,笔者尝试把一个较为抽象的命题分解为具体的题目去问学生,便于引导学生"有话可说",发挥出较好的口语水平。针对"Do you like reading and what do you read in you spare time?""How do you like paper books and e-books?""What books do you prefer to read online and why?"等一系列具体的小问题,学生们普遍反映良好,能够迅速开始思考,组织思想和语言,较为顺利地回答。笔者基于上述问题引导学生整合思路,进行语言学习的同时,也帮学生掌握了如何用金字塔思维(pyramid thinking)来解决问题。本案例也是笔者对大学阶段的英语教育应该从"授人以鱼"向"授人以渔"转变这一理念的践行。

结语

大学英语教学任重道远,笔者结合20年一线教学经验,经过观察和思考,针对"互联网+"环境下的大学英语教学进行了分析和探讨。笔者根据大学英语的教学特点提出了学生、教师、教学管理部门应该承担的责任和转变,旨在进一步认识和适应"互联网+"环境带来的深刻巨变和大学英语教学面临的机遇和挑战,供大家参考和讨论。

参考文献

[1]叶玲,姚艳丹,韩叶.基于翻转课堂的大学英语教师发展研究[J].中国医学教育技术,2020(34):146-149.

[2]石照霞.互联网信息技术与大学英语教学融合的研究[J].外语翻译,2020(6):161-162.

[3]左亚娟."互联网+"背景下混合式教学模式在大学英语教学中的运用策略探究[J].课程教育研究,2019(48):116-117.

[4]黄明洁,马媛馨.互联网+时代背景下大学英语视听说教学模式的研究与实践[J].湖北开放职业学院学报,2020(12):173-175.

[5]李林鸿.互联网+环境下的大学英语慕课教学模式探讨[J].佳木斯职业学院学报,2020(2):164-165.

疫情防控下高校线上教学实践与探索
——以基于超星泛雅平台和腾讯会议的中级法语课程为例

于晨琦[*]

(首都经济贸易大学 北京 100070)

摘 要: 新冠肺炎疫情突如其来,打破了高校的传统授课模式,2020年3月,笔者所在的首都经济贸易大学全面开启网络教学。本研究基于笔者本学期的线上授课经验,在介绍中级法语课程网络授课方案的同时,对网络教学的平台、特点、利弊等方面进行探讨。另外,通过分析超星泛雅平台的学习数据,以及对学生问卷调查进行结果统计,笔者亦对首次线上教学进行反思与总结,并对网络授课的改进方向提出建议。与传统的教学方式不同,网络授课有自己的优势和不足,教师应充分利用线上教学的优势,为学生提供良好的课堂效果和学习体验。

关键词: 新冠疫情;网络教学;中级法语;超星泛雅平台;腾讯会议

引言

2020年初,新冠肺炎疫情突如其来,打破了宁静的校园生活。1月27日,教育部发布《关于2020年春季学期延期开学的通知》,明确规定全国各大、中、小学延期开学,推迟返校;1月29日,教育部对各学校春季学期的教学做出相应部署,倡导利用网络平台授课,即"停课不停教",并于2月4日发布具体指导意见。疫情就是命令,防控就是责任。为响应国家号召,我校教务处于2月6日建立"教师网络教学微信群",并于11日和18日在线上举行了两次网络教学平台的操作培训。2月17日,教务处对春季学期网络教学相关事项发布正式通知,规定任课教师应于26日前上报授课方式等方案,并于28日前完成师生对接,3月

---

[*] [作者简介]于晨琦(1992—),女,黑龙江人,首都经济贸易大学外国语学院副教授,研究方向为法语教学法、中法文化交流史、法国自传文学。

2日正式开学。根据官方数据统计,开学以来,我校有89%的本科课程和62.6%的研究生课程采取了网络教学形式;具体到笔者所在的外国语学院,这两个数据分别为96%和90%。至此,一场出乎意料的疫情将我国的教育产业加速推入"互联网+"的浪潮之中。回顾本学期的教学工作,从开始的陌生到后来的娴熟,再到现在的常态化,可以说,网络教学这种新形式给每一位教师都带来了许多新的认识和思考。

一、中级法语网络授课情况

笔者的中级法语课程授课对象是我校法语专业的大二学生,他们每周有6个课时的法语课程学习。笔者本学期的教学计划是在完成法语初级阶段学习任务的基础上,适当带领学生备考专业四级考试。在本学期的线上教学中,笔者选用了超星泛雅和腾讯会议作为网络授课平台:超星泛雅平台主要用于日常教学,包括授课、活动、作业、考试等;腾讯会议主要用于在线答疑。经过一学期的测试,两个平台总体上用户体验良好,期末对学生的问卷调查也表明,大多数同学对本学期的网络授课平台感到满意。

众所周知,网络教学与线下教学存在诸多不同:首先,网络教学在很大程度上依赖于学生的自制力和自控力,学生长时间在线学习很容易分散注意力;其次,网络教学效果也与学生的自主学习能力息息相关,与传统课堂相比,线上教学师生互动效果有所减弱。基于以上两点,在网络教学的过程中,应注意启发学生学习兴趣,培养其自主学习的能力;另外,每次网络授课的时间不宜过长,以使学生能在有效学习时间内更好地集中精力,避免事倍功半。因此,在本学期的中级法语线上课堂中,笔者根据网络教学的相关特点,相应调整了授课方法。

首先,笔者在教学中增加了"法语角"的模块,以培养学生自主学习法语的兴趣。利用超星泛雅平台的小组、收藏、专题创作三个板块,在为学生分享趣味法语资源的同时,引导学生自己进行相关专题创作。多数老师对超星泛雅平台的使用局限在课程板块,对其他板块往往开发利用不足。平台的小组板块可以上传趣味法语资源,如音乐剧、歌曲、电影、配音等,而平台的收藏板块中有一些法国名著,可以用来引导学生阅读法国文学作品。为充分利用以上两个板块多种多样的法语资源,笔者要求学生在本学期每人进行一个专题创作——可以是读书笔记、影评、法语配音、法语歌曲等,并将自己的创作上传至超星泛雅平台。这样,班级里的每一位学生都能够看到其他同学的作品,在互动交流中更增强了学习法语的兴趣和动力。相比于传统的线下教学,网络授课的优点是资源整合的便捷性和互动评论的开放性。借助于平台功能，教师可以将希望呈现给学生的资源汇集展示，学生也可以在网络平台对其他人的作品进行点评，这为增强学生学习兴趣并培养学生自主学习能力提供了许多便利。

其次，在本学期原定教学内容的基础上，利用超星泛雅平台的功能，笔者增加了签到、随堂练习和抢答三项活动，这样能够在保证学生基本学习时长的同时，通过抢答积分的方式增加学生的学习动力。在教学内容的设计方面，笔者采取的是录播后上传平台的方式。超星泛雅平台的"全国课程资源中心"中有全国各地各学科教师的授课资源，可以在备课时将其中相应部分有机融合于自己的课堂教学中。因为学生在网络学习时难以长时间集中注意力，这就要求教师上传的录播视频尽量短小精炼，不能完全照搬传统教学的课堂讲授模式。基于上述要求，笔者的每个录播视频长度都在30分钟以内，并且在讲解的过程中注意精炼重点，避免重复讲解。通过期末的问卷调查了解到，学生对这种讲授方式的满意度很高。他们认为，录播课相对于直播课的优点在于录播视频可以反复观看，有助于夯实知识点和课后进行复习。

再次，利用腾讯会议，笔者会在每周的固定时间为学生统一线上答疑。在答疑前利用超星泛雅平台的投票和讨论功能，提前收集学生具有代表性的问题，这样能够使答疑更为精准，更有针对性。笔者每周的答疑也是与学生交流学习感受和生活状态的机会。突如其来的疫情使全国大部分人长期禁足家中，对学生的心理和情绪会造成一定的影响，所以笔者也利用每周的答疑机会和学生讨论疫情，叮嘱大家在做好防护的同时心怀希望，对学生进行适当的心理疏导。在特殊时期，教师的职责不仅局限于传道授业解惑，也要利用自己的生活阅历和教师身份对学生进行人文关怀和心理辅导，确保学生以健康的身心状态投入到网络学习中。

最后，基于本学期网络教学的特点，笔者改变了课程传统的期末考试形式，代之以形式多样的过程性考核。通过设置活动环节（包括签到、随堂练习、抢答）、观看录播视频完成任务、作业和平时测试，将考核安插到平时教学的过程之中。另外，将"法语角"中的专题创作作为考核的附加分项，以鼓励学生在了解课外知识的过程中形成自己的思考。以上几种考核方式相结合，一方面能够在一定程度上督促学生紧跟教师进度，完成学习任务；另一方面，多样的考核方式也能激起学生的学习兴趣，避免考核方式单一造成的偏颇及不公。在进行考核的过程中，超星泛雅平台的统计功能起到了重要作用：平台可以设置期末成绩中各项考核所占的百分比，为实施多样化过程性考核的结果统计提供了很大帮助。当然，通过本学期中的几次平时测试,笔者也发现了一些平台功能的不完善之处。超星泛雅的考试模块对填空题和选择题设计十分友好,不仅可以自动批阅,还有错题统计功能;不足之处在于平台提供的各类题型均无法修改题干,不利于试卷的设计和学生对考试内容的理解。另外,平台的容量有限也一直是影响考试顺利进行的因素:在正常上课时间进行的平时测试经常会因平台容量不足而出现卡顿,有时甚至出现直接退出或不能进入考试模块的状况,在一定程度上影响了教师的教学计划和学生的积极性。

二、超星泛雅平台及学生问卷调查的数据分析

网络教学的一大优点在于,教师能够借助授课平台强大的统计功能,查看每一位学生的学习报告及班级整体的学习情况,据此对教学进行相应的调整,并为每一位同学制订个性化的学习方案。通过对本学期超星泛雅平台上学生的学习数据进行分析,笔者总结出中级法语网络教学有待改进的方面有以下几点:第一,授课班级期末成绩整体偏高,这一方面反映了学生本学期的学习效果良好,但另一方面也说明教师应在一定程度上加大期末测试的难度;第二,学生3、4月份的学习次数统计(见图1)显示出大多数学生的学习时间集中在周一和周五,而周中学习次数较少。对此,教师应采取控制随堂练习时间、任务完成期限及作业提交时间等措施,督促学生将学习时间平均分配到一周当中。

最后,笔者将学生的学习次数与期末成绩对比后发现二者具有很强的正相关性。相应地,教师需关注学习次数较少的学生,及时与他们沟通学习状态和学习中产生的困难,做到一人一策,必要时也可通过平台对自制力不强的学生发出学习预警。

在本学期即将结束之际,笔者对中级法语课程班上的学生进行了一次问卷调查,以期了解学生本学期的网络学习体验和建议,从而更好地对网络教学进行改进。本次调查共收回有效问卷32份,其中女生24份,男生8份,调查主体为20岁左右的法语专业大二学生。这次问卷调查的结果反映出学生对网络教学的体验和建议主要有以下几点:

第一,根据问卷的学习时间及满意度调查,班内女生的周平均自主学习时长普遍高于男生(见表1),且女生的学习满意度也普遍较高。由此可以看出,班级内女生的自主学习意识要明显高于男生。由于网络对于男生的吸引力要普遍大于女生,因此,如何使男生在网络教学当中保持较高的听课质量和专注度仍是一个值得探讨的问题。

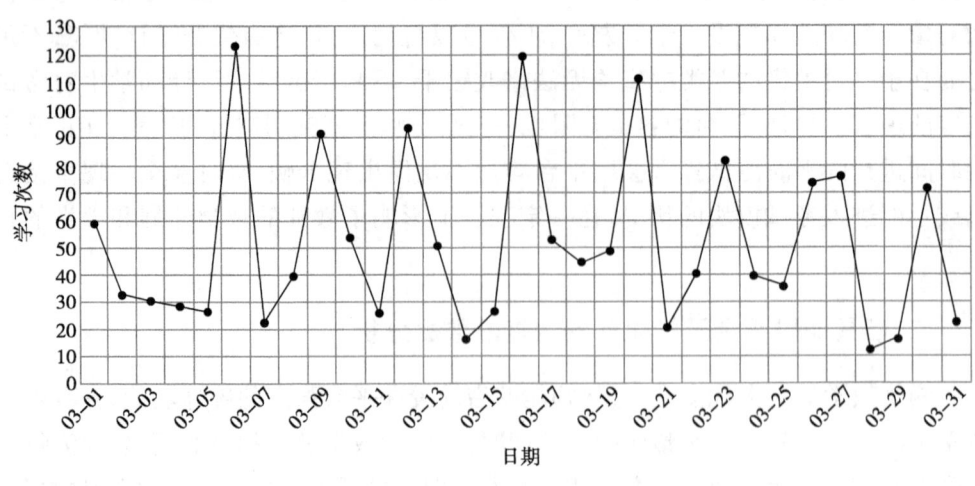

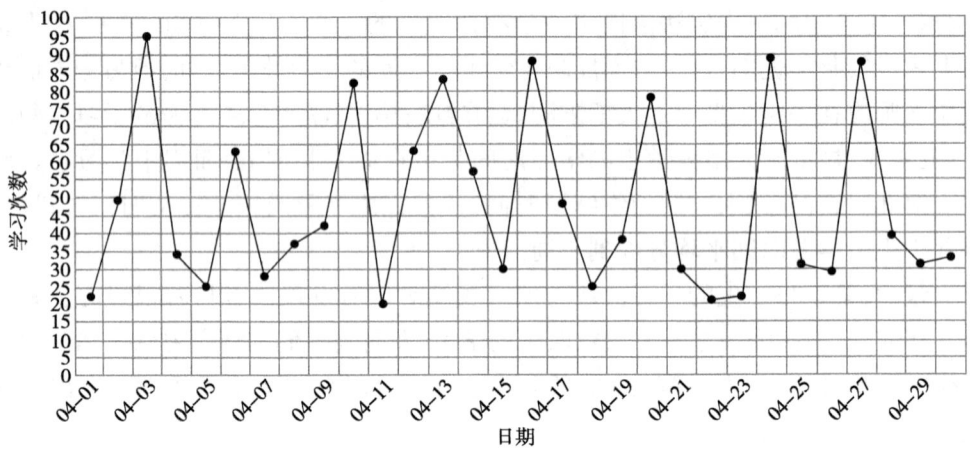

图1 学生学习课程章节的次数

表1 自主学习法语课程时间

第9题:除任课教师布置的学习任务外,你每周自主学习中级法语课程相关内容的时间是:(单选题)

X\Y	2小时以下	2~4小时	4~6小时	6小时以上	小计
男	25%	37.5%	37.5%	0.00%	8
女	4.17%	33.33%	54.17%	8.33%	24

第二,与传统的线下教学相比,学生对线上教学的体验在各方面都大同小异

(见表2)。从该表可以看出,数据相差较大的几个方面分别是教师讲授、作业提交与讲解,以及讨论与互动。多数学生认可教师录播的讲授形式,认为可以反复观看视频,便于知识点的理解与复习;而线上作业提交的截止时间相比于线下教学较长,这样学生可以根据自己的情况灵活自由地安排适合自己的学习计划。但在讨论与互动方面,多数学生认为与传统教学相比,网络授课的互动效果不尽如人意。对此,教师可以灵活运用超星泛雅活动板块中的主题讨论与分组任务功能,加强师生以及生生之间的交流与合作。然而对于网络授课而言,与学生之间的互动确实是一个有待解决的问题,这一点笔者在本学期的教学工作中也深有体会。

表2 线上教学与线下教学的学习体验对比表

第5题:在本学期中级法语的线上教学中,你的学习体验与线下教学相比:[矩阵多选题]

题目\选项	学习环境	教师讲授	师生关系	提问与回答	讨论与互动	作业提交与讲解	考试	其他
比线下教学好的方面	18 (56.25%)	18 (56.25%)	13 (40.63%)	13 (40.63%)	6 (18.75%)	18 (56.25%)	14 (43.75%)	5 (15.63%)
比线下教学差的方面	13 (40.63%)	7 (21.88%)	9 (28.13%)	16 (50%)	22 (68.75%)	9 (28.13%)	14 (43.75%)	2 (6.25%)

除此之外,这次问卷调查还反映出了网络授课的一个较大的缺点:部分学生对线上学习的负面体验主要集中在缺乏学习氛围和个人自制力差。针对这一部分学生,笔者认为可以考虑采用直播与录屏剪辑相结合的方式进行网络教学。自制力不强的同学可以按照原课表时间按时参加教师的直播课程,教师在直播的同时进行录屏,课后经过剪辑将视频上传至教学平台,以供全体同学反复观看。

结语

正如加拿大阿尔伯塔大学理学院院长所说:"传统教育教学方法也许只是冰山一角,影响教学效果更多取决于冰山之下的评价方法(如形成性评价和总结性评价)、学生学习行为、游戏化学习、知识编辑策略。换言之,当知识传播方式发生改变后,教学不仅取决于知识传授方式,更多取决于知识展现形式。"(薛成龙和李文,2020:12-17)与传统的线下教学相比,线上教学具有自己的特点。教师只有根据这些特点及时调整教学方式,才能更好地适应网络教学。另外,网络教学为培养学生的自主学习能力提供了契机。众所周知,授人以鱼不如授人以渔。教师应利用网络教学的机会,改变传统的以教师为主的授课方式,多在课堂中加入引导性和讨论性内容,启发并培养学生自主学习的能力。最后,任何事物都具有两面性。通过调查分析可知,网络教学也是优点与缺点并存。教师应充分利用网络教学的优势,尽量规避其缺点,并在适当情况下与传统线下教学相结合,双管齐下,才能为学生呈现最好的教学效果。

参考文献

[1]陈大伟.线上教学中的坚守与改变[J].教育与教学研究,2020,34(4):67－77.

[2]高忠虎,吴忠铁,吴云,等.新冠疫情防控期基于腾讯课堂和超星泛雅平台的高校线上教学实践与探索[J].中国多媒体与网络教学学报,2020(6):12－13.

[3]薛成龙,李文.国外三所大学线上教学的经验与启示[J].中国高教研究,2020(4):12－17.

[4]周翔.疫情下高校"停课不停学"线上教学可持续发展的探讨[J].福建教育学院学报,2020(4):75－77.

> # 建构性作答方式英语听力课堂测评
任务设计原则及方法初探
——以研究生公共英语听力网络录播课为例

孙 桐 高建平*

(首都经济贸易大学 北京 100070)

摘 要:听力测试中的建构性作答方式任务主要包括听写题、简答题和填空题等类别,具体有多种多样的任务设计形式。这类任务虽然应用广泛,但相关研究有限,对于优质任务设计的原则和方法尚处于初步探索阶段。为了对课堂测评环境中的建构性作答方式听力测试任务设计提供科学系统的指导,本研究对相关原则和方法进行了梳理和总结。在此基础上,笔者在新冠肺炎疫情期间,从主讲的研究生公共英语听力网络录播课中选取了5个不同类型的任务作为案例,分析了该类任务的设计思路及原理。

关键词:建构性作答方式;听力测试;课堂测评;任务设计;研究生公共英语;案例分析

引言

听力测试中的听写题、简答题和填空题都属于建构性作答方式任务,这类任务内容形式繁多,用途广泛,真实性强,项目区分度好,是标准化测试和听力教学中常用任务类型。但迄今为止,有关该类任务的研究数量及内容有限,缺乏系统性。对于优质任务设计的原则和方法,近年来虽有文献(Geranpayeh& Taylor,2013;Green,

---

* [作者简介](第一作者兼通讯作者)孙桐(1987—),男,吉林长春人,首都经济贸易大学外国语学院讲师,博士,主要研究方向为应用语言学/语言测试、外语教学、词汇学。
(第二作者)(1970—),男,山东籍,首都经济贸易大学外国语学院副教授,博士,研究方向为外语教学、语言测试、英汉跨文化研究等。

2017)初步涉及,但建构性作答方式听力任务设计有其复杂性,现有研究难以为其提供科学系统的指导。笔者试图在现有理论和实践的基础上,对听力素材的处理和试题设计的原则进行系统的整理和归纳;并以2020年新冠肺炎疫情期间研究生公共英语听力网络录播课中的5个建构性作答方式任务为案例,分析并展示句子填空题、简答题、部分听写、摘要填空题、笔记填空题等5种听力任务的设计原理和思路。

一、听力测试建构性作答方式任务

(一)定义及分类

建构性作答方式(constructed response format)是语言测试项目或任务的一类设计形式,要求考生以口语或写作的形式回答问题,而非在题目给出的若干答案中做选择(Davis et al,2002:32;Richards & Schmidt,2010:123)。听力测试中的建构性作答方式任务主要有两大类别:第一类需要考生以简答或填空的方式写出简短的答案(Elliott & Wilson,2013:167);第二类是复合任务类型,如结合听说、听写和听读写等技能的任务(如ETS,2012),需要考生提供更为复杂的回答,往往需要产出完整的语篇。第二类任务的构想不再局限于听力技能本身,能否归类为听力任务尚有争议,在本研究中不做详细讨论;本研究提及的建构性作答方式听力任务属于第一类任务,虽然考生需要在答题中运用简单的写作能力,但任务本身仅以考察听力技能为目的。

上述"第一类任务"在标准化国际英语测试和课堂测评中运用广泛,常见类型包括简答题(short answer questions)、句子填空题(sentence completion)、部分听写(partial dictation)、笔记填空题(note completion)、摘要填空题(summary completion)、流程图填空题(flow-chart completion)、表格填空题(table completion)以及图片填空题(plan/map/diagram completion)(Cai,2013;Geranpayeh & Taylor,2013;Cambridge University Press and Cambridge Assessment English,2019)。这些任务的共同特点是考生对每个题项只需给出简短的回答[①]。

(二)主要特色

建构性作答方式听力任务受其设计形式影响,主要有五个方面的特点:首先,该类任务要求考生根据听力语篇的内容直接给出答案,无须从可能的答案中选择,往往被认定具有较强的真实性(Elliott & Wilson,2013)。第二,建构性作答方式任

---

① 格林(Green,2017)甚至把全部这些任务类型都统称为"short answer questions",以突出仅做简短回答的任务要求,但该分类方法在名称上容易产生混淆,本研究统一使用"建构性作答方式"这一表达。

务有利于避免考生猜测推断正确答案,因此项目一般具有较好的区分度(Green,2017)。第三,该类任务的设计具有良好的灵活性,可用于测量多个层次的听力理解能力(Green,2017)。第四,简答和填空等形式可引导考生更多运用词汇检索,把握语篇中关键性的细节性信息(Field,2012,2013;Elliott & Wilson,2013)。最后,由于该类听力任务答案一般来自语篇中直接出现的信息,其在课堂教学中有利于提升学生语音加工的精准度。

(三)研究现状及现存问题

建构性作答方式听力任务虽然应用广泛,但学界对其研究不够全面深入。现存问题主要体现在三个方面:第一,相关实证研究和综述涵盖了一定范围的任务类型,包括简答题(Buck,1991;Buck & Tatsuoka,1998)、句子和摘要填空题(Boroughs,2003)、听写(Cai,2013;Weir et al,2013;沈蕾,2013)、笔记填空题(Field,2011,2012;Wang,2017)等有限类型;其中除了听写和笔记填空题以外,其他任务类型仅有所使用或简单提及,并未作为研究重点。第二,现有研究所涉内容并不全面,主要集中在标准化测试任务的开发和改进(如 Weir et al.,2013)和效度研究(如 Wang,2017)等话题上。有关任务设计的方法和原则,仅有部分学者的著作(Geranpayeh & Taylor,2013;Green,2017)有所涉及,另有个别关注评分方法和标准的研究(如 Harding and Ryan,2009),相关知识还不够系统,尚有一些争议,有待进一步探索。第三,对于该类任务的使用环境,目前的探讨局限于大规模标准化测试或纯粹实验操作,尚未与课堂测评、教学任务设计及教材开发等英语教学领域的研究话题接轨。基于以上三个方面的研究空缺,本研究以新冠疫情期间研究生公共英语听力网络录播课中的任务设计为实例,对建构性作答方式英语听力课堂测评任务的设计原则及方法展开探索。

二、任务设计基本原则

本研究参照格林(Green 2017),吉兰帕伊和泰勒(Geranpayeh & Taylor,2013)等著作中有关不同类别听力任务设计细则,并结合听力课堂测评的背景,围绕选材、使用方法和试题设计等方面,总结了听力建构性作答方式任务设计的普遍原则。以下将主要以列表的方式具体呈现。

(一)听力材料的筛选和使用规划

英语教师在备课过程中不难获取形式多样的海量听力资源(如网络资源、英语听力教材、标准化考试资料),但只有对获取的素材有准确的鉴别和规划能力,才能合理利用资源,为高效的课堂教学奠定基础。具体而言,对于建构性作答方式听力任务的设计,什么样的听力材料适合选用？可以测量哪些方面的能力？应选用何种任务类型？听力材料的选取及使用的原则如表1所示。

表1 听力材料的选取及使用的原则

考虑事项	具体原则
听力材料的适切性	A1 听力材料应具有较高真实性①,内容积极健康,不涉及存有严重争议的政治敏感或意识形态问题
	A2 听力材料语言内容难度应符合学生当前水平,语速不宜过快,无特殊口音,发音清晰,语言使用规范,不宜掺杂太过响亮的背景噪声
	A3 听力材料用时不宜过长,一般不超过10分钟,过长的材料应考虑重点截取一些片段
	A4 对于视频听力材料,应尽量选择视频内容辅助听力理解的材料,排除易导致分散注意力的材料(如体育比赛、动作片片段)
	A5 对于初步选定的素材,一定要完整听过之后再决定是否在课堂中使用(推荐做笔记),不应仅以转录文本内容为选择依据。
测量目标的设定	B1 在仔细分析听力材料结构和内容基础上,再决定听力任务所考察的具体听力技能
	B2 单个项目可用于测量对细节性信息的获取和理解,对主旨、观点、态度及事实性信息的理解等不同层次的听力能力,但一个题项只对应一种测量目标
任务类型的选择	C1 句子填空题、简答题和部分听写等任务类型对听力语篇的结构和内容一般没有特殊要求,属于"百搭题型",但容易引导考生过度关注细节性信息,使用应谨慎
	C2 摘要填空题、笔记填空题、表格类填空题、流程图填空题以及图片填空题有助于从整体上呈现听力语篇的整体结构,但这些任务对听力材料的内容有特殊要求,设计者应慎重考虑
	C3 若符合教学需要,且材料合适,同样的听力语篇可考虑同时设计不同类型的建构性作答方式任务

① "真实性"并非绝对的概念。一般来讲,BBC、VOA新闻听力、TED演讲、经典英文电影原声片段以及某些国际标准化英文测试中(如IELTS、TOEFL iBT)的听力材料的真实性不容易被质疑。

根据表1分析,设计建构性作答方式听力任务时,应有合适的选材、合理的测量目标设定和具体的任务类型选择,在此基础上才能进一步开展试题设计。其中,A1—A5的内容反映了选材的原则;B1—B2是测试量目标设定的原则;C1—C3是任务类型选择的原则。教师在选材或规划任务设计的过程中,可根据教学需要,将此表内容按照具体原则改编为核查清单,以评价试题设计准备工作是否完善。表中的三类原则是环环相扣的,首先必须确认"听力材料的适切性(A)";在此基础上,才能进行"测量目标的设定(B)";若前两项内容都没有问题,最后完成"任务类型的选择(C)"。

(二)试题设计普遍原则

在选择了合适的听力材料,且对任务设计进行了初步规划之后,接下来应考虑任务设计的具体问题。对于建构性作答方式听力任务的试题设计,应重点考虑五个方面的问题:任务说明如何编写?项目的设置和撰写应注意哪些问题?正确答案的设置应参考什么原则?如何设定评分标准?如何使用及改进已有题目?建构性作答方式听力任务试题设计原则如表2所示。

表2　建构性作答方式听力任务试题设计原则

考虑事项	具体原则
任务说明的编写	D1 任务说明的开头应该清晰简要地总结听力语篇的话题或主要内容,若用于教学目的,教师可考虑写一个简明的话题引入
	D2 任务说明中应简述任务设计形式及对作答的要求,如完成句子、回答问题、完成笔记等
	D3 建构性作答方式任务应对答案的字数设定明确的限制,一般情况下每个答案建议不超过4个词(包含或排除数字可自选)①,否则考生难以作答,且会为评分带来困难。部分听写任务的填空词数限制可适当放宽,但一般不超过一个完整句子
	D4 如果学生对选用的任务类型比较陌生,教师可考虑在试题之前设置一个示例题项和答案,作为示范

---

① 格林(Green,2017)建议每个答案不超过5个词,但考虑到在词数限制过宽的情况下,正确答案的表达也会增多,容易给评分带来不确定性,故此本研究对这一标准做了更严格的限定。

续表

考虑事项	具体原则
项目编写	E1 一个独立任务中项目编号的顺序应该与其对应的听力原文中关键信息出现的顺序一致
	E2 对于测量高层次听力理解能力的项目（如对主旨、主要观点的理解），答案字数限制应适当放宽（与D3不冲突），一般不用"仅填一词"的设定
	E3 题干内容尽量复述其对应的语篇中关键信息的内容，关键词可用近义词替换，不直接拷贝原文内容（部分听写任务除外）
	E4 题干的用词尽量简洁、精准，不能引发产生歧义的答案
	E5 在句子的中后段和结尾处设置填空，尽量避免将其设置在句子开头（不排除少数例外），这样设置符合考生在听力语篇中获取关键信息的习惯，且有利于避免猜测答案
	E6 各题项的答案在听力语篇中对应的信息不应过于密集，避免为学生的作答带来过多认知负担
	E7 一组题项中不能混搭不同任务类型（如简答题和填空题），但可分别将其设置为基于同一语篇的不同任务
答案设置	F1 设置答案时应全面考虑到每个题项可能存在不同的正确答案
	F2 每个题项的正确答案应尽量选择听力原文中直接出现的表达，词数不超过任务说明中限定的范围
	F3 为避免产生混淆，一组题项不要重复使用同样的答案
评分标准	G1 常规情况下，某题项的正确答案判定标准为学生应答与参考答案（或其中之一）完全一致（用词、拼写、语法都正确）
	G2 对于初级或中等水平的学生，答案中不引起歧义的轻微拼写或语法错误可以选择判定正确或取得部分分数
试题核查	H1 初次完成的试题设计应一边播放听力材料，一边检查任务设计，修正其中的错误或不完善之处，若条件具备，应请同行协助检查
	H2 对于已经设置了练习题的听力材料，若试题设计明显违背上述原则（DEFG四类），应考虑对题目重新设计或加以改编；对于权威性标准化听力测试（如剑桥系列）中的测试任务，若符合教学目的，可直接使用

表2总结了建构性作答方式听力任务的具体设计原则，主要包括任务说明、项

目编写、答案设置、评分标准和对已有试题的借鉴和改进等方面的详细事项。其中,D1—D4反映了对任务说明的要求;E1—E7为项目编写的具体原则;F1—F3是答案设置的原则;G1—G2反映了评分标准的要求;H1—H2为试题检查和改进的注意事项。该表所列的原则是基于英语课堂测评任务设计的考虑,个别标准化听力测试中的重要设置不在讨论范围之内,如任务说明的录音、播放次数等问题,教师可在课堂教学中灵活掌控这些问题。表2内容可作为简答题、部分听写以及各类填空题任务设计的重要参考,虽然并不是绝对的"金科玉律",但对于不符原则的设计,教师一定要谨慎思考其对听力任务效度及学习效果的影响,再做决定。

三、任务设计具体方法及课堂测评案例分析

笔者于2020年春季学期承担学校的研究生公共英语教学任务①。在疫情暴发后的特殊时期,受教育部"停课不停学"的倡导,笔者与教研组其他任课教师利用超星学习通平台,为学校的非英语专业研究生组开设了网络英语课程(共建课,录播形式)。笔者利用三个独立的教学周,选取了真实的音频和视频英语听力资源,为学生开设了一系列网络听力课程。

本节展示研究生公共英语网络录播课中设计的建构性作答方式听力任务,共提供5个案例,涵盖句子填空题、简答题、部分听写、摘要填空题、笔记填空题等任务类型。针对每个案例,主要介绍听力材料的来源、语篇主要内容、教学重点、测量目标的设定及任务类型的选择依据。

(一)句子填空题

例1是一段视听材料,选自TED-Ed视听资源,名为"我们能否摆脱标准化测试?"。

Task 1:Should We Get Rid of Standardized Testing(节选)

Instructions:What are standardized tests? Why do we have to take them? How should we understand their usefulness and limitations? Let's watch a TED ed video focusing on the nature of standardized testing and complete each of the following sentences with NO MORE THAN THREE WORDS AND/OR A NUMBER.

(1)According to the video, the first standardized tests were designed and used in China _____ .

---

① 2020年春季学期研究生公共英语课程形式为共建课,课程安排由本研究第二作者(高建平)策划,听力录播课由本研究第一作者(孙桐)主讲。

(2) Some standardized tests provide scores only in relation to those achieved by _____.

(3) Some standardized tests measure performances according to _____ criteria.

Keys:1. (over/in) 2 000 years ago;2. other test takers;3. predetermined

该听力语篇围绕"标准化测试"的话题,剖析了测评的本质,介绍了一系列有关考试的基本概念。除了训练听力技能以外,视听材料中一些测试学知识点也特别值得学生学习。因此,依据该材料内容,其配套听力练习适宜考查学生对语篇中关键信息的理解,句子填空题是一种合适的选择。

(二)简答题

例2的听力材料是比尔·盖茨2015年的著名TED演讲"The Next Outbreak? We Are not Ready"。该听力任务基于新冠疫情期间的防控背景,回顾演讲者5年前极具预见性的观点,对任务名称进行了调整。

Task 2:Bill Gates—The "Oracle" of the Coronavirus(节选)

Instructions:Five years ago,Bill Gates make a TED lecture to warn us that we had not been ready for the next outbreak,unfortunately he was right! Now let's watch it get ready to answer each of the following questions with NO MORE THAN FOUR WORDS.

1. What could kill over 10 million people in the next few decades?

Answer:_____

2. What are people lack of in dealing with the outbreak of the Ebola?

Answer:_____

3. What are the problems of the case reports of an spreading epidemic on the newspaper?

Answer:_____

Keys:1. a highly infectious virus/an infectious virus/ a virus;2. a (response) system;3. delayed and (extremely) inaccurate.

该演讲围绕流行病防控的话题,从社会的层面分析总结了政府应采取的必要措施,并指出了当时政府防疫准备工作的不足之处,对当下全世界新冠肺炎疫情的防治很有参考价值。在训练听力技能的同时,语篇中提及的一些重要事实性信息和对流行病防控的建议非常值得学习。因此,配套练习题重点考查学生对重要事实性信息的理解,选择使用简答题,并将每个问题答案的字数限制放宽。

(三)部分听写

例3选自《研究生学术英语视听说教程》(2016)中Special Topic 3中第二部分

Test & School 中的 Lecture Watching 部分的视听材料。笔者根据教学需要，依据原材料对听力练习进行了重新设计。

Task 3：The Crisis in Education（节选）

Instructions： This TED lecture is a lengthy speech on the problems of education. There are a few clips of the transcript of the lecture, but some pieces of key information are missing. Please listen to the lecture and complete all the gaps as what the speaker has said.

Clip #2

Let me ask you something you may (6)_____. How many of you here are over the age of 25? That's not what you take for granted, I'm sure you're familiar with that. Are there any people here (7)_____? Great. Now, those over 25, could you put your hands up if you're wearing your wristwatch? Now that's a great deal of us, isn't it? Ask a room full of teenagers the same thing. Teenagers do not wear wristwatches. I don't mean they can't, (8)_____. And the reason is we were brought up in a pre-digital culture, those of us over 25. And so for us, if you want to know the time, you have to wear something to tell it. Kids now live in a world which is digitized, and the time, for them, is (9)_____. They see no reason to do this. And by the way, you don't need either; it's just that you've always done it and you carry on doing it. My daughter never wears a watch, my daughter Kate, who's 20. She doesn't see the point. As she says, "(10)_____" "Like, how lame is that?" And I say, "No, no, it tells the date as well." "It has multiple functions."

Keys： 6. take for granted；7. under the age of 25；8. they just often choose not to；9. everywhere；10. It's a single-function device.

这段 TED 演讲结合生动的实例讲解了当代教育面临的主要问题。该讲话时间较长，其间讲话者有很多即兴发挥的内容。讲话者讲解了一些深入浅出的例子，学生能否领会，取决于对一些关键性信息的理解。因此，配套练习题选用部分听写任务，主要考查学生对语篇中细节性信息的获取能力，以及对重要观点的把握能力。

（四）摘要填空题

例 4 选自《研究生学术英语视听说教程》（2016）中 Special Topic 2 中第一部分 Animals & Conservationists 中的 Movie Watching 部分的影视片段。所选片段为《里约大冒险》中的对话片段，笔者根据材料内容的特点对听力练习进行了重新设计。

Task 4:The Dilemma of Keeping or Freeing Animals(节选)

Instructions: Let's watch a movie clip from *Rio*, a 3D computer – animated musical adventure – comedy film, named after its setting, Rio in Brazil. The film is based on a story of Blu, the only male Spix's macaw(金刚鹦鹉) in its species, who is taken to Rio de Janeiro for mating. Please complete the plot summary by filling each of the gaps with ONLY ONE WORD OR A NUMBER. Please pay attention to the grammar when filling the gaps.

Plot summary:

When Linda opened the door of her bookstore, she saw a man fell on the ground, who came in at once and claimed that he had not adapted to the (1)_____. This strange man, whose name was Dr. Tulio Monteiro, had actually travelled (2) _____ miles only looking for Blu. He showed a great interest in the bird and tried to (3) _____ with him, but Blu was confused at his

attempt. Then Tulio went on to introduce that Blu was a very (4)_____ bird because he was the only (5) _____ of his species.

Keys:1. weather;2. 6 000;3. communicate;4. special;5. male

该影视片段的主要内容是两位主要角色的对话,他们因为对金刚鹦鹉 Blu 应该寻求配偶还是作为宠物照顾产生了冲突。这段材料通过对话的形式结合视频内容,情节性很强,适合学生抓住语篇中一些重要信息,对故事情节进行复述。故此配套练习题选用摘要填空题,主要考查学生对反映故事情节的重要信息的获取能力。

(五)笔记填空题

例 5 选自《研究生学术英语视听说教程》(2016)中 Special Topic 3 中第一部分 Education Matters 中的 Video Watching 部分的视听材料。这段材料是 IELTS 官方网站中的考试介绍视频,笔者根据材料内容的特点和教学需要对任务进行了重新设计。

Task5:The IELTS Reading Test(节选)

Instructions: In order to be a better test taker, it is highly advisable to get familiar with the test itself and to be equipped with practical strategies to get your answers right. Watch a video introducing the IELTS reading test and complete the notes below with NO MORE THAN TWO WORDS for each blank.

Some Advice to Prepare for the Reading Test
➢ practice fast reading skills
a. skimming
1) To identify key themes and (3)＿＿＿＿＿＿—a "bird's eye view".
E. g. pay attention to titles, subtitles, key words, (4)＿＿＿＿＿＿, etc.
b. scanning
1) To look for specific information—"swooping down for specific detail".
E. g. a name, a date, etc.
2) No need to read (5)＿＿＿＿＿＿ in the article.
Keys：3. general ideas；4. topic sentences；5. every/each word

该视频的主要内容为雅思阅读测试的介绍，并讲解了重要的阅读策略和考试答题策略，结构十分清晰，包含了很多实用的知识点讲解。该语篇不但可以帮助学生了解提高英语技能的方法和途径，且有助于学生积累考试经验，同时还能让学生学习一种清晰的讲话结构。因此，听力练习设计选用笔记填空题，重点考查学生对语篇中关键细节性信息的理解能力。

结语

本研究针对听力测试中的建构性作答方式任务，归纳了听力材料的处理和试题设计的主要原则和方法，并以研究生公共英语网络共建课中5个不同类型的课堂测评任务为案例进行分析，展示了该类任务的多样性、灵活性及任务设计规范。本研究在格林（Green，2017）及吉兰帕伊和泰勒（Geranpayeh & Taylor，2013）等著作的基础上，对建构性作答方式听力任务设计开发的细则进行了更为细致和全面地总结，但当前的框架处于初步探索阶段，有待未来进一步修正完善。由于建构性作答方式听力任务种类繁多，本研究无法全部展示，还有一些特殊任务类型（如表格填空题、图片填空题）的设计有待后续研究进一步讨论。最后需要指出，建构性作答方式听力任务作为多样化题型设置中的一种选择，有其固有特色，但也有一些局限性，如作答中涉及某些不相关因素（如阅读和写作能力、语法知识），答案词数限制引发的疑问等①，建议在听力教学中与选择性作答方式（selected response format）

---

① 简答题、填空题等任务的字数限制如果过宽或不存在，容易为题项的评分带来困难，从而影响任务的信度和效度；若限制过严，则会影响测量目标的灵活性，难以编写测量高层次听力理解能力的题项。测试开发者可根据实际需要追求两者之间的平衡，但无法消除这个矛盾。

的任务类型搭配使用(如选择题、多项匹配题),取长补短。

参考文献

[1] BOROUGHS R. The change process at the paper level. paper 4,listening[C]// WEIR,C J, MILANOVIC M. Continuity and Innovation:Revising the Cambridge Proficiency in English Examination 1913 - 2002. Cambridge:Cambridge University Press, 2003,315 - 353.

[2] BUCK G. The Testing of Listening Comprehension:an Introspective Study[J]. Language Testing,1991,8(1):67 - 91.

[3] BUCK G. ,TATSUOKA K. Application of the Rule - space Procedure to Language Testing:Examining Attributes of a Free Response Listening Test[J]. Language Testing,1998,15(2):119 - 157.

[4] CAI H. Partial Dictation as a Measure of EFL Listening Proficiency:Evidence from Confirmatory Factor Analysis[J]. Language Testing, 2013,30(2):177 - 199.

[5] CAMBRIDGE University Press & Cambridge Assessment English. IELTS Academic with Answers:Authentic Practice Tests 14[M]. Cambridge:Cambridge University Press,2019.

[6] DAVIS A,et al. Dictionary of Language Testing[M]. Beijing:Foreign Language Teaching and Research Press,2002.

[7] ELLIOT M. , WILSON J. Context validity [C]//Geranpayeh A, Taylor L. Examining Listening: Research and Practice in Assessing Second Language Listening. Cambridge:Cambridge University Press,2013:152 - 241.

[8] ETS. The Official Guide to the TOEFL Test[M]. (4th ed.) New York:The McGraw - Hill Companies,2012.

[9] FIELD J. Into the Mind of the Academic Listener[J]. Journal of English for Academic Purposes,2011,10(2):102 - 112.

[10] FIELD J. The cognitive validity of the lecture - based question in the IELTS listening paper[C]//TAYLOR L,WEIR C J. IELTS Collected Papers 2:Research in Reading and Listening Assessment. Cambridge:Cambridge University Press,2012, 391 - 442.

[11] FIELD J. Cognitive validity[C]//GERANPAYEH A,TAYLOR L. Examining Listening:Research and Practice in Assessing Second Language Listening. Cambridge:

Cambridge University Press,2013:77~151.

[12]GERANPAYEH A,TAYLOR L. Examining Listening:Research and Practice in Assessing Second Language Listening[M]. Cambridge:Cambridge University Press,2013.

[13]GREEN R. Designing Listening Tests:a Practical Approach[M]. London:Palgrave Macmillan,2017.

[14]HARDING L,RYAN K. Decision making in marking open – ended listening test items:the case of the OET[C]//JOHNSON J S,Lagergren E. Spaan Fellow Working Papers in Second or Foreign Language Assessment. Washington:English Language Institute University of Michigan,2009:99 – 113.

[15]RICHARDS J C,SCHMIDT R. Longman Dictionary of Language Teaching and Applied Linguistics[M]. 4th ed. Edinburgh:Pearson Education Limited,2010.

[16]WANG H. Testing Lecture Comprehension Through Listening – to – summarize Cloze Tasks:The Trio of Task Demands,Cognitive Processes and Language Competence [M]. Singapore:Springer,2017.

[17]WEIR C J,et al. Measured Constructs:a History of Cambridge English Language Examinations 1913 – 2012[M]. Cambridge:Cambridge University Press,2013.

[18]沈蕾. 大学英语考试复合式听写的效度研究[M]. 南京:南京大学出版社,2013.

[19]王筱晶. 研究生学术英语视听说教程[M]. 北京:中国人民大学出版社,2016.

思政元素融入大学英语课堂之我见

刘燕梅*

(首都经济贸易大学 北京 100070)

摘　要:本研究从课程思政提出的背景引出其在大学英语教学中的意义,探究了课程思政元素在大学英语教学中的融入因素和体现的角度的可行性。

关键词:思政;大学英语学习;融入;教学;实施

引言

《高等学校课程思政建设指导纲要》中明确指出:公共基础课要"重点建设一批提高大学生思想道德修养、人文素质、科学精神、宪法法治意识、国家安全意识和认知能力的课程,注重在潜移默化中坚定学生理想信念、厚植爱国主义情怀、加强品德修养、增长知识见识、培养奋斗精神,提升学生综合素质。"

高校大学英语课的指导性文件——《大学英语课程教学要求》对基础课阶段的大学公共英语的描述为"承担着为适应我国经济发展和未来国际交流的需要,通过传授英语语言知识与应用技能,培养学生在学习策略和跨文化交际、英语综合应用技能方面的能力的任务"。

因此,如何在大学英语教学中践行"现代化、国际化、多科性、有特色的国内一流、国际知名财经大学"的要求,培养适应当代经济和社会发展、德智体全面发展、理论基础扎实、知识面较宽、富有创新精神和实践能力的高素质应用型、创新型人才是首都经济贸易大学公共英语教师的首先要思考的问题之一。

---

* [作者简介]刘燕梅(1966—),女,北京人,首都经济贸易大学副教授,研究方向为语言教学、跨文化交际等。

一、思政元素在大学英语课程中的意义

学校是立德树人的地方,正所谓"十年树木,百年树人"。大学生时期是青年学生世界观养成的重要阶段,如何在传授知识的同时帮助青年学生养成正确的世界观、人生观和价值观是当代大学的主要任务。《高等学校课程思政建设指导纲要》中指出:"落实立德树人根本任务,必须将价值塑造、知识传授和能力培养三者融为一体、不可割裂。"开设大学英语课的目的是通过英语学习,让学生了解国外经济、科技发展,有助于传播中华文化,增进交往,进而提升国家软实力。由此可见,大学英语课程的学习会对大学生的未来发展产生深远影响,有助于学生树立世界眼光,培养国际意识,提高人文素养。大学英语课程思政的重要性可见一斑。

首先,大学英语课程内容丰富,题材广泛,涉及社会、人文、历史和科技经济发展。在讲述英语国家这些知识的同时注重强化中华文明,融合我们优秀的社会制度特点、筑牢学生的中华民族意识正是思政的目的之一。其次,大学英语课作为大学一、二年级的必修课有着课时多、学分高、持续时间长的特点。抓住思政教育的契机,在教学中自然融入思政元素,使学生在英语听、说、读、写、译的学习过程中提高思想政治觉悟,有助于解决"培养什么人、如何培养人、为谁培养人"的问题,从而达到立德树人的目的。最后,针对学生积极、上进、有理想、有担当的特点,应通过英语知识的传授营造良好的校园和课堂文化氛围,鼓励学生为实现中华民族的伟大复兴而努力学习。

二、思政元素在大学英语课程中的诸多体现

思政元素在大学英语课程中的融入主要体现在教学目标、教学方法和教学实践等方面。

(一)教学目标

习近平总书记在党的十九大报告中指出:"青年兴则国家兴,青年强则国家强。青年一代有理想、有本领、有担当,国家就有前途,民族就有希望。"《大学英语课程教学要求》提出"高校开设大学英语课程,一方面是满足国家战略需求,为国家改革开放和经济社会发展服务,另一方面,是满足学生专业学习、国际交流、继续深造、工作就业等方面的需要"。作为高校人文教育的重要组成部分,大学英语课程的工具性和人文性是重要的教学内容。

大学英语学习的目的不仅是培养学生的英语应用能力,提高跨文化交际意识和能力,而且是增强学生多元文化素养,为学生将来的学习、生活、社会交往和未来工作中"能够有效地使用英语,满足国家、社会、学校和个人发展的需要"打下基础。而课程思政的核心之一就是提高大学生思想道德修养、人文素质,厚植爱国主义情怀,加强品德修养,增长见识,培养奋斗精神,提升学生综合素质。

(二)教学方法

语言教学的发展经历了从传统的古典人文主义到科学主义再到现代人文主义复归的轨迹,即古典人文主义——科学主义——现代人文主义。

在这一演变过程中,社会发展、经济、政治和教育背景都对教学方法有着不可估量的影响。近年来,随着中国科技、经济等诸方面的不断进步,社会对语言教学的要求越来越高,在这样的背景下,交际教学法在大学英语教学中获得蓬勃发展。大学英语课程中思政元素的融入与人文主义教学的回归和交际教学法的发展也会起到相辅相成的作用。

(三)教学实践

课堂教学是"构建全员全程全方位育人大格局中的主渠道"。大学英语课作为基础课中的重头戏,教学目标、要求、教材和教案都是落实课程思政的重要环节。

《大学英语课程教学要求》提出"大学英语教学以英语的实际使用为导向,以培养学生的英语应用能力为重点"。无论是语言知识的传授、语言应用能力的落实,还是跨文化交际能力的养成,都是课堂教学中必不可少的环节。

因材施教是教学要求的指导性原则。作为北京市属大学,首都经济贸易大学坚持"以培养适应当代经济和社会发展需要、德智体全面发展、理论基础扎实、知识面较宽、富有创新精神和实践能力的高素质应用型、创新型人才为目标"。为配合《高等学校课程思政建设指导纲要》的实施,教学材料的选择和教学课件、教案的准备都应该挖掘、体现思政元素,寓思政教育于教材、教案和课件中。

三、思政元素在大学英语课上的可行性

在充分挖掘各类课程思想政治资源,发挥好每门课程的育人作用和全面提高人才培养质量思想的指导下,"全面推进课程思政建设工作,坚持知识传授和价值引领相统一"为思政元素在大学英语课上的实施奠定了理论和政策基础,其可行性体现在课程思政建设氛围、教师素质和学生观念等方面。

(一)课程思政建设氛围

我国改革开放政策的深入实施,在社会文化、思想道德、价值观体系等诸多方面给中国社会,尤其是青年人的思想带来了极大的冲击。爱国主义情怀、社会责任担当、主流价值观等都是大学生思想道德教育的重点。2020 年 6 月教育报印发的《高等学校课程思政建设指导纲要》明确了要科学设计课程思政教学体系,结合学科专业特点推进课程思政建设。在此指导思想引领下,各级各类高等院校积极响应,为课程思政融入高校人才培养创造了良好的建设氛围。

(二)教师素质

作为课堂的主导者之一,教师自觉主动建设课程思政和把握教学内容与思政中心点的内在逻辑契合是有效融入思政元素的关键。新时代的教师,应在教学实践中秉承教书育人的职业道德,主动探索大学英语课与思政教育的内在联系,自然地把专业育人和立德树人结合起来,提高大学生思想道德修养、人文素质。

(三)学生观念

在传统的思维导向中,学生在大学英语课堂上通过听、说、读、写、译获得语言知识并付诸实践即达到了学习目的。而思政元素的融入是要寓价值观引导于知识传授和能力培养之中。这就需要教师对学生的价值观取向、专业知识需求和其他相关因素有更深入明晰的了解,在课程中自然地导入思政元素,在潜移默化中转变学生传统的学习观念,在传授语言知识的同时帮助学生塑造正确的世界观、人生观、价值观。

四、课程思政在大学英语课上的实施

大学英语课作为大学一、二年级的基础必修课是课程思政建设的一个重要阵地。落实课程思政需要兼顾教材和教法两方面。

(一)进行教材思政建设

现有的大学公共英语多以外语教学与研究出版社、上海外语教育出版社和高等教育出版社的课本为主流教材。这些教材在内容编排上基本采用的是主题式单元模式,即一个单元一个主题,经过听、说、读、写、译等多方面的学习和训练来达到培养学生语言应用能力的目的。

课程思政建设可以根据单元主题,深入挖掘其体现在社会历史进程、道德意识引领、不同政体分析、文化差异、社会经济发展、未来职业思考等方面的内容,结合当前国内外和现实生活中的重大事件,融入跨文化交际元素,培养学生的批判性思维,通过过程学习提高学生的英语水平,树立中国文化自信,培养民族自豪感和爱国主义情怀。

(二)采用多维度教学方法搭建大学英语课程思政建设平台

语言学习是通过听、说、读、写、译等多角度实现的。课程思政的建设也应该遵从语言学习规律,全面开花。

1. 听力与阅读。作为语言输入的两大渠道,听力和阅读除了传授语言知识外,还可以直接传递包括道德标准、人文素养、文化引领、家国情怀等诸多信息。大学生性格特点鲜明,思想活跃且易于接受新鲜事物,如果社会、家庭和学校引领不当,他们极有可能发生世界观、人生观和价值观的错位。因此,应在听力和阅读教学中给予学生正确引导,自然融入课程思政元素,于潜移默化中帮助学生在获取语言知识的同时树立正确的世界观、人生观和价值观。

现代教育技术的发展为听力和阅读学习提供了极大的便利。以往的听力和阅读材料的获取通常以外国媒体为主,这在一定程度上忽略了传统文化和中国元素的传播。在课程思政的大环境下,可以选取弘扬中国社会政治、经济、文化特色等方面的材料,培养学生爱党、爱国、爱校的美德。

2. 口语、写作和翻译。在听力和阅读课堂的指导下,根据因材施教的原则,要求学生把语言知识通过口语表达、篇章写作和翻译进行产出是大学公共英语课的目的之一。

在中国文化走出去,走向世界的战略背景下,大学英语学习中的口语、写作和翻译日趋凸显其重要性。

在多媒体教学遍地开花,慕课(MOOC)翻转课堂等教学手段为越来越多的高校所应用的今天,不光传统教学受到冲击,也使大学生思维更为活跃。这就要求教师在大学英语教学过程中更加注重每个学生的语言输出,观察其思想变化,适时通过课程思政对学生给予关注、关心和关怀。根据语言学习目标对课程产出需要来提供正确的思政方面的引导,帮助学生树立社会主义核心价值观,批判性地学习英语语言和文化。

结语

大学英语教学中融入课程思政元素是国家、社会和培养社会主义接班人的需要,对高校、教师和学生都是一个极具挑战性的教学实践。在落实过程中高校需要指引、协调教师和学生在课程思政方面遇到的问题和困难;教师需要不断提高自己的思想、政治水平和业务能力来圆满地完成教学任务;学生需要在正确的世界观、人生观和价值观的引领下,发挥积极向上、勤奋好学,有激情、家国情怀和勇于担当的特性,主动配合以实现大学阶段的人生目标。

参考文献

[1]肖礼泉.英语教学方法论[M].北京:外语教学与研究出版社,2006:16.

论生生互动在高级英语课程中的作用*

高建平**

(首都经济贸易大学 北京 100071)

摘 要：本研究以建构主义教学理念为指导，分析了英语专业本科生"高级英语"课程中运用生生互动教学手段的意义。如果运用得当，该课程相关生生互动活动可以帮助提高课程内容的针对性，增强课堂过程的趣味性，并为切实提高学生的实际交流能力，提供高效、实用的练习环境。

关键词：高级英语课；生生互动；建构主义

引言

外语学习的目标之一，可认为是提高学习者使用某种目标语言的交际能力。而即便对于英语专业高年级本科生，真正实现这一目标也非易事。无论在英语专业或公共英语课堂上，还是在本科或者研究生层次的外语教学中，笔者常常发现这样的问题：貌似简单的交际任务，往往给学生带来实质性的困难。为帮助解决这一问题，笔者结合建构主义教育观思想，在"高级英语"课程内，初步探索了"生生互动"这一教学手段可能存在的巨大价值。本研究中的"生生互动"，是指学生与学生之间，就课程相关内容而进行的有组织的互动性课堂活动。

瑞士心理学家、教育学家让·皮亚杰主张，知识并非来自主体或客体，而是来自主客体间的互动，通过同化与顺应的过程而逐渐构建起来。苏联心理学家、教育学家维果茨基也认为，人的交往最初表现为外部形式，以后内化为内部心理形式。

---

* [基金项目]本研究为2020年度首都经济贸易大学教改立项项目"'生生互动'视域下互动式'高级英语'课程教改研究"的部分成果。
** [作者简介]高建平(1970—)，男，山东籍，首都经济贸易大学外国语学院副教授，博士，研究方向为外语教学、语言测试、英汉跨文化研究等。

这可以反映出人类语言交际能力的发展过程。基于建构主义,意义的阐释或者信息的传递并非独立于主体而存在的,而应该源于主体对意义或者信息的逐步建构。由此,外语学习者只有成为积极的信息加工主体,即主动的意义建构者,而不是被动的灌输对象,才能真正培养出自身的外语交际能力(Communicative Competence in a Foreign Language)。具体来说,在"高级英语"课程内应用生生互动,至少在提高教学针对性,增强教学过程趣味性,以及提高学生获取信息的能力等三方面,具有较为重大的意义。

一、生生互动有利于提高教学针对性

教学上的常见困难之一是教师缺乏对学生实际情况的准确把握。具体就"高级英语"课程而言,学生的实际情况既包括学生的既有英语知识水平、语言技能水平,也包括学生的学习方法偏好和交流话题偏好等,教师如果不能掌握上述重要信息,教学目标、教学方式乃至教学活动的设计等一系列问题,可能都会出现偏差。"失之毫厘,谬以千里",如此教学,很难想象能达到最佳教学效果。

学生既有的英语知识水平和语言技能水平,是否可以通过类似"分级考试"等方式准确获取呢?理论上,教师通过组织较高质量的综合性"分级考试"(placement test),可以较为高效地获得某一时间节点上的截面信息。但学生的实际情况往往是动态的、不断演进的,而频繁的"分级考试"显然会打乱课程节奏,给学生增加了额外课业负担,甚至会由于客观上增加了学生的焦虑感,而在教学效果上适得其反。再者,分级考试多针对较大范围的群体而设计,并非针对已分好班的学生;该类考试还会受限于题目数量、题目范围、做题时间和答题方式等因素,对于具体某班的某门课程来说,其评测结果的分辨率往往较低;其对于"因材施教"的指导意义可能也流于形式,不够精细。换言之,考试仅仅是一个抽样检测过程。限于样本数量,对于语言知识或语言应用能力这种范围相对宽泛的领域而言,尤其对具体学生在某课程内所涉及的某种知识或技能而言,普通分级考试很难让教师准确把握学生的实际情况。

学生的学习方法偏好和交流话题偏好问题,是否可以通过开课前或学期初的问卷调查解决呢?从笔者自身授课经验来看,该类问卷一般仅能提供某种程度的参考,很难让教师对学生真实情况有十足把握。一方面,该类问卷一般形成于教师对学生有一定了解之前,问卷本身虽具客观性,但针对性明显不足。另一方面,学生面对问卷时不一定能做到认真合作,而当设计者对调查对象缺乏了解、问题内容或提问方式不够严谨的时候,更难采集到所需要的准确信息。此外,外语学习者大多不是外语学习过程的研究者,上"高级英语"课的英语专业的学生亦是如此。由于教师和学生在外语学习理念、学习方法以及语言相关的知识技能体系等方面广泛地存在信息不对称,即便学生主观认真配合问卷调查,其对某些问题的回答也可能会凭"一时的感觉",并不一定真实反映其在外语学习过程中某个阶段的实际情况。换言之,学生并不一定总能够准确描述自己的"问题"或"水平"。这时,经验丰富的教师所给出的专业判断可能会更贴近实际情况。

合理的生生互动,恰好可以在课堂内为学生提供一个相对放松的交流环境,同时为教师提供一个了解学生实际情况的窗口。首先,在教师与学生间互动过程中,由于互动主体身份不同,学生较多情况下处于较为被动的状态;而生生互动中双方身份相同,视角接近,彼此间关系更为平等,有益于创造出更放松的互动氛围。在这种氛围中,学生无须做作,更容易展现出真实的交际水平。换言之,更容易展现出较为真实的语言知识水平和语言技能。只要安排得当,同学之间的交流内容会更自然,更接近于学生的生活和日常语言使用情况。对这些更为真实的现场语言使用,有经验的教师以旁观者视角加以收集、分析和总结,一般会得到更贴近事实的学生语言状况。在该过程中,教师可能会发现实际语境中的真实问题。其次,生生互动实时发生于课堂内,对发现的问题可以进行核实或进一步明确,这显然是师生互动无法企及的优势。另外,"高级英语"课在英语专业本科学习阶段中位置较为特殊。其一,学生在选该课时大都已经过本科一、二年级的学习,打下了较好的语言知识、应用基础;同时这些学生又不同于面临毕业的四年级同学,没有紧迫的论文、考研或就业问题分散精力。从这个角度讲,他们最具备做好生生互动的内在能力和外部条件。其二,基于同样原因,"高级英语"课上的学生经由多年不同学习方法、学习态度和各方面综合因素的塑造,在英语知识和技能乃至学习方法偏好等诸多方面,彼此间的差异已经非常大。有鉴于此,如果要做到"因材施教",最大化课堂效果,客观上就要求通过生生互动这种教学手段,相对准确地获取学生动态的外语学习水平。只有以更为准确的相关信息为基础,教师才可能更有针对性地安排课堂内容、选择教学方式和组织课堂活动。

二、生生互动有利于提高教学过程的趣味性

生动的课堂是很多外语教师追求的目标之一,这不仅因为课堂是否生动,将直接关系到该门课程能否受到学生的欢迎;更重要的是,生动的课堂大多要求更高的学生参与度,而参与度会直接体现学生在课堂内的语言交际能力。对于"高级英语"这门课程而言,生动的课堂尤其具有特殊意义。众所周知,"高级英语"是英语

专业高年级的最后一门语言本体课程,选材语言难度较大,篇幅较长,内容较为艰深。鉴于课程选材的特殊性,客观上要求教师运用各种方法,激发学生对教学内容的兴趣。

当然,激发学生兴趣的渠道很多。例如,提高教师讲解的精彩程度,加强课件的视觉吸引力,以及优化课堂活动安排等,都能发挥一定作用。但生生互动方式,着眼于提高学生参与度从而激发学生学习兴趣,具有三个不同于上述方法的重要优势:其一,生生互动可以使形式与内容更好地统一,使形式更好地服务于内容。"高级英语"课显然不是以愉悦观众为主要目标的"脱口秀"节目,它肩负着切实提高学生高阶语言知识和技能的任务。这就要求"生动的课堂"必须服务于"艰深的任务"。而基于生生互动这一方式,教师可以鼓励同学之间互相协作,彼此启发,共担压力,同享收获,从而愉悦地完成复杂任务。其二,生生互动可以把学生在语言知识和技能方面的个体差异,转化成共同协作中的"取长补短",从而完成某些个体学生难以单独胜任的任务,使其更早体验到成功的快乐和协作的意义。从某种意义上说,这还有利于帮助学生建立应对困难的信心。其三,生生互动可以展现同一问题的不同视角,学生在多方位思维的碰撞中体会到思路开阔的乐趣。无论教师如何博学多才或视角独特,其一人的思维广度,也无法匹敌众多学生的思维广度。此外,年龄、阅历相仿的学生之间,对感兴趣的视角或话题会更容易产生共鸣。

通过优化安排的生生互动,有助于提高教学过程的趣味性,降低学生对复杂教学材料的焦虑感,在彼此的协作中,使原本沉闷的课堂变得生动有趣。

三、生生互动有助于提高学生的实际交际能力

我国英语学习者常被诟病的一个问题是,"用外语进行实际交际的能力较弱"。尽管无论是教师还是学生,在英语上投入的精力和热情不少,但与英语相关的"强项",似乎过长地停留在"长于做题"或"擅长考试"这一褊狭的领域。为何如此?如果认真反思,我们不难发现,教师和学生会把大量的时间和精力,习惯性地置于"做题""考试"抑或与二者高度相关的内容之中。因此,产生实际交际能力薄弱的问题也就不足为怪了。也就是说,我们的课堂并未真正着力于交际能力的培养。受到一贯重视的"做题与考试",尽管某种程度上也可能有助于知识与理论素养的积累,但显然很难在语言技能培养方面产生令人满意的效用。

毫无疑问,从更广阔的社会视角观察,学生学习外语的更重要目标不应该是"应对考试",而应该是获得实实在在的外语交流技能,从而有助于国际交流合作、

贸易往来,有助于国人更好地了解世界,更顺畅地弘扬中华民族文化。从笔者实际教学经验来看,即使对于英语本科高年级修习"高级英语"课程的同学而言,要实现上述目标仍有较大差距。这实际上也是笔者力推生生互动这一教学活动的重要原因。

  首先,生生互动可以在现有条件下,比较高效地创造有实际意义的语言交流环境。实际使用语言是提高语言能力的最佳途径之一。多语地区居民习得某种外语的效率往往较高,比如,欧洲某些非英语母语地区的居民,往往可以用较少的时间和精力成本,熟练掌握英语语言技能。这固然是多种因素综合作用的结果,但语言的实际应用(或者说有意义运用,而非无实际意义的语言结构操练)也扮演了重要角色。结合实际情况来讲,如果"高级英语"课程紧密联系教材内容,为学生创设更多有意义的语言交流环境(而不是机械的语言形式操练环境),使其进行更多的有意义的语言操练,学生的实际交流能力应该可以逐步提高。限于篇幅,本研究暂不展开讨论创设课内交流环境的问题。

  其次,生生互动可以帮助学生掌握具体的语言交际技巧。比如,如何通过提出适切问题,高效获取所需信息。需要特别指出,鉴于中、英两种语言文化差异,同学之间如何主动提问、恰当提问、高效提问,仍是"高级英语"课上广泛存在的问题。运用好生生互动这一手段,是现有条件下突破学生交际技能瓶颈的关键。

  最后,适当设计生生互动活动,有助于学生锻炼发现问题的能力。这不仅有益于培养学生的洞察力和批判性思维,更重要的是可以锻炼学生共同寻找问题并通过求同存异探索答案的能力。通过这方面的不断锻炼,学生未来面对更为复杂的国际交流时,更容易适应环境,从而更好地完成相关工作。

四、组织生生互动活动的常用策略

  针对不同课程以及不同层次的学生,教师需要使用不同的策略安排生生互动活动,发挥这一教学手段的最佳功效,以期实现更好的课堂教学效果。针对"高级英语"课程,笔者主要采用以下三种策略:

  其一,语言方面必须提供及时帮助(scaffolding)。教师在设计互动活动时不能过于主观,应切合学生实际情况,进行必要的语言知识补充,安排提问技能操练活动。限于既往英语学习经历,并非所有学生都知道如何适切提问,对于诸如怎样使用恰当的英语,简练、准确地描述问题在教材中的位置之类的问题,不可仅凭教师的主观臆测就简单忽略。笔者通过观察分析发现,互动初期的语言焦虑往往会严重影响互动效果。

其二，思路方面应适度提示。所谓"适度"，即既不可没有提示，也不能提示过细。前者可能会使活动开端受阻，后者可能会限制学生的发挥。诚然，学生思路活跃，想象力丰富，但这并不意味着互动活动中听任学生信马由缰，毕竟课堂时间有限，而且需要完成既定教学任务。所以，在布置生生互动任务之前，抑或在教师巡视分组互动情况期间，教师应该给适当的思路引导。

其三，及时给予语用提示。这里的语用提示，主要是指语言的文体（比如正式程度）、色彩（比如褒贬）和英语交际礼仪方面的指导。限于客观条件，多数情况下互动活动中并无母语使用者参与，所以教师应该补充相应的语言文体、词汇色彩乃至文化差异方面的信息，不但要帮助学生使用合乎语法的语言，更要提示学生使用得体的语言。一方面，这可以帮助学生更好地理解不同语用和文化差异，帮助其更好地适应未来跨文化交流；另一方面，这也可以调节互动气氛，从而达到更好的互动效果。

结语

总之，生生互动是基于建构主义教育理念的一种重要教学手段；如果运用得当，它有助于提高课程内容的针对性，增强教学过程的趣味性，也可以提供难得的课内语言交际机会，培养学生的实际外语沟通能力。当然，针对不同层次的学生或不同的课程，应该采用差异化的设计策略。这样，才有可能发挥出生生互动教学的最佳效果。

参考文献

[1] ELLIS R. Second Language Acquisition[M]. Shanghai：Shanghai Foreign Language Education Press，2000.

[2] GOODMAN N. Of Mind and Other Matters [M]. Cambridge Mass：Harvard University Press，1984.

[3] 崔景贵. 建构主义教育观述评[J]. 当代教育科学，2003(1).

[4] 何莲珍. 新时代大学外语教育的历史使命[J]. 外语界，2019(1)：8-12.

[5] 周季鸣，万江波. 大学英语课堂口头报告的评价标准[J]. 外语教学，2019(4)：66-71.

非英语专业大学生写作错误引发的思考以及问题解决方法探析

白云红*

(首都经济贸易大学外国语学院,北京,100102)

摘 要: 写作在非英语专业大学英语教学中一直是难点,不仅任课教师没有足够的时间和精力兼顾到写作教学,而且学生写作中出现的问题多年来具有惊人的相似性。受中式思维的影响,学生所呈现的写作方面的错误相当一部分为 Chinglish。本研究旨在呈现学生进行写作时所出现的问题,尤其是多年来困扰笔者的问题,分析并探讨解决相应问题的途径。期望在未来的教学中能逐步帮助学生切实有效提高写作水平,提高应用语言能力。

关键词: 写作错误;写作教学;英语语感;解决方法;应用能力

引言

对于中国非英语专业的大学生而言,英语写作一直并非易事。词汇量不足、英语输入阅读量过少、中式思维的习惯等困扰了千千万万大学生,使得他们在进行英语写作时自信心不足。多年来受制于升学压力,学生没有更多精力或兴趣进行英语书籍或报刊的阅读,而在这方面投入的时间和精力不足,会导致学生语言输入严重不足,其后果是学生在书面表达时力不从心,词汇量不够,缺乏自信。

笔者在本研究中将重点关注学生在写作方面出现的问题,进行总结,并针对不同问题进行深入的探索,以期在未来教学中进行更加有效的指导,切实帮助学生解决写作常见的问题,进一步提高学生的写作质量,提升其书面应用英语的能力。

---

* [作者简介]白云红(1966—),女,首都经济贸易大学外国语学院副教授,研究方向为教学理论与实践研究、大学生英语应用能力培养

一、大学英语教学要求

《大学英语教学指南》(以下简称《指南》)确定了大学阶段的英语教学要求分为三个层次,即一般要求、较高要求以及更高要求。这三个不同层次的要求是我国各大高等院校非英语专业大学毕业生经过大学阶段的英语学习与实践应当达到的英语水平标准。其中,一般要求是每个大学毕业生必须达到的目标,较高要求和更高要求不列为本研究的目标。教学要求包括了英语语言知识、应用技能、学习策略和跨文化交际等方面的内容。大学英语教学的指导思想强调培养学生的英语听说能力,以及读、写、译等英语综合应用能力等;提倡因材施教,以适应立体化、网络化、个性化英语教学和学习的实际需要。

笔者所教的一年级新生来自经济学院、管理工程学院以及城市经济与公共管理学院,属于非英语专业学生。一般要求是高等院校非英语专业本科毕业生应达到的基本要求,本研究主要探讨学生英语学习中的写作问题,因此笔者重点关注一般要求。一般要求中针对书面表达能力的要求为:能用常见的应用文体完成一半的写作任务;能描述个人经历、事件、观感、情感等;能就一般性话题在半小时内写出 120 词的短文;内容基本完整,用词恰当,语篇连贯;能在一般或应用写作中运用恰当的写作技能。

二、大学英语教学中的写作教学现状

众所周知,英语学习的顺序被界定为"听—说—读—写",很多专家基本都认为"写"应该被置于最后的位置。因为写作是一种学习者把输入内容进行内化的表达形式,"听""说""读"三者对于"写"的水平提高而言都是大有裨益的,因此,师生在前三项中投入的精力和时间占整个学期的绝大部分,而且写作只是置于精读教学过程中,并没有独立的课时用于写作教学。另外,任课教师要完成统一规定的整学期单元教学任务,这也使得教师没有充分的课堂时间进行写作方面的指导。综上所述,英语应用能力表现形式之一的书面表达能力亟须得到更多的重视。

学生在写作教学课时不够、平时语言输入量也远远不足的情况之下,面对任课教师布置的写作任务,往往手足无措,词不达意,语法结构错误百出,痛苦不已。

三、学生写作方面问题之呈现

(一)大数据报告中统计的学生写作的问题

根据 2015 年中国高校英语写作教学联盟发布的《百万同题——英语写作大数

据报告》(以下简称《报告》),学生写作方面的错误可以划分为这几大类:词性误用、拼写、句子结构问题等。

本研究将重点关注学生句子使用的问题。《报告》的数据显示,在由全国各地高校学生参与完成的109万篇以上文章的写作中,学生错误总数量达到430多万次,句子错误问题总计出现121.8万次。按照错误出现频次从高到低排序如下:

1. 主谓一致问题。主谓一致问题出现54.6万次,所占比例之大一目了然。错误句子如:So I think reading and practice is inseparable. 主谓一致问题在笔者教过的学生写作中也很常见。例如:第三人称单数主语对应使用复数动词。

2. 不规范用法问题。该问题出现47.8万次。错误句子如:Reference books can growth our field of vision. 其中也存在学生对单词属性记忆不清的问题。

3. 成分确失问题。该问题出现13.4万次,此类的错误存在率比较高。错误句子如:A good book maybe among the best of friends. 经过多年的英语学习,学生对句子结构的了解还不够清晰,这无疑是教学过程中需要大力改进的一个方面。

4. 成分冗余问题。问题出现4.6万次,也是高频出现的问题类型。

5. 时态错误问题。相对于主谓一致的问题,时态错误情况不甚严重,但也属于常见错误。错误句子如:Helen was getting happier every day.

6. 语态错误问题。错误句子如:John got injured in the accident which was happened yesterday. 语态错误在学生写作中发生率很高,因为学生对一些词或短语的理解不够,而且非英语专业学生的英语学习缺乏连贯性,知识掌握不够牢固。

(二)与笔者学生写作问题的比较

笔者教学过程中总结的学生写作中的错误与《报告》既有相似之处,也有差异。

1. 主谓一致问题。学生涉及此问题的句子结构不甚相同,如:Colleges begin expanding enrollment is another reason. 学生可能把一个完整句子用作主语,也可能频繁地把动词用作句子的主语,如:Improve our values is the most important. 学生对于有哪些属性的词、短语或从句可以用作句子主语不甚了解,因此类似的错误句子频繁出现。以上错误句子中的第一句可以更正为:That colleges begin expanding enrollment is another reason. 或者 Another reason is that colleges begin expanding enrollment. Improving our values is the most important. 第二句可以更正为:The most important is to improve our values.

2. 不规范用法问题(或不合英语逻辑的表达问题)。例句:College students are hard to find jobs. While doing the translation exercise, there must be a good dictionary. 此类不符合英语逻辑表达的句型在学生写作中也不少见。以上错误句子可以更正

为:It's hard for college students to find jobs. While doing the translation exercise, we need to have a good dictionary.

3. 成分确失问题。此类问题具有普遍性,例句:Women's capability is lower than men. 用于比较句型中的类似错误比较常见。在学生写作中,成分缺失问题较严重。

其他常见错误在历届学生作文中频繁出现,特别是对于常用句型表达错误具有普遍性,而且对于学生用错的句型结构,任课教师纠正的难度很大;或者说经过多次纠正,仍然有相当一部分的学生混淆句型,记不清正确的表达。

4. 更多错误示例类型。

(1)例句:There are many students cannot find an ideal job. (误)There are about millions of college students graduate every year. (误) There be 句型的错误使用在学生写作以及口语表达过程中很常见。以上错误句子中的第一句可以更正为:There are many students who cannot find an ideal job. 或者 There are many students unable to find an ideal job. About millions of college students graduate every year. 第二句可以更正为:There are about a million of college students graduating every year.

(2)例句:She suffers a certain disease, always has the same nightmare. (误)He works out every day, not allow himself the thought of not winning the game. (误)学生对于非谓语形式的短语在句子中的使用错误百出。以上错误句子中的第一句可以更正为:She suffers a certain disease, always having the same nightmare. 第二句可以更正为:He works out every day, not allowing himself the thought of not winning the game.

(3)例句:Gender inequality makes women cannot find jobs they want. (误)学生在写作过程中对补足语的使用没有清晰的概念。该句可以更正为:Gender inequality makes it hard for women to find a job they want. 或者 Gender inequality makes women unable to find a job they want.

(4)例句:How to solve the problem? (误) He doesn't intend to take the job. Because this job is not satisfactory to him. (误) Because 从句常被学生认为是完整的句子,问题也具有普遍性。以上错句可以更正为:How can they solve the problem? He doesn't intend to take the job, because this job is not satisfactory to him.

四、学生写作问题出现的可能性原因

1. "听说领先"的指导性原则导致学生口语表达训练所占据的时间远远多于书面语言表达训练占据的时间。学生进行口语表达时的错误会呈现在其书面语表达内容中,因为教师倾向于鼓励学生表达自己的思想,从而不会过多地纠正其口语表达过程中出现的问题。而作为学生英语应用能力之书面表达能力——写作能力的培养在实际教学过程中一直是难点。

2. 学生进入大学阶段之前的英语教学围绕应试展开,即:教师课堂上讲语法,学生做练习巩固所学语法知识。此种模式下的教学比较机械,学生吸收语法知识的效果不高,从而直接导致学生的写作水平难以提高。

3. 由于多年来承受升学的压力,为了应对考试,学生会把精力用于记忆单词,进行题海战,无暇顾及英语材料的阅读,这对于英语思维的培养有诸多不利之处。学生的书面表达受中式思维影响,所使用的句子不太符合英语的表达习惯。

4. 近些年来,时有英语学界人士提倡看英文电影学地道英语,但口语表达与书面输出的语言差异性使得看英文电影未必对英语写作有很大作用。

结语

作为公共基础课的大学英语课程,集视、听、说及读写训练于一体,专门的英语写作课程并未开设。如何有效提高学生语言输出能力,对于大学英语教学来说的确是个难题。但教师精心设计课上教学活动并与课下训练任务有效结合,可以作为帮助学生提升写作水平的有益尝试。但学生必须提升英语语感,多了解英语思维模式后才可以有效提高语言输出能力。英语学界普遍认同的能提高学生英语语感的方法如下:多读英语原版文章,多听原声音像材料,大声朗读经典文章等。学生可以在课下大声朗读,关注重音、语调、语言的节奏,感受文章所传递的情感和思想(Zhou Guangming,2006)。因此,提高学生语言输出能力的关键在于英语语感的培养。

在"听说领先"的指导性原则下,课堂活动的设计可以兼顾听说与读写,可以采用"以说促写""以说代写""以读促写"的方式。根据目前的班级人数设置,适宜增加听说活动,根据所学话题安排学生小组计时完成听说任务;学生讨论结果经过任课教师纠正后,学生可以课下进行写作。这种"以说促写"的方式能帮助学生进行语言材料的整理,从而帮助学生做到有效的书面输出。"以说代写"的方式类似于"口头作文",也是训练英语思维的有效做法,能避免学生频繁进行书面表达的枯燥感。"以读促写"要求学生多进行原文阅读,增加语言输入量,逐步增强学生的英语语感,这是要求学生必须做到的。教师只有采用灵活多变的教学手段,采用有效的教学方法,促使学生进行规律的英语学习,不断提高英语语感,才能使学生进行高质量、有效的语言输出成为可能,才能提高学生的应用能力。

英语教学质量的提高也亟须任课教师不断学习更加有效的理论及教学方法。英语教学改革需要从学生早期接受英语学习开始,只有系统改革中国学生的学习方法和教师的教学方法,才能真正实现让学生自由、顺畅地用英语表达自己的思想的愿景。长路漫漫,师生学习之路无止境。

参考文献

[1]中国高校英语写作教学联盟.百万同题:英语写作大数据报告[R].北京:北京语言智能协同研究院,2015.

[2]周广明.重视英语朗读提高学生语言能力[J].福建教育学院,2006(8).

[3]白云红.提高大学生英语应用能力的实践探索:从英语写作教学谈起[G]//首都经济贸易大学外国语学院.外国语言、文学与文化研究论文集.北京:首都经济贸易大学出版社,2016.

高校英语专业教学中的体验式学习模式探析

郝 莉[*]

(首都经济贸易大学 北京 100070)

摘 要:体验式学习模式在英语专业教学中通常应用于语言技能实训,然而,随着时代的发展,英语专业教学更加注重思维能力的培养。体验式学习模式与作为人文学科的英语专业教学相结合,需要探索新的实施路径。通过掌握内容与技能、近转移和远转移三个步骤,体验式学习模式实现对学生的批判性思维、系统性思维和创造性思维的培养,提高学生的文化敏捷性,使学生成长为社会需要的复合型人才。

关键词:体验式学习;英语专业教学;批判性思维;系统性思维;创造性思维;文化敏捷性

引言

在传统教育的模式下,高等教育的主要目的是传授知识与技能,目前大多数高校的课程设置和教学方法也依然将传播知识和信息等作为重点。但是近几十年来,尤其是21世纪以来,人工智能的发展正在颠覆这种教育模式,知识的获取在网络发达的今天变得轻松而简单,仅靠掌握一定的专业知识和技术已经无法应对未来社会的挑战。因此,教育应该将重心转向培养机器无法替代的能力。

一、新形势下教学理念的转变

世界经济论坛(World Economic Forum)于2015年发布的《教育新视野:解锁技术潜能》(*New Vision for Education: Unlocking the Potential of Technology*)中提出,21世纪的能力教育有三种:基本素养、综合能力和性格养成。其中,基本素养包括读

---

[*] [作者简介]郝莉,女,首都经济贸易大学外国语学院讲师,博士,硕士生导师,主要研究领域为英语教学、翻译学。

写能力、计算能力、科学素养、信息技术素养、理财素养和文化及公民素养,综合能力包括思辨能力、创新能力、交际能力和合作能力,而性格养成包括好奇心、主动性、毅力、适应力、领导力、社会和文化意识。美国高等教育政策的研究者、著名教育学家约瑟夫·E.奥恩也指出,高等教育应培养新一代的创造者,使他们能够利用我们这个时代的科技奇迹,在被人工智能机器改变的经济体系和社会体系中蓬勃发展。要达到这样的目标,学生需要掌握"新读写能力",同时要开发出人工智能所不具备的思维方式,也称为"认知能力"。奥恩认为新读写能力与传统的书面语言读写能力不同,是在数字环境中更复杂的读写能力,包括科技素养、数据素养和人文素养。这些使我们不仅能与他人交流,而且能够与机器沟通。认知能力则是掌控高度科技化的世界所需的更高层次的能力,它包括批判性思维、系统性思维、创业精神和文化敏捷性。批判性思维是对想法进行分析,然后理解并运用事实解决问题的能力。系统性思维是将信息运用不同情境中的能力;创业精神要求学生在机器不断取代现存工作岗位的前提下,不断开拓新的产业和市场,并且开发高科技尚未掌控的新领域。文化敏捷性则对于跨越国界解决问题至关重要,它需要人们对不同文化有足够深入的了解,能够完全融入多元文化的团队。在不同环境下适应不同角色,并取得成功。在高等教育阶段培养学生的新读写能力是基础,而培养认知能力则是重要目标。

在这样的新形势下,一轮又一轮的课堂教学改革也在进行着,传统的以教师为中心、知识传授为主要目标的教学模式正在转换为以学生为主体,以培养学生各项认知能力为主要目标的自主学习模式。近年来翻转课堂、慕课(MOOC)等的兴起,尤其是新冠肺炎疫情发生以来的线上教学模式的普及,极大地改变了整个社会对教育的认知与理解,学生已然成为课程学习的中心,而教师应及时转变传统的教学理念,有效使用不同媒体和信息技术进行教学设计和教学模式创新,激发学生的自主学习能力和思维能力。

二、体验式学习的概念与特征

(一)体验式学习的概念

关于体验式学习的讨论已经进行了上千年。经验主义者认为,对现实的认识必须从体验的情境当中获得。美国著名教育家约翰·杜威亦主张建立一种基于生活体验的教育模式,从经验中学习,之后进行反思性思维。当代最具影响力的体验式学习理论于20世纪80年代由美国组织行为学教授大卫·库伯提出,他认为体验式学习的基本特征是"作为一个学习过程,而不是结果;体验学习是以体验为基础的持续过程;体验学习是在辩证对立方式中解决冲突的过程;体验学习是一个适应世界的完整过程;体验学习是个体与环境不断的交互作用过程;体验学习是一个创造知识的过程。"在当代学者奥恩看来,体验式学习的意义在于将实践置于全新的情境之下,有意识地将自我与现实世界结合,不断地检查、测试和完善他们的知识。体验式学习模式可以有力地抵御机器人和人工智能带来的威胁(奥恩,2019:100 - 102)。

(二)体验式学习的特征

与传统的教学模式相比,体验式学习具有以下几个突出的特点:

1. 有开放的学习空间。体验式学习将课堂与真实世界紧密相连,让整个世界都成为潜在的学习空间。相关研究表明,灵活开放的学习空间可以提升学生的成绩,促进师生之间的互动,增强学生的学习体验,从而达到良好的学习效果。体验式学习包括专业实习、勤工俭学、合作项目等,其外延可以扩展到任何形式的课堂环境之外的学习。

2. 能进行个性化主题学习。体验式学习主要基于不同的项目和主题展开,学生对于不同项目和主题的参与方式与角度会呈现出个性化的特点。在体验的过程中,学生充分发挥主观能动性,成为真正的学习主体,并依据自身经验对所学知识进行创新性的拓展与应用,从而解决真实世界中的实际问题。

3. 设立多元化评价机制。体验式学习注重学习的过程,而不是结果的反思。因此评价的方式也更为多元,以形成性评价为主。学生对课堂知识掌握的程度只是评估的一个方面,教师应更为注重学生在实践中的参与程度、创新意识、领导力等,对体现出的批判性思维、系统性思维、创新性思维进行评价与反馈,从而提高学生的文化敏捷性,促进学生综合认知能力的发展。

三、英语专业教学中的体验式学习模式

体验式学习的理念虽然已经引起广泛讨论,并且在多个学科各个层次的教学中均付诸实践,但目前看来,体验式学习模式基本被看作是实训教学的一种形式,是从实践出发,再回到实践的一个过程,其研究与实践普遍认为适用于商科、工程等应用学科。在英语专业课程的学习中,针对语言技能的实训也有部分教师进行了体验式教学的尝试(周彦君,2016:19 - 20;余倩、祁雯,2017:214 - 215)。然而在目前的国内外形势下,单纯的语言技能培养显然已经远远不能满足社会对人才的要求。在我国传统英语专业的教学中,教学内容主要侧重于英语的实用技能,即听、说、读、写、译等方面的实践能力,而学生的人文素养、思辨能力等综合性能力则

一度被忽视。在此框架下，英语只是作为一种应用性的工具，其学科地位和专业的独立性均受到一定质疑。有专家指出，目前英语专业方面的课程设置过于集中于语言学和文学等与语言紧密相关的学科，这些课程并不能培养真正的复合型人才。英语专业应实现与其他学科如商务、法律、医学或工程等的交叉，"用功能语言学、语类理论和元话语理论去研究医学和工程等另一学科的理论内容和知识是如何用英语建构和传播的"（蔡基刚，2020），这样培养出的学生才是社会真正需要的复合型人才。然而这样设置的"英语＋医学""英语＋工程"等专业实际上分别是医学类专业和工程类专业，并非真正意义上的英语专业，英语专业作为人文学科的内核不应改变，作为英语专业学科基础的语言学、文学等课程仍应继续保留与发展，培养学生的人文素养、批判性思维、系统性思维、创业精神和文化敏捷性等能力，以抵御人工智能冲击。

英语教学与研究界经过深刻反思，认为英语专业在发展过程中最为根本的问题是对学生素质培养的忽视，英语专业的教学改革也应朝这个方向发展。2020年4月《普通高等学校本科英语专业教学指南》（以下（简称《指南》）正式颁布出版，其中明确提出针对英语专业本科生的能力要求为："本专业学生应具有良好的英语语言运用能力、英语文学赏析能力、英汉口笔译能力和跨文化能力；具有良好的思辨能力，终身学习能力、信息技术应用能力、创新创业能力和一定的研究能力；具有良好的汉语表达能力和一定的第二外语运用能力。"

可以看出，《指南》对思辨能力、创新创业能力和跨文化能力等方面的要求与前面提出的国际教育理念不谋而合，对于应对新形势下的人才培养目标具有一定的指导意义。而这些能力的培养均与社会实践有着密切的关系。体验式学习模式在应用于技能实训的基础上，亦可与培养批判性思维、系统性思维、创造性思维及文化敏捷性的目标相结合，增加学习空间的开放性和灵活性，将课堂所学知识充分应用于社会实践。

四、英语专业体验式学习的实施路径

由于以往的研究主要将体验式学习模式与应用型学科相结合，将实践作为学习的源泉与最终目的，因此对于体验式学习的实施路径，国内外相关研究通常依据的是大卫·库伯的学习过程四个阶段周期理论：第一阶段为具体经历阶段，学习者从实践开始，形成具体的体验；第二阶段为反思观察阶段，通过比较和评价对体验进行分析和反思；第三阶段为抽象概念化阶段，从感性认识上升到理性认识，建构起抽象的理论模型；第四阶段为主动实践阶段，测试抽象概念在新情景下的应用和意义。这四个阶段从实践开始,最终又回到实践,循环往复,学习不间断继续。对于实践性强的应用型学科,此理论尤为适用;对于作为人文学科的英语专业来说,课堂上的知识内容与相关技能是学习的基础,应作为学习的第一阶段,而体验与实践应结合内容与技能,实现在不同的情境中解决相关实际问题。

因此,英语专业课程的学习过程应遵循奥恩提出的体验式学习的三个顺序:首先,学习者应掌握学科的内容技能;其次,学习者应在实践中将内容结合到给定的环境中。这种情境通常是相似的,这种应用能力通常称为"近转移"。最后,学习者需要具备转移的能力,将所学的理论、概念或知识体系运用到差异较大的情境中,这种转移称为"远转移"。

(一)掌握内容与技能

在传统的英语专业教学中,听说读写技能、语言学相关知识与文学知识是核心内容,教材一直是知识讲解与技能训练的重要依据。在新形势下,教师应认识到教材内容的滞后性和局限性,积极地拓展教学内容,与时俱进。首先,对于课程中较为陈旧的文章与内容,应鼓励学生用发展的眼光来对待,向学生提供更新更全面的学习资料,并引导学生从新的视角创造性地理解主题内容。其次,教师应紧跟学科理论发展趋势,将最新的专业理论与思想带到教学中来。再次,在加强专业学科理论学习的同时,应针对批判性思维和创造性思维进行元理论讲解与指导,从思辨的基本特点和理论框架入手,结合教学内容,帮助学生掌握思考的规律与方法,系统训练学生的批判性思维能力,最终养成良好的思维习惯。

(二)实现近转移

"近转移"是指"学生将一个理论、概念或知识体系在一个新的,但大体上熟悉的情境下付诸实践"。这里的情境可以是抽象的虚拟情境,可以通过案例、情境模拟、角色扮演、小组讨论、辩论等形式进行深化学习。比如,在学习短篇小说《莳萝泡菜》(*A Dill Pickle*)的过程中,教师首先要帮助学生了解20世纪20年代西方的女性主义思想;然后让学生阅读同时期的另一篇小说,让他们对其中体现的女性主义思想进行挖掘和分析,也可对同时期不同国家的作品中体现的女性主义思想进行比较,或者对不同时期的女性主义思想作纵向的比较。在分析和比较的过程中,学生的批判性思维可以得到充分锻炼,而且文学作品中对文化背景的真实再现也可以帮助学生提升文化敏捷性。"情境"可以是具体的真实情境,可以采取社会调查、实地参观或者企业实习的形式"付诸实践"。比如,在媒体公司实习的学生可能需要用英语进行文案写作,学生需要用到课堂中学到的写作技能,并且根据公司的实际情况做出适应性调整,对内容和格式进行加工。在完成写作项目的过程中,学生需要对工作内容与环境进行综合评估,这样就锻炼了系统性思维的能力。

(三)实现远转移

远转移是指学生在差异很大的全新环境中,能够使用掌握的知识解决实际问题。一些教育家认为,远转移应该是教育的最终目标,而且远转移的能力在很大程度上取决于创造性思维的能力和思维灵活性,而这些能力正是机器人和人工智能所缺乏的,是提升学生在未来社会中的竞争力的重要保障。

英语专业本身便具有跨学科基础,如前所述,其培养目标是"复合型人才",而实际生活中,英语专业人才也在从事着各种千差万别的工作,具有较强的远转移能力无疑对事业发展起着至关重要的推动作用。远转移能力指学生将本专业所学的研究方法应用于全新情境的能力。对此,奥恩(2018)曾举例说明:他认识的一位英语专业的大学生为某云计算公司作财务分析,这位学生认为财务分析和文学分析非常相似:"当你读一首诗或一本小说时,你的教授会告诉你在文本之间寻找任何蛛丝马迹,并尽可能地挖掘出作者想说的一切。当你看着一个数字电子表格时,你在做同样的事情:这些数字试图告诉我什么?"除此之外,远转移也可以是不同技能的综合运用,比如使用新的技术方法对专业知识进行整合,进行创新研究,尤其是信息技术和人工智能技术的应用。"我们不仅可以开设以外语专业为主,信息技术或人工智能技术相关专业为辅的外语专业跨学科专业,而且可以将与大数据技术、信息技术或人工智能技术相关的课程融入现有外语专业课程体系之中,以培养学生的信息技术素养。"(胡开宝,2020:17)

结语

在目前的教育背景下,为了培养社会急需的创新型人才,在英语专业的教学中,新型的体验式学习模式可以与目前较为先进的慕课(MOOC)、翻转课堂、混合式教学模式等结合起来,通过在课堂中掌握内容与技能、在相关实践中实现近转移、继续拓展实践领域实现远转移等三个结构顺序,将内容与实践相结合,超越传统的语言技能训练模式,转而培养学生的批判性思维、系统性思维及创新型思维能力。

参考文献

[1] WORLD ECONOMIC FORUM. New Vision for Education: Unlocking the potential of Technology [EB/OL]. [2020-06-22]. http://widgets.weforum.org/nve-2015/.

[2] 普通高等学校本科英语专业教学委员会. 普通高等学校本科外国语言文学类专业教学指南[M]. 北京:外语教学与研究出版社,2020.

[3] 奥恩. 教育的未来:人工智能时代的教育变革[M]. 李海燕,王秦晖,译. 北京:机械工业出版社,2019

[4] 蔡基刚. 高校英语专业定位的挑战与颠覆:普通高等学校本科英语专业教学指南颁布思考[J/OL]. 东北师大学报(哲学社会科学版),https://kns.cnki.net/kcms/detail/22.1062.C.20200609.1713.002.html.2020-6-10

[5] 库伯. 体验学习:让体验成为学习和发展的源泉[M]. 王灿明,等译. 上海:华东师范大学出版社,2008

[6] 胡开宝. 新文科视域下外语学科的建设与发展:理念与路径[J]. 中国外语,2020,17(3):14-19

[7] 余倩,祁雯. 英语人文素质教学的体验式教学模式研究:以茶文化为切入点[J]. 福建茶叶,2017,39(1):214-215

[8] 周彦君. 阅读体验视角下外国文学教学研究[J]. 语文建设,2016(14):19-20

浅析机考对大学英语教学的反拨作用*

侯燕玫**

（首都经济贸易大学外国语学院　北京　100070）

摘　要：无纸化考试是现在高校大学英语课程的主要考试形式,本研究以反拨作用为理论基础,研究首都经济贸易大学英语机考,指出机考的优势,以及机考对大学英语教学产生的正、负反拨作用,为之后进一步量化研究提供了基础,也为英语教学改革提供了有效的建议。

关键词：机考；英语教学；反拨作用；教学改革

引言

基于计算机的语言测试（Computer–based Language Testing, CBLT），国内又称为机考或无纸化考试,是由计算机化调适性语言测试（Computerized Adaptive Language Testing, CALT）发展而来的（杨安良,2008:73）。21 世纪初,随着托福、雅思等国外大型外语考试开始在全球范围内进行机考,机考这一新兴考核形式在国内外语界也越来越得到重视（邓斯芮,周杰,2019:107）。2008 年我国开始进行四六级英语机考试点,随着信息技术和人工智能越来越普及,目前大多数院校已经在大学英语课程中广泛使用机考。

一、英语机考现状

从 2015 年至今,我校采用的是北京外研讯飞教育科技有限公司开发的"讯飞

---

* [基金项目]本研究是 2018 年度首都经济贸易大学教改立项项目——"大学英语机考对外语教学的反拨作用的实证研究"的部分成果。

** [作者简介]侯燕玫(1987—　)，女,北京人,首都经济贸易大学外国语学院中级工程师,硕士,研究方向为教育管理和语言测试研究。

AI考试系统",考试前由各教研室主任对各自年级学生定级、组卷、审核、归档,每场考试有考生约1 300人,考试结束后两三个工作日,可以由系统自动完成全部阅卷工作。每学年学校会统一组织大型考试5次,包括大一新生分级测试1次、大一年级期末考试2次、大二年级期末考试2次。

二、大学英语机考试题的设计原则

在基础题库之上,结合学校教学安排增加与大学英语综合教程和视听说教程相关试题内容,生成首都经济贸易大学校本题库。试题主要分为一、二、三、四和六级难度;题型与四级题型基本一致;题目选材广泛,包括人物传记、新闻报道、英美文化、日常知识、科普常识等。

三、英语机考与纸质考试的对比

结合考试实际情况,机考与纸质考试相比,有以下特点:一是绿色环保。机考可以节省大量纸张,有利于环境保护;取消了试卷印刷环节,减少了环境污染。二是组卷操作简单。试卷准备工作变得简单,只需要在题库之中抽取或者替换题目即可。三是试卷多样。依靠庞大的题库,可以根据题型需要随机抽题和组卷,因此能够产生多种组合的试卷集。四是全题型智能评阅。讯飞AI考试系统利用口语评测引擎及翻译、作文评阅引擎支持系统实现全题型智能评阅,教师可以选择不参与或者进行二次自适应调整,确保学生成绩公平、有效。五是数据安全。运用考生数据全生命周期保护技术,确保在整个考试流程中数据不可伪造、不可篡改。考试数据可以依据学校需求年限保存,不占用空间,不必担心储存方式。六是统计分析便捷。考试数据随考试结束完成收集,方便快捷。讯飞AI考试系统提供基础的数据分析功能,可为外语测试量化分析研究提供可靠数据。

四、英语机考对大学英语教学的反拨作用

反拨作用是指语言测试对语言教学与学习的影响,一般分为正面作用和负面作用(陈琳,2012:48)。测试过程和结果会影响教师的教学方式、教学内容和教学策略,会影响学生的学习动机、学习方式和学习态度,而这些又会反作用于测试的实施和测试结果。

(一)英语机考对大学英语教学有正反拨作用

英语机考在很多方面都产生了正反拨作用,主要体现在以下几方面:
1. 学习材料丰富。试题材料来源于国内外多种媒体资源,涉及访谈、新闻报

道、演讲、对话等。题材也是多种多样,包括科技、教育、社会、健康、经济、文化、时事等。这就要求教师和学生在课堂之外大量阅读和畅听相关资料,保持对前沿信息的敏感度。这让英语学习材料变得丰富,在英语学习的同时收获多方面的知识,对学生综合知识素质的培养起到推动作用。

2. 激发学习动机,提高学习兴趣。英语学习不应该是枯燥无味的单词和词汇背诵,应通过丰富的口笔试试题提升英语学习的乐趣,从而激发学习动机,提高英语学习的趣味感和成就感(宁静,张志杰,2013:51)。

3. 推动教学,提高教学质量。英语学习的目标不仅仅是应试,机考的实施只是想通过口笔试检验学生的学习效果以及教师的教学水平,尤其帮助教师发现教学不足之处,不断改进教学方法,提高教学质量。

4. 增强语言能力的培养。机考较纸质考试的优势之一就是提供口语解决方案,在听力、阅读、写作和翻译基础上增加对口语能力的考察,激发口语学习的积极性,提升口语交际能力,增强语言能力的培养。

(二)英语机考对大学英语教学有负反拨作用

任何事物都具有两面性,机考对大学英语教学的负反拨作用也很明显,主要体现在:

1. 设备要求高。由于考试过程中,尤其是听力部分对计算机和网络的依赖比较大,机考对硬件设备和网络环境要求比较高(黄立安,2013:234;宋宝梅等,2015:49)。在我校,最高并发量达到1 200人。这要求考试系统性能稳定,并发量高。考试过程中对计算机性能高要求的同时,鼠标、键盘、耳机等配件也要保证能百分之百正常使用。

2. 计算机操作熟练度要求高。目前,纸质考试为考试方式的主流。学生习惯于手写,而翻译和写作需要在短时间内敲击键盘进行输入,无疑给学生答卷增加了难度,要求学生在英语学习的同时,还要重视办公能力的提升,这也符合用人单位对学生的基本要求。

3. 教师存在感和责任感降低。由于使用口语评测引擎及翻译、作文评阅引擎支持系统,系统可以实现考试全题型的智能评阅,繁重的阅卷工作不再需要教师全程参与。这就有可能让教师从考评中脱离,从而忽略对学生答卷的分析和指导,造成教学和考评无法衔接。这就要求教师提升自己的责任感,重视机考结果的分析,发挥学、评、教三者之间的促进作用。

结语

著名语言学家戴维斯(Davies)曾经说过:"一种好的考试方式可以成为促进英

语有效教学的途径。"(陈明辉,黄峥峥,2013:144)英语机考对大学英语教学产生的正反拨作用远大于负反拨作用,通过英语机考对大学英语教学的反拨作用促进大学英语教学的改革,发挥教师引导优势的同时,提升学生的自主学习能力,建立良好的英语学习和评估环境,从而促进英语综合能力的提高。

参考文献

[1]杨安良,田少华.我国计算机化调适性语言测试(CALT)研究现状[J].外语界,2008(2):73,77,96.

[2]邓斯芮,周杰.我国英语无纸化考试研究综述[J].教育文化论坛,2019,11(3):106-111.

[3]陈琳.语言测试反拨作用研究述评[J].重庆电子工程职业学院学报,2012,21(5):48-51.

[4]宁静,张志杰.CET机考对大学英语教学的预期反拨作用探析[J].吉林省教育学院学报,2013(7):50-51.

[5]黄立安,赵彤,房冰.论大学英语机考利弊及其反拨作用[J].成功(教育),2013(22):234.

[6]宋宝梅,侯飞,孙善飞.四级机考对大学英语教学的反拨作用[J].林区教学,2015(11):48-49.

[7]陈明辉,黄峥峥.英语口语机考对教学的反拨作用:以海南师范大学为例[J].南昌教育学院学报,2013,28(4):143-144.

疫情期间高校线上教学的几点心得

徐丽群*

(首都经济贸易大学 北京 100070)

摘 要：突如其来的疫情打乱了高校正常的教学计划，各高校纷纷采取线上教学的方式，教学的时间和空间都发生了巨大变化，教学计划、教学内容、教学考核也发生了根本性变化，教师和学生都手忙脚乱。现疫情平稳，课堂教学已恢复正常，可以对线上教学效果做进一步思考与讨论：如何利用这个特殊的机会进行教学改革？如何让线上教学和课堂教学相辅相成？除教学外，在线讨论、线上讲座、线上科研会给我们带来什么样的契机？

关键词：线上教学；课堂教学；教学改革

引言

2020年一场突如其来的疫情，打乱了我们的生活秩序，教育界也受到了巨大的冲击。高校被迫延期开学，根据教育部"停课不停教，停课不停学"的指导思想，改变了传统的教学模式，采取线上教学的方式，利用微信、钉钉、腾讯会议等平台开展教学活动。教师仓促上阵，既不了解线上教学，也不懂网络资源平台，更不懂直播技术；学生也十分茫然。师生克服重重困难，线上教学终于启动。教师教学从原来的线下"心领神会"到现在的线上"单向灌输"；学生的学习场所从课堂转为各自的居住地，大家借助各种网络平台，开始了新学期的学习。这是一个与以往完全不同的学期。

一、教学模式改变

在传统的教学模式中，教师和学生在课堂上进行面对面的沟通，教师能够及

---

* [作者简介]徐丽群(1987—)，女，北京人，首都经济贸易大学外国语学院教师，硕士，研究方向为外语教学。

时了解学生的学习动态,能够及时为学生答疑解惑;同样,学生能及时提出疑问,并能及时和老师进行交流,和同学进行沟通,也可以随时进行课堂讨论、辩论,从而获得满意的答案。疫情来临,各校纷纷开展线上教学模式,而线上教学不再有知识传授的现场感和真实感,教师面对着电脑屏幕进行讲课,学生们"躲在屏幕后"进行学习,没有了课堂教学中的心领神会,也没有了和学生的眼神交流、心灵沟通,隔空交流也不大可能产生灵感。一时之间,教师难以适应,学生们也不能很快进入状态。

新的授课方式对于广大的教师是一个巨大的挑战。所有的教师都要重新梳理教学内容和教学计划,充分利用现有的资源和资料,网上的各类慕课课程、网络公开课、网络精品课的优势充分发挥。主流高校也开放了很多优质课程资源。远程授课方式各有不同。一些教师采取直播的方式进行教学,师生同时在线,上课的主要模式是教师讲,学生听,偶尔有学生提问。但授课时容易掉线,常常伴有杂音,教师对着屏幕讲课会略感枯燥。还有一些教师采取"学生自学 + 教师指导 + 师生互动"的方式进行教学,强调以学生自学为主,教师讲授为辅,让学生先行熟悉和掌握相关内容,完成相关阅读与写作任务,教师讲解并解答重点问题;若还有遗留问题,在恢复课堂教学后集中进行讲解和整理。尽管面临着非常大的困难,但在疫情严重时期,教学活动依然正常进行。教师积极努力教学,教学任务圆满完成;学生也表现积极。总之,教学效果还是比较好的。

二、教学内容改变

疫情期间,教学内容有了很大的变化,线上教学不是简单地把线下教学内容全盘搬到线上,或者将教学内容进行 PPT 录屏,而是重新整合教学内容,线上指导学生自主学习。如何将教师积累的教学资料与各类平台的网络资源更好地进行融合,这是教师面临的最大课题。不同学校、不同学科间有很大的不同,一些学校的语言文学专业教师考虑到人文学科的特点,不开设网课,而是鼓励学生在家阅读和写作,让学生利用宝贵的时间静下心来阅读和思考,多记一些读书笔记。这样自学学生也会有很大的收获。学生可以利用这段时间多看一些国外经典的著作和电影,既能练习听说读写能力,也能提高自身的文学素养。在学生自主学习的过程中,教师并没有缺位,而是随时指导学生并答疑解惑。

疫情平稳后,课堂教学恢复正常,线上教学用到的各种资料可以作为课堂教学的补充。教师在授课时以课堂教学为主,线上教学为辅,并各有侧重。线上教学为传统的课堂增加了很多背景知识、重点提示等内容,还有教师对该理论和知识的深层次地解读,这些对学生都大有裨益。学生既可以在课堂教学后获取线上深层次的资源,也可以在课堂教学前提前了解相关内容,带着疑问和想法去参加课堂学习,这样的方式使线上教学和课堂教学得到有效的互补。

就目前来看,优质线上资源的建设仍然不足,在资源开发上仍有较大提升空间,国家层次开发建设的课程数量还不够;国外的著名大学开放了一些公开的课程资源,我们应该积极地去借鉴。我们可以参考国外的优质资源,但不能直接照搬。只有与教学目标和内容密切相关,并与学习者的能力相匹配的课程资源,才能够有效地促进学习。面对学生个性化、多样化的学习需求,高校教师还需更加努力,不断优化课程,以达到最佳授课效果。

三、教学效果和教学评价方式改变

线上教学受到多方条件限制,想要达到理想的效果,还需多方努力。线上教学效果与学生的自学能力和自我约束能力密切相关,不同高校、不同层次的学生自主学习能力差异明显,在线上课堂教学中能够自我约束、自主学习的学生表现尚好,但是自我约束能力差的学生,在缺乏教师引导和管制的情况下学习效果差,甚至出现边游戏边听课的现象。与传统教学相比,线上教学容易使学生之间出现较大的分层。另外,由于教师和学生在空间上处于分离状态,所以存在部分学生代刷课的现象,一些学生并没有认真观看视频,在线讨论也存在着模仿和抄袭的问题。除网络直播课程外,大多数线上课程可以由学生自己安排时间学习,学生的上课的空间也自主决定,学习的时空错位,使学生无法产生真实感,不能很快进入学习状态,会有一种疲惫感。疫情过后教学秩序恢复正常,学生们欢呼雀跃返回校园,充分表达了对课堂教学的渴望。

线上教学还受制于网络通信条件,同一时间段的直播、点播或下载,会使网络出现拥堵或瘫痪现象,使师生交流迟缓,影响教学质量。

与传统的课堂教学不同,疫情期间的教学考核方式也发生了很大的变化,目前高校线上教学平台多数都带有对学生的评分功能,但是完整的评价机制还没有形成。多数教师采取的是平时成绩和期末作业评分相结合的方式来考核,教师根据课堂的需要自行设置各部分权重比例,最终形成学生的线上课程成绩。这就要求教师及时收集和准确地分析教学数据,对学生实现多维度的教学监测管理,通过掌握学生出勤率、预习完成度和师生互动指标等,了解学生的在线学习状态,为在线教学提供有效的监督。高校要利用信息化手段,探索推进基于学习过程的全程化考核方式,全方位、多维度反映学生的整体学习情况,帮助学生培养良好的学习习惯,最终提高学习效率。

四、其他教学方式改变

除教学外,基于网络平台的其他教学科研活动在疫情期间得到了极大的促进,在线讨论、线上讲座、科研会议等活动都通过线上方式开展,给学生提供了丰富的学习材料。小组讨论作为课堂教学的重要手段,逐渐成为许多大学课程的重要部分,其形式也已从线下转移到了线上,不仅打破了空间的限制,也为学生提供了充足的思考时间,克服了课堂讨论时间紧张的弊端,弥补了课堂教学的不足。

线上讲座不拘于地点,能够让更多的人参与其中,能够更加方便地听到各地名家乃至外国专家的讲座,也便于使用多样的方式,如截屏、录屏等准确、全面地记录信息。例如,山东大学外国语学院为庆祝建院90周年举行了高端论坛,采取的就是线上形式,三天时间组织了3个主论坛和6个分论坛,邀请了上百位知名专家,举办了103场主题讲座,给广大的外语工作者和学生带来了一次高端的外语教学体验。

结语

现在疫情仍没有结束,不论是管理者还是教育者都在对线上教学做更深入的思考,仓促上阵的线上教学也给我们带来了许多启发。无论是线上教学还是课堂教学,都有其不足之处,将二者有机融合,有利于提高教学效果与学习效率,是高校教学改革的目标与方向。教师应从课程授课计划、课程整体设计、教学方式方法、教学评价等多层次进行线上教学与课堂教学的对接和互补实践,促进二者的融合,真正将以学生为中心的教学理念落实到日常的教学实践和教学管理中。

参考文献

[1]郭英剑. 疫情防控时期的线上教学:问题、对策与反思[J]. 当代外语研究,2020(1).

[2]郭英剑. 当学生"隐入"屏幕,教学该怎样进行[J]. 中国科学报,2020(3):16.

[3]刘志伟. 高校线上教学存在困境与提升策略研究[J]. 新教育时代(教师版),2020(19)

[4] 房林. 浅谈高校"线上教学"的现状、问题及嵌入路径[J]. 市场研究,2018(12).
[5] 姜先亮. 疫情下线上教学与教研的路径优化[N]. 江苏教育报,2020-04-03.
[6] 郭英剑. 疫情期间如何保障线上教学质量[N]. 中国科学报,2020-03-24.

商务英语线上线下混合课建设与实践*

刘重霄**

(首都经济贸易大学　北京　100102)

摘　要：课程是人才培养的基本载体,是教学的核心环节。本研究以"商务英语"课程为对象,从课程建设历程、课程教学设计以及流程再造、课程内涵特征、考核体系、课程应用以及社会反馈等方面,分析了混合式课程建设内容及问题,为现代化数字课程建设提供参考。

关键词：线上线下混合课;实践分析

一、课程开发背景及发展历程

作为本校最早开发的线上线下混合课程之一,"商务英语"课程在公共外语教学改革和国际化人才培养中发挥了重要作用。课程发展经历了三个阶段:

(一)初创期

2013年,学校进行综合性教学改革,开发新时代数字化校本课程,创新教学模式,目标是建设一门具有较强实用性、学生就业即可应用的商务英语课程。

课程组认真进行课程策划,编写脚本,选择传媒公司,录制拍摄,经过3年不间断的努力,基本完成"大学财经英语"课程建设,于2016年在首都经济贸易大学试行,上线外国语学院网站课程平台,同时上线学校教务处精品课程网站即超星泛雅网络教学资源平台,总点击量达20 397人次,课程评分为5.0。

(二)拓展期

2017年,外国语学院与高等教育出版社签订合作协议,共建"数字化课程建设

---

* [基金项目]本研究为2020年首都经济贸易大学校级重点教改立项、项目"基于深度学习模式建构与应用的财经高校混合式大学英语'金课'建设研究"的阶段性研究成果。

** [作者简介]刘重霄(1971—　),男,河北人,首都经济贸易大学外国语学院教授,博士,硕士生导师,研究方向为英语教学、跨文化商务交际。

示范基地","大学财经英语"课程被高等教育出版社评为"优秀网络课程",于同年上线高教社 iSmart 智能学习平台。课程增加了更多国际视野和全球化视角内容,更名为"财经英语看世界"。

2018 年,学校与中国大学慕课(MOOC)合作,课程上线爱课程(icourse)平台,至 2020 年已经运行五期,学习者达 29 556 余人,课程评分为 4.6,反馈良好。

(三)升华期

2019 年,"财经英语看世界"课程开启小规模限制性在线课程(Small Private Online Course,SPOC)教学探索,努力打造线上+线下混合教学英语"金课"。同年出版有声视频教材。课程进一步拓展了内涵与外延,加入了中国商务文化元素,渗透了"金课"理念(吴岩,2018),同时扩大了授课覆盖面。

针对疫情期间"停课不停教,停课不停学"的倡导,课程于 2020 年初开启第五期教学,满足疫情期间网络学习需求,同时开启校内 SPOC 教学。作为全校为数不多的全英文慕课,"财经英语看世界"被推荐给教育部工商管理教指委,并上报到教育部;被北京高校大学英语教育发展中心推荐到教育部高教司文科处,供世界各地学校学习。

本课程最初为本科生自学选修课程,目前已纳入大学英语必修模块课程,并且作为提升研究生财经英语知识和国际商务交流能力的补充,被列为研究生选修课程。同时,本课程也是学校进行外语翻转课堂教学改革的试点课程。自 2013 年以来,学校以英语教学改革为抓手,进行了基于翻转课堂和慕课建设的教学改革,先后建设了"英语语音"等 7 门网络视频课程,服务全校学生的英语自主学习,学习者达 2 500 余人次/学期,为学习本课程在语言与文化层面奠定了先修基础。作为翻转课堂的主要学习与讨论内容,该课程在提升学生的全球思维、跨文化国际商务交际能力方面发挥了重要作用。

二、课程内容、教学设计及流程再造

(一)课程目标定位

本课程旨在通过创建优质的现代商务英语"金课",帮助学生融汇商务英语专业知识与相关理论,系统掌握国际商务领域的发展脉络,培养学生的英语语言技能与跨文化商务沟通能力,助力培养"具有国际视野、通晓国际规则、能够参与国际事务与竞争的素质型人才",为北京国际化都市建设提供人才资源。

(二)课程内容概述

课程内容紧紧把握社会发展和时代脉搏,既能提升学生的西方文化素养,也服务于学生未来的职业发展和学业规划,同时传播中华文明。作为财经类高校的一门全英文公共课,本课程将本校开发的"财经英语看世界"慕课(MOOC)作为线上学习内容,融入实体课堂教学,形成本课程完整的内容体系,包括企业建构概论、跨国公司、国际金融与投资、国际贸易、新兴产业、中西商务文化、跨文化交际等七大板块内容,具体为商业概论(Introduction to Business),跨国公司职业生涯(Working for a Multinational Corporation),国际贸易(International Trade),金融危机(Financial Crisis),金融衍生品(Derivatives),个人理财(Personal Finance),新业产业(Emerging Industries),银行学(Banking),人力资源管理(Human Resource Management),生产管理(Production Management),商务文化(Business Culture),跨文化沟通(Cross-cultural Communication)十二大部分。话题涉及经济形势分析、投资、中国商务文化、跨文化交际等,注重国际商务职场日常会话与常用知识的输入。课程内容强调经典性、前沿性、思想性和时代特征,注重动态更新。主要通过三个渠道,建设课程内容资源库:以国外经典教材《商业概论》(Introduction to Business)为实体课程的主体内容,保证课程内容的系统性和经典性;以本校建设的"财经英语看世界"MOOC、中国大学MOOC的国家精品课程资源为网络课程的主体内容,保证课程内容的前沿性与挑战度;以《中国日报》《经济学人》《时代周刊》等国内外影响力较大的经管类英文媒体报道及学术期刊文章为辅助内容,保证课程的时效性。

(三)课程教学设计与流程重塑

课程采用线上+线下混合教学模式,充分发挥实体课堂和网络慕课合二为一的互补优势;全方位利用现代化教育技术手段,实现师生线上线下双向交互和生生在线即时交互;营造全英文商务学习环境,提供经典学习资源,分析最新真实案例,进行项目化实践教学。通过实体课堂的知识获取、语言习得和专业技能培养,线上慕课的信息输入、自主学习和问题意识培育,实现对国际贸易实务、中西商务文化、新兴业态、跨文化交际等现代国际商务知识体系的理解、吸收与自我建构,并通过线上线下双向的系统化、辩证性评价及反馈,实现完整的授课模式重塑如图1所示,有效提升学生的国际商务交际能力及语言运用能力和综合人文素质。

鉴于兼具文化交流和商业实务的特点,本课程在教学过程中注重实践教学。首先,在教学设计上,落实实践教学理念,采用多样化的教学手段予以实施;其次,从考核评价机制上,实践教学占有一定比例的分值;最后,从软硬件设施及环境上,依托北京高等学校语言教学示范中心商务英语实验平台、模拟环境以及各种语言

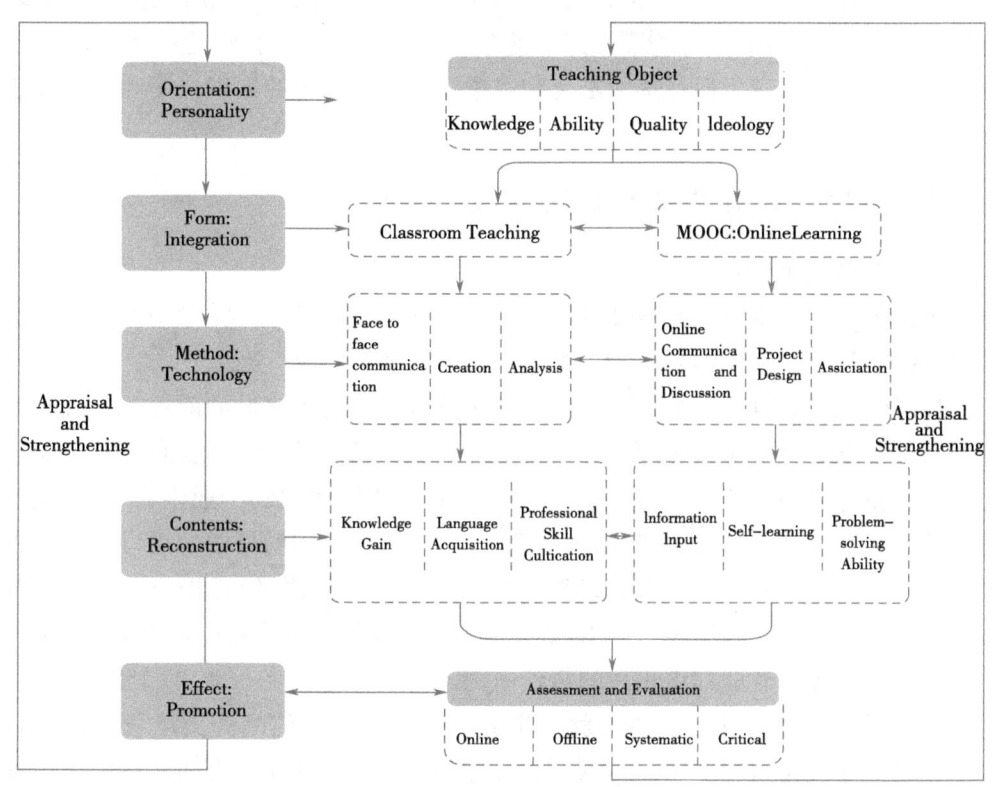

图 1 课程的教学设计与流程重塑结构

能力训练系统,提升学生跨文化商务交际能力。

1. 充分利用校友或校外导师等企业资源,开展校企联合教学。每学期邀请三个跨国公司(如联想)、独角兽企业(如阿里巴巴)等企业领导人走进课堂,以访谈形式讲授国际商务相关重要概念,分析企业发展和运转的真实情况,与学生进行直接对话和探讨,让学生对未来职业有全面的了解。

2. 采用"线上+线下"的SPOC教学模式,开展基于内容的案例式教学。每个教学单元均提供具体案例,要求学生做文献研究或社会调查,深刻体会课堂讲授问题的现实背景与解决策略;课堂以小组为教学单位,依据教学内容开展实时线上教学研讨与交流;学生每人每学期进行不少于1次的课堂展示,展示对问题的独特思考过程,并提供解决问题的创意性方案。

3. 搭建各种竞赛平台,进行能力提升的实训教学。每学期给学生提供参加"国际商务英语大赛""全国大学生英语竞赛""北京市英语演讲比赛"等不同维度、不同内容、不同层次竞赛的机会,将竞赛视为课程实践教学的构成部分,竞赛结果与课程考核挂钩,占有一定分数比例,意在鼓励学生参与。教师全程参与竞赛辅导,提供及时反馈,学生通过赛前准备和赛中实践提升自身的知识应用和语言表达能力。

三、课程内涵建构、考核体系及应用情况分析

(一)课程内涵建构

该课程是以学生、社会、教师的需求分析为基础,以建构主义(俞理明、郭鸿杰,2003)为指导,充分利用信息技术打造的一门现代商务英语"金课"。

1. 受众分析需求化。需求分析(管春林,2003)是课程建设的前提和基础。本课程目标受众为经贸类高校学生,既包括经贸类专业学生,也包括英语类专业学生。课程设计启动之前,对首都经济贸易大学的许多在校生和毕业生,以及其他财经类院校学生进行了需求调查,结果发现,大家对未来工作场景中常用口语有较大需求,如外企中的沟通交流用语、外贸交流口语和谈判用语、银行柜员英语等。教师根据学生需求及其外语表达能力、经贸专业知识水平,在授课过程中努力寻求外语表达能力和经贸专业知识讲授的最佳平衡。

2. 课程内容本土化。民族的就是世界的。区别于其他商务类课程以西方跨国公司和商业文化为主要内容,本课程在讲授西方商务的同时,更加注重中国传统商业文化、当代中国企业文化以及中国特色商业概念和术语的英语表达,如古代晋商文化的传承,当前中国跨国商业活动的开展等,让学生在学习国际商务的同时,掌握讲中国商业故事的本领和技巧,也为国际学生学习和了解中国商业打开了一扇窗。

3. 教学手段信息化。该课程利用信息技术,保证教学材料的真实性、知识获取与能力培养的交互性和学习效果检测的过程性的有效结合。

该课程力争教学手段丰富有趣,线上线下有机结合。线上授课团队进行牵引式研讨和定期答疑,线下实施翻转课程教学。突破传统授课形式,通过网络平台扩大授课范围,初步形成围绕课程内容的校际学生课题论坛与学习社区。通过网络观看视频进行预习、在线阅读文章现场消化、课后平台完成复习任务等,形成课前、课中、课后完整的体系化网络学习。课程上线 iSmart 平台,实现课程资源的社会共享。

4. 学习方式生活化。课程定性为具有实操性的应用型课程。线上课程突出以短视频呈现、学生自学的特点,在 10 分钟左右的时间内呈现 8 至 10 个知

识点,详略得当,相对独立,以教师讲授、实景演出、文化脱口秀、互动游戏等形式进行多样化呈现,激发学生的学习兴趣。课程强调专业、前沿和时效,紧扣社会需求;形式上将日常对话训练、独立长案例分析和讨论穿插交错,并通过信息技术实现学习内容的自我选择;邀请实业界人士到课堂现身说法,与师生直接对话。

(二)多元化课程考核体系

充分利用信息技术,采用"线上+线下"的考核方式,"主观题+客观题"的考核形式,重点考查慕课教学内容+实体课堂教学内容+实践教学内容,辅之以学科竞赛、国际化考试成绩的折合计算,具体表现形式为单元测试、平时表现、实践教学评价、期末考试及学科竞赛和国际化考试,形成最终成绩。考核强调学习的过程性。按照"金课"的要求,课程测试在内容上和形式上均有一定难度。

单元测试占30%,以标准性试题为主,旨在有效检测学生对课程内容(慕课+实体课堂)的学习情况,帮助学生了解课程要点及自身学习的薄弱点。

平时表现占20%,以主观题为主,主要考查学生在学习过程中参与讨论以及交流的情况。讨论题的设置,能够让学生深刻反思现实生活,并将所学知识与现实生活中的实例紧密联系,从而体现课程学习的实际价值,同时培养学生的系统思维和辩证看待问题的能力。

实践教学评价占10%,以学生提交的讨论记录和案例分析报告为考核材料,主要检查学生的实践参与、分析及解决问题的能力。

期末考试占40%,涉及客观题和主观题,全面检测学生对课程整体内容系统掌握和应用财经英语知识及技能的情况,促进学生进一步深刻了解国际金融和经济发展状况。

学科竞赛、国际化考试成绩按照比例折合计算,作为附加分数。

(三)课程应用情况分析

自实施线上课程和线上线下相结合的混合式课程以来,课程在超星泛雅平台运行4年,点击量达20 397人次;在中国大学MOOC开设五期,学习者达29 556余人。线下课程3门,5个学期,涉及工商管理、人力资源、新闻传播、国际汉语、商务英语、MBA等多个专业,面授学生335人。具体情况见表1和表2。

分析发现,线上课程作为整体课程的一部分,并未考虑到学生的个体性差异,而面授课程恰好弥补了这一缺陷。

表1 线上课程数据信息表

课程开设情况			
开设学期	起止时间	选课人数(人)	课程链接
1	2018-09-03—2018-11-02	6 416	http://www.icourse163.org/course/CUEB-1002986005?tid=1003177008
2	2018-11-12—2019-01-25	7 833	http://www.icourse163.org/course/CUEB-1002986005?tid=1003710006
3	2019-04-15—2019-06-20	5 788	http://www.icourse163.org/course/CUEB-1002986005?tid=1206199211
4	2019-09-23—2019-12-17	3414	http://www.icourse163.org/collegeAdmin/termManage/1206947232
5	2020-02-23—2020-07-20	6 105	https://www.icourse163.org/course/CUEB-1002986005

表2 线上课程数据信息表

数据项		第(2)学期	第(3)学期
授课视频	总数量(个)	50	50
	总时长(分钟)	401	401
非视频资源	数量(个)		0
课程公告	数量(次)		3
测验和作业	总次数(次)	20	20
	习题总数(道)	300	300
	参与人数(人)	107	95
互动交流情况	发帖总数(帖)	853	608
	教师发帖数(帖)	72	67
	参与互动人数(人)	95	84
考核(试)	次数(次)	0	1
	试题总数(题)	0	30
	参与人数(人)	0	24
	课程通过人数(人)	38	22

表 3　线下课程数据信息表

班级	学期	人数(人)	学时
大学英语(商务英语)	2017—2018(Ⅱ)	101	32
国际商务英语	2018—2019(Ⅰ)	20	32
MBA(商务英语)	2018—2019(Ⅱ)	42	32
大学英语(商务英语)	2019—2020(Ⅰ)	124	32
大学英语(商务英语)(SPOC)	2019—2020(Ⅰ)	48	32

四、社会性反馈及评价

在针对已修读本课程的本校学生所进行的后续调研中发现,受访学生表示本课程的对话设计较好地还原了现实生活中涉外业务的情景,其中的知识性内容对其了解职场业务知识有直接帮助。课程内容的制定契合了当前学生关注的热点,让学生在学习课程的同时,也对课程所涉及的某一领域的文化进行了更深层次的了解与掌握。

商务英语"金课"受到了多家用人机构的广泛认可。经过电话调查,中国银行、毕马威等企业对课程效果给予积极反馈,认为该课程提高了学生的财经类英语的应用水平,缩短了员工入职前的培训时间,降低了企业培训员工的成本,并表示更有意愿雇佣掌握财经英语的学生。

在"北京地区高校英语类专业联席会第五届年会""大学英语信息化教学论坛"等研讨会上,本课程也受到了多家学术机构和业界专家的高度认可,希望该课程在商务英语人才培养上发挥作用。

参考文献

[1]管春林. 试论需求分析在经贸英语专业课程设置中的意义和方法[J]. 外语与外语教学,2005(3):37-40.

[2]吴岩. 建设中国"金课"[J]. 中国大学教学,2018(12):5-9.

[3]俞理明、郭鸿杰. 因特网在外语学习中的应用:建构主义学习观[J]. 外语语言文学,2003(1):5-10.

Promoting Autonomy and Learning Effect of EFL Learners via Online Learning

Wang Hongyu

(Capital University of Economics and Business, Beijing 100070, China)

Abstract: Online learning programs and autonomy has increased substantially nowadays due to the shut down or close down of a great many of schools caused by the breakout of worldwide pandemic. Thanks to the advanced technology and diverse learning platforms provided by schools and educational organizations, students - centered pedagogy and autonomous learning is more emphasized than before. Although online learning platforms and services provide a large variety of rich learning resources for students to self - study, what learning effect will be produced or achieved compared to face - to - face learning in the classroom environment? It is really hard to evaluate the result of online learning. However, during the special time, like the breakout of coronavirus or the future time of emergency, large scale of online learning is a top concern for promoting autonomous learning and learning effect. How to improve autonomy and learning effect is the priority to be considered by teachers when it comes to distance learning. This paper aims to give some suggestions on how to make good use of online learning resources under the detailed guidance from the teachers to enhance autonomy and learning effect by means of online learning so as to promote students' lifelong learning competency.

Key words: EFL learners, online learning, autonomy, learning effect

1. Introduction

Traditionally, as is well - known that distance learning usually occurs to those who are inconvenient and inaccessible to schools due to working or far away from school or low tuition and so on. Nowadays, an urgent call for a worldwide scale of on - line teaching and learning is badly needed for Covid – 19 emergency. Whether technology and preparedness is possible, it is on the way. In China, as we look to the future, we recognize the imperative for developing on – line teaching to a higher level and maturity, especially higher education serving as the basis of students' future career. Compared to American higher education institutes, Chinese universities normally can't provide internal, systematic, and powerful online interactive platforms with powerful functions for teachers to post learning material, give announcements, assign homework, link library resources, email to all, etc. ; for students to submit assignments, present peer – feedback, check grades progress, evaluate teaching and so on. Especially, embedding system like Zoom meeting can be easily done in any school during an emergency. For example, University of Oregon adopts "Canvas" system for teachers to interact with students; Michigan State University is using "Angel" as an interactive platform. Therefore it is urgent for Chinese higher education institutes to innovate and establish stable, systematic, and powerful platforms for teachers and students to interact for shifting teaching pedagogy both online, offline and blended teaching easily.

Besides, It has been highly recognized that developing learner's autonomy based on online learning not only involves posting appropriate learning materials even a lot of learning materials in front of a student, but guidelines are very indispensible for helping the student develop the skills and state of mind leading to successful self – disciplined and self – regulated language study.

Moreover, the dramatic increase in online resources, network services, and educational software, together provide new opportunities for self – directed learning. In the last few years, developments in mobile technology and the explosion in social media use have accelerated the level of interest (Godwin – Jones, 2011). The areas of autonomy and technology in language education have a potentially very close but in practice often also uneasy relationship. In a narrow sense, technology is a tool that helps learners and educators to achieve certain educational goals. Autonomy can be one of those goals. (Hayo Reinders, 2011)

2. Learning Resources

It is well known that online learning material comes flooding to students with the advent of digital technology like smart phone, ipad, and notebook computers etc. The most influential site worldly is YouTube which provides a large amount of learning material for learners. In February of 2005, Steve Chen, Chad Hurley, and Jawed Karim founded YouTube with the domain name http://www.youtube.com. The site was created as a forum for people to create and share short video clips online. One year later Google purchased YouTube for $1.65 billion. How popular is YouTube now? Consider that on a daily basis there are more than two billion views (YouTube Facts & Figures). In addition, 51 percent of YouTube viewers go to YouTube weekly, and 52 percent of 18 to 34 year-olds often share videos with other people (YouTube Fact Sheet). (Joseph M. Terantino, 2011)

YouTube offers fast and fun access to language and culture-based videos and instruction from all over the globe. It provides an outlet for student and teacher-created videos, and most importantly, YouTube videos provide students with an opportunity to engage meaningfully in the target language. (Terantino, 2011).

Technology has revealed the extent and importance of the social networks learners engage in, and their effect on what and how people learn. As cited in Han's (2019), Mobile learning, including mobile-assisted language learning, focuses on using portable devices to facilitate learning (Ducate & Lomicka, 2013; Stockwell, 2016). Besides YouTube, other online social services such as Google, Baidu and all sorts of software serve as various learning platforms that students can consult in. What's more, many other channels in different countries and regions provide various online learning outlets, too. How to make good use of them will benefit students lifelong under enough guidance and learning strategies from the teachers.

To conclude, as Brown and Lee (2015) note that by "technologies" we refer not only to web-based tools like YouTube, Wikipedia, and Moodle, but also to independent software such as Rosetta Stone and Adobe Connect Pro. Furthermore, teachers need to be aware of the challenge of maintaining up-to-date information, knowledge, and resources available on the internet. Thus students effectively learn relevant, latest and meaningful material with strategies both individually and collaboratively online.

3. Student's Autonomy

Student's learning autonomy refers to self-disciplined and self-regulated learning with strategies effectively. However this automaticity needs training and fostering under the guidelines of the teacher systematically. Strategies for autonomous learning will be cultivated by both teacher and student gradually, which play a significant part in automaticity in order to guarantee successful learning.

As Godwin – Jones (2011) notes that language learning autonomy is more crucial for the student to develop effective strategies for promoting individual learning, while being willing and able to change and improve those strategies over time, as the language learning progresses. Moreover, Reinders (2011) states that the areas of autonomy and technology in language education have a potentially very close but in practice often also uneasy relationship. In a narrow sense, technology is a tool that helps learners and educators to achieve certain educational goals. Autonomy can be one of those goals. Student's learning autonomy is the crucial point to whether a student can be successful in learning finally.

Studies show that incorporating self – regulated learning (SRL) strategies into foreign language teaching encourages the development of autonomous learners. Quantitative analyses indicated that although participants reported moderate to low levels of SRL use, it is a significant predictor of foreign language achievement and had significant correlations with language achievement. The results are meant to draw attention to the importance of SRL research within the foreign language teaching field as well as foster SRL implementation in language instruction. (Seker, 2016)

To sum up, students' learning autonomy is one of the important goals of online learning. Self – discipline and self – regulation as well as self – learning strategies should be emphasized and enhanced by teachers little by little by means of detailed plan. According to Brow and Lee (2015), the principles of using technology include: promote active and collaborative learning activities using technology; provide scaffolding for successful task completion; keep paragraphs concise and use bulleted lists for online reading texts, especially on mobile devices; be aware of the challenge of maintaining up – to – date information, knowledge, and resources available on the internet.

4. Teaching Mode

Teaching mode online varies a lot from person to person. It can be streamline lectures in Zoom or Tencent with discussions and group work, or task - based project assigned by the teacher with appropriately designated reading material and PPT scripts and then submit homework in writing or video or other form as you prefer.

As cited by Malgorzata Kurek, Jan Dlugosz, Andreas Müller - Hartmann, Pädagogische Hochschule Heidelberg (2019), given the ongoing advances of various types of online and blended instruction based on participants' active engagement rather than on transmission pedagogy, it is becoming vital to equip future teachers with adequate competences (Brandl, 2017; Guichon, 2009; Guikema & Menke, 2014). Actually, the higher percentage of students who drop or fail online courses compared to face - to - face courses points to the lack of preparedness of many students in terms of time management, online skills, and effective learning strategies (Godwin - Jones, 2011). Therefore in order to guarantee student's automaticity and learning effect, appropriate learning resources, helpful guidelines from the teachers, along with enough preparedness from the students will surely result in the success of autonomy and learning effect via online learning.

Lan (2020) points out that different approaches are viewed as learner - centered activities, such as collaborative or cooperative learning, problem - based learning, discovery learning, project - based learning, and task - based learning. Teachers act not as knowledge providers but as learning facilitators in learner - centered activities (Bhattacharjee, 2015) by organizing activities that assist learners in developing new insights and to connect them with their previous learning. How to achieve the goals listed above is very challenging.

In addition, Yang(2011) notes that previous studies have emphasized the relationship between student's engagement and learning performance, and yet the context in which the student and teacher interact to engage each other has been ignored. In order to engage college students who are learning English as a foreign language (EFL) in the context of a big class, this study developed a system, which is an online situated language learning environment, to support the students, the teachers, and the teaching assistants (TAs) to communicate synchronously and asynchronously in and after class. In this study, the behavioral, emotional, and cognitive dimensions of students' intensive and reciprocal engagement were observed and recorded in the system for students to reflect on their language usage and further improve their language learning and for the teachers and the TAs to get experience.

What's more, O'Byrne and Pytash (2015) argue that hybrid or blended learning is defined as a pedagogical approach that includes a combination of face – to – face instruction with computer – mediated instruction. The terms blended learning, hybrid learning, and mixed – mode learning are used interchangeably in current research; however, in the United States, hybrid learning is used most often. Although hybrid learning can be diverse in how it is implemented, educators agree that this approach has the opportunity to provide personalized instruction with some element of student control over path, pace, time, and place. Educators and students need to be given the latitude to teach and learn in these hybrid spaces while being protected and supported by schools. Ultimately, teachers and students bear an equal responsibility as they collaboratively learn and experiment in these evolving spaces.

5. Learning Effect

Han (2019) states that a similar study was conducted by the same authors (Herronet al. , 2002) with intermediate – level French learners. By watching eight videos during the semester, intermediate learners also did significantly better on the post – test than the pre – test. Additionally, the intermediate post video – viewing free recall test showed that students learned significantly more cultural practices than products from the videos. These findings support using multimedia resources such as video and language classrooms to enhance the awareness and retention of both big – C and especially little – c knowledge. Most of the previous findings or pedagogical suggestions focus on the effectiveness of noticing and retaining information of practices and products from multimedia.

Lan (2020) concludes that virtual reality (VR) is not only attracting the attention of the information and computer technology (ICT) industry (Shirer & Torchia, 2017), especially in the production of consumer VR hardware, but also that of educators. Furthermore, mixing VR with physical environments allows the learners' spaces to be redesigned and expanded (Adams Becker et al. , 2018). The online Cambridge Dictionary defines VR as "a set of images and sounds, produced by a computer, that seem to represent a place or a situation that a person can take part in". Such an environment can be either authentic or imaginative. The research done by Lan (2020) shows the essential components of successful language learning could be satisfied by mediating the three specific characteristics of VR through learner-centered language activities and how to match the essential components of successful language learning to the specific characteristics.

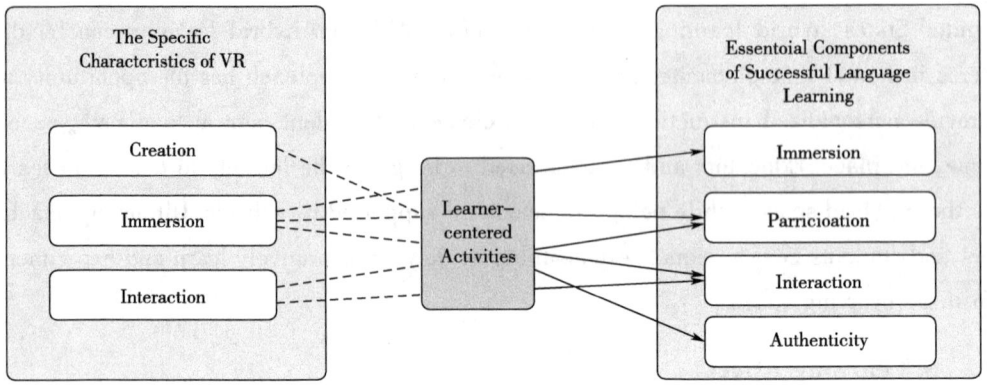

Figure 1. Leaner-centered Activities Diagram by Lan(2020)

6. Conclusion

To sum up, computer-aided language learning is highly valued nowadays, but developing learner's autonomy does not mean laying a hill of material before a student. The crucial point is to help the student develop the skills and mindset that can lead to successful self-directed language learning by means of constructing purposeful self-reflection, developing effective strategies as well as individual learning. Although most distance learning is delivered in the virtual environment, individual teacher plays a meaningful role in providing appropriate and up-to-date learning material and learning guidance in order to foster student time management, online skills and effective learning strategies. Moreover, autonomy does not mean being alone but a process of the teacher-student dynamic interaction, student's online collaboration, peer network and a powerful mechanism for deep language acquisition. What's more, a crucial part of that process is leading students to be self-reflective in their use of language in virtual environment. Obviously, learner autonomy ultimately should provide the ability to choose modes of learning of significance to the individual. Learner autonomy will look different in different cultures, so teachers need to adapt to local, regional and national contexts.

Reference

[1] HAYO R, CYNTHIA W. Learner Autonomy and New Learning Environments [OL] Special Issue Commentary, 2011, 15 (3): 1 - 3. http://IIt. msu. deu/issures/october - 2011.

[2] HICKEY T. The Role of Input and Interaction: Working Papers in Educational Linguistics [J]. Distance learning and Second Language Acquisition, 1991, 7(1): 39 - 49.

[3] JOSEPH M, TERANTION. Youtube For Foreign Languages: You Have To See This Video, Language Learning & Technology [J]. Emerging Technologies, 2011, 15 (1): 10 - 16.

[4] MALGORZATA K, JAN D, ANDREAS M H, et al. The Formative Role of Teaching Presence in Blended Virtual Exchange [J]. Language Learning & Technology, 2019, 23 (3): 5 -273.

[5] O'BYRNE, W. I. , PYTASH, et al. Hybrid and blended learning: Modifying Pedagogy across Path, Pace, Time, and Place [J]. Adolescent & Adult Literacy, 2015, 59 (2): 137.

[6] ROBERT G J. Emerging Technologies: Autonomous Language Learning [OL]. Language Learning & Technology, 2011, 15(3): 4 - 11.

[7] SEKER, M. The Use of Self - Regulation Strategies by Foreign Language Learners and Its Role in Language Achievement [J]. Language Teaching Research, 2016, 20(5): 600 - 618.

[8] YANG, Y. Engaging Students in An Online Situated Language Learning Environment [OL]. Computer Assisted Language Learning, 2011, 24(2): 181.

[9] YITING HAN. Exploring Multimedia, Mobile Learning, and Place - Based Learning in Linguacultural Education [J]. Language Teaching and Technology Forum, 2019, 23(3): 29 - 38.

[10] YU - JU LAN. Bringing virtual reality into FL learning, Language Learning & Technology [J]. Immersion, Interaction, and Experience - Oriented Learning, 2020, 24 (1): 1 - 15.

通过在线学习提高英语学习者的自主性和学习效果

王宏玉*

(首都经济贸易大学 北京 100070)

摘 要:目前,全球疫情的暴发导致很多学校关闭,推行在线学习计划和自主学习模式势在必行。得益于学校和教育机构提供的先进技术和多样化的学习平台,以学生为中心的教学方法和自主学习模式比以往任何时候都显得更加重要。尽管在线学习平台和服务为学生提供了多种丰富的学习资源,但与课堂环境中的面对面学习相比,是否会产生同样的学习效果呢?然而,在特殊时期,如疫情期间或未来的紧急时刻,大规模的在线学习不可避免。在线学习过程中,教师应优先考虑如何提高自主性和学习效果。本研究旨在通过教师的详细指导,就如何充分利用网络学习资源,提高英语学习者的自主性和学习效果提出建设性的意见,从而使学生在自主学习上终身受益。

关键词:英语学习者;在线学习;自主性;学习效果

---

* [作者简介]王宏玉(1966—),女,北京人,首都经济贸易大学外国语学院副教授,硕士,硕士生导师,研究方向为应用语言学、跨文化交际。

The Strategies of Improving College Students' intercultural communicative Competence

Yang Jing

(Capital University of Economics and Business, Beijing, 100102)

Abstract: With the trend of globalization, College English Curriculum Requirements (2007) proposes that students will be able to enhance their ability to use English in an all-round way and improve their cultural quality so as to meet the needs of China's social development and international exchanges; however it becomes more urgent to improve college students' intercultural communicative competence. By many years of teaching and the studies of all kinds of teaching experiments, the author has explored several strategies for college students to improve their intercultural communicative competence (ICC).

Key words: strategy; College student; intercultural communicator; ICC

1. Introduction

At a time when global markets, communication technologies, and transportation systems have vastly increased multicultural contact in our daily lives, it is essential that "we develop communication skills and abilities that are appropriate to a multicultural society and to life in a global village" (Samovar & Porter, 2000). Therefore, in a world of international interdependence, the ability to understand and communicate effectively with people from other cultures takes on extremely urgency. According to College English Curriculum Requirements (2007), the objective of College English is "to develop students' ability to use English in an all-round way, especially in listening and speaking, so that in their future work and social interactions they will be able to exchange information effectively through both spoken and written channels, and the same time they will be able to enhance their ability to study independently and improve their cultural quality so as to meet the needs of China's social development and international exchanges". Therefore, in the college English teaching, we need to explore more methods and strategies to improve students' Intercultural communicative competence (ICC).

2. The definition of ICC

Spitzberg suggests that intercultural communication competence is simply "behavior that is appropriate and effective in a given context" (Spitzberg, 2000: 375. Cited in Gudykunst, 2003: 199). Kim (1992) in utilizing a systems – theory approach to examine intercultural communication competence, defines this construct in terms of one's "adaptive capacity" comprised of cognitive ("sense – making"), affective (including emotional and aesthetic tendencies, motivational and attitudinal predispositions), and operational/behavioral (flexible and resourceful) dimensions. Chen and Starosta (1999) define intercultural communication competence as "the ability to effectively and appropriately execute communication behaviors that negotiate each other's cultural identity or identities in a culturally diverse environment." Wiseman (2001) suggests that intercultural communication competence is comprised of knowledge, skills, and motivation needed to interact effectively and appropriately with persons from different cultures. Samovar and Porter (2001) note that being a competent communicator means you have the ability to analyze the situation and select the appropriate mode of behavior.

3. Basic components of ICC

The term communicative competence has been further developed by researchers such as Canale and Swain (1980) and Canale (1983), Bachman (1990) and Celce – Murcia et al. (1995), who attempted to define the specific components of the construct of communicative competence. The widely cited model by Canale and Swain (1980), later expanded by Canale (1983), includes four competencies under the heading of communicative competence: grammatical competence (i. e. knowledge of the language code); sociolinguistic competence (i. e. knowledge of the sociocultural rules of use in a particular context); strategic competence (i. e. knowledge of how to use communication strategies to handle breakdowns in communication) and discourse competence (i. e. knowledge of achieving coherence and cohesion in a spoken or written text).

Spitzberg and Cupach (1984) isolate three components of ICC: knowledge, motivation, and skills, which indicate three levels of ICC: cognitive level, affective level, and behavioral level, and has been widely quoted and accepted so far. Motivation refers to our desire to communicate appropriately and effectively with others. Knowledge refers to our awareness or understanding of what need to be done in order to communicate appropriately and effectively. Skills refer to the actual performance of the behaviors felt to be effective and appropriate in the communication context. Knowledge is the base for intercultural communication. Skills transform knowledge and motivation into actual performance. Motivation, bridging the two components, functions throughout the process. Without motivation, no efforts would be made to learn about knowledge and get involved in real communication. Each of these components alone is insufficient to achieve intercultural communication competence.

Chen and Starosta (1999) outline three key components of intercultural communication competence: intercultural sensitivity (affective process), intercultural awareness (cognitive process), and intercultural adroitness (behavioral process), defined as verbal and nonverbal skills needed to act effectively in intercultural interactions. Intercultural sensitivity is the affective dimension of ICC that refers to the emotional desire of a person to acknowledge, appreciate, and accept cultural differences. Intercultural awareness is the cognitive dimension of ICC that refers to a person's ability to understand similarities and differences of others' cultures. Intercultural adroitness is the behavioral dimension of ICC that refers to an individual's ability to reach communication goals while interacting with people from other cultures.

Samovar, Porter and McDaniel (2007:314) suggested that a competent intercultural communicator should be one who is "(1) motivated, (2) have a fund of knowledge to draw upon, (3) possess requisite communication skills", and (4) are of good character. While most of the literature dealing with communication competency includes only three components (motivation, knowledge and skills), they (Samovar, Porter & McDaniel) believe that one more feature needs to be added to the profile of a competent communicator. That attribute is character. Their idea is that if you are not perceived by your communication partner as a person of good character your chances for success will be diminished. The single most important trait associated with people of character is their trustworthiness. Characteristics often associated with the trustworthy person are integrity, honor, altruism, sincerity, and goodwill (Samovar, Porter & McDaniel,2007:316).

4. Strategies of improving students' ICC

Through many years of teaching and the studies of all kinds of teaching experiments, the author deems that students need to improve their ICC by such following strategies: improving their communicative skills, enhancing their confidence, and improving their intercultural knowledge.

4.1 Communicative skills improvement

In order to improve students' ICC, they should enhance their communicative skills, so as to have the abilities to interact appropriately, effectively and satisfactorily in an intercultural communication. Students should improve the ability to be mindful, the ability to manage anxiety, the ability to employ empathy.

4.1.1 Ability to be mindful

In order to have an appropriate and effective interaction in nonverbal communication, students needed to be mindful. Mindfulness (Thich,1991) means paying attention to one's internal assumptions, cognitions and emotions, and at the same time, becoming attuned to the other's conflict assumptions, cognitions, and emotions (Ting-Toomey, 1999:267). When we are consciously aware of our communication behavior, we become mindful to some extent. Mindfulness involves "(1) creation of new categories;(2) openness to new information; and (3) awareness of more than one perspective" (Langer, 1989:62). Being mindful involves making more, not fewer, distinctions. When students are mindless, for example, they tend to use broad categories to predict others' behavior (e.g. their ethnicities, genders, or roles).

Ting-Toomey suggests that to be mindful of intercultural differences, we have to learn to see the unfamiliar behavior from a fresh context. On a general level, mindfulness demands creative thinking and living (Ting-Toomey,1999:268). For example, in an intercultural misunderstanding situation, when two individuals couldn't agree with each other, how can they solve the problem? They have to learn to help each other and solve the problem from a mutual-interest perspective and collaboratively learn to develop a creative, synergistic solution. Mindfulness can help us to arrive at the cognitive and affective "readiness" stage to interact with people who are different from ourselves (Ting-

Toomey,1999:269). It can help us to put our own ethnocentric motivations in check. It can prompt us to examine the motivational needs and bases from the other persons' frame of reference or standpoint. Mindfulness is the mediating step in linking knowledge with skillful practice. Ting – Toomey (1999) suggests that many communication skills are useful in enhancing intercultural communicative competence. There are four core communication skills that are worth using in a diverse range of intercultural situations. They are mindful observation, mindful listening, identity confirmation, and collaborative dialogue.

4.1.2 Ability to manage anxiety

When we interact with strangers, our ability to communicate effectively is based, at least in part, on our ability to manage our anxiety and uncertainty (Gudykunst,1995). If they could improve the ability of managing their anxiety, they would improve their communicative skills. There are three factors affecting students' anxiety and uncertainty. Firstly, when students interact with strangers, they feel uncertain or anxious, due to their personality characteristics, a particular anxiety – provoking stimulus and the persistent and multi – faceted nature of some anxieties. Secondly, when students met some people from other cultures, they might feel uncertain and anxious and didn't know how to start the communication, due to the fact that they couldn't predict strangers' behaviors and responses. Uncertainty reduction theory (Berger & Calabrese,1975) suggests that we are unlikely to experience uncertainty about communicating with another individual, especially when we are unable to predict or explain a stranger's behaviors. Uncertainty hinders the quantity and quality of communication. The less certain we are about another individual's behaviors, the more anxious we are. However, if students knew more intercultural knowledge, it might be better for them to reduce the anxiety. Gudykunst (2003:34) suggests our culture and linguistic knowledge of strangers' culture helps us predict their behavior. The more we understand and can speak the strangers' language and more knowledge we have of their culture, the more our uncertainty will be reduced. Thirdly, we Chinese came from high – UAI cultures. Hofstede creates an uncertainty avoidance index (UAI) to assess a culture's relative location along the uncertainty avoidance dimension. Hofstede summarizes the view of people in high uncertainty avoidance cultures as "what is difficult, is dangerous", and the credo of in low uncertainty avoidance cultures as "what is different, is curious." (Hofstede,1991:119)

4.1.3 Ability to employ empathy

Empathy, also called telepathic or intuition sensitivity (Gardner, 1962), refers to the ability to step into one's culturally different counterparts' mind to develop the same thoughts and emotions in interaction. Empathic persons have been found to be more concerned for others' feelings and reactions, more accurate in observing the internal states of their counterparts, and more able to show affect displays, active listening, and understanding in intercultural communication situation (Davis, 1983; Parks, 1994). In other words, the more empathic one is, the more intercultural sensitive one will be. Alternatively, those who lack empathy, and who therefore indicate little or no awareness of even the most obvious feelings and thoughts of others, will not be perceived as competent. Empathy does not mean "putting yourself in the shoes of another". It is both physically and psychologically impossible to do so. However, it is possible for people to be sufficiently interested and aware of others that they appear to be putting themselves in other's shoes. So the ability to empathy is the capacity to behave as if one understands the world as others do (Lustig & Koester, 2006:75).

Therefore, if students could interact with intercultural encounters effectively and appropriately, they needed to involve (1) carefully listening to their contact partners, (2) understanding contact partners' feelings, (3) being interesting in what contact partners say, (4) being sensitive to contact partners' needs, and (5) understanding contact partners points of view, (6) being attentive to contact partners' nonverbal behavior. In sum, if students could employ the empathy well, their communicative skills would improve rapidly.

4.2 Confidence Enhancement

When Students interact with foreigners, they lack of confidence. That might derive from anxiety and uncertainty, intercultural knowledge, communicative skills and good character. To enhance their confidence they need to be self – esteem, self – knowledge.

4.2.1 Self – esteem

One way to improve students' confidence is to enhance students' ability to be self – esteem. Self – esteem is one of the essential elements of intercultural sensibility. When students viewed themselves positively, they tended to feel confident and worthy, and then they might be more likely to interact with their contact partners, so with an optimistic outlook and confidence in interaction, students could not only establish a sense of self –

value and self-worth, but also more able to deal with the feeling of alienation, frustration, and stress caused by the ambiguous situation in the process of intercultural communication (Chen & Starosta, 1997). Self-esteem is an aspect of self-concept, which is assumed to mediate all behavioral choices. Thus, positive self-evaluation tends to motivate individuals to do well in dealing with others, including those who have different cultural backgrounds. This, in turn, will lead the person to develop a positive motivation and emotion to recognize and respect situational differences in intercultural encounters.

Self-esteem is the positive or negative feelings students have about themselves. The greater self-esteem they are, the better they can manage their anxiety about interacting with strangers. In order to maintain and enhance self-esteem, Rosenberg (1981) suggested that one way is when individuals have a low self-esteem, they may act in ways that increase it so that they feel better and more satisfied. Another way is for individuals to redefine situations, generating a new, more positive impression of themselves. Still another way to enhance self-esteem is through association with individuals that validate and confirm one's positive identity (Swann, 1990).

4.2.2 The importance of self-knowledge

Before the students got to know intercultural encounters' culture, they needed to know their personal attitude, prejudices, and opinions of some bias. By doing so, they could interact confidently with the people who came from other cultures. Suntzu, the Chinese martial philosopher, said about 2 000 years ago: know yourself; know your enemies; one hundred battles; one hundred victories. "Know yourself" is advice handed down from ancient philosophers in many cultures. To understand the other person you have to understand yourself. This isn't as easy as it may seem at first; most of what makes up a culture is absorbed unconsciously in the growing-up process of socialization. So the first step is to recognize the self-reference criterion that makes our understanding of another culture opaque; that is we tend to understand the unfamiliar in terms of what we already perceive as normal from our own point of view.

Know yourself is a crucial element in becoming a competent intercultural communicator. Know yourself means you need to know your culture, know your perceptions, know how to act out your perceptions and monitor yourself. Knowing your likes, dislikes, and degrees of personal ethnocentrism enables you to place them out in the open so you can detect the ways in which these attitudes influence communication (Samovar, Porter &

McDaniel,2003:338). We can know ourselves through self – monitor. The process of self – observation and self – analysis is often called "self – monitoring." Some of the advantages of self – monitoring are discovering the appropriate behaviors in each situation, having control of your emotional reactions, creating good impression, and modifying your behavior as you move from situation to situation (Samovar, Porter & McDaniel,2003: 340). It is essential for students to know themselves through self – observation and self – analysis, so that they can become more competent to interact with encounters and enhance their confidence.

4.3 Intercultural Knowledge Improvement

Some students lacked the knowledge of cultural differences, so they couldn't communicate smoothly with their partners. Such as the knowledge of non – verbal communication they need to learn more. They can learn the culture knowledge through lectures, mass media, magazines, newspapers, proverbs, jokes, folktales, legends, myths and art.

Students can also be exposed to large amounts of cultural facts through the Internet. They can read many e – books, e – magazines and e – newspaper through the Internet, because much culture knowledge that is not usually found in a textbook is presented in the newspaper and magazines, for instance, *China Daily*, *21st Century*, *New York Times*, *Washington Post*, *Studio Classroom and Crazy English*, etc. The teacher can ask students to compare some items in the foreign newspaper with its equivalent in Chinese newspapers. Some good cultural insights can readily be found in headlines, advertisement, editorials, sport pages, comics, even in the weather report. The teacher can also introduce some films filled with intercultural stories, and then ask students to find out anything special and anything different from their own culture. In addition, it is necessary for students to have more interpersonal contact with students from other countries. Through interaction and observation they can acquire more specific knowledge about other cultures. In sum, acquiring cultural knowledge is a good first step when they are preparing themselves to enter into any new culture. By having good command of more culture knowledge students can communicate more smoothly with foreigners, thus, their intercultural competence can be further enhanced.

5. Conclusion

With the increasing tendency of globalization, it is getting more important to improve students' intercultural communicative competence. In order to achieve this objective, the author found out that students' ICC has much room to be improved. College students still need to improve their intercultural communicative skills by being mindful and managing anxiety; need to build up their intercultural communicative confidence by self – esteem, and self – knowledge; need to enhance the culture knowledge. Furthermore, they can be an efficient intercultural communicator like Ting – Toomey (2007) suggests that in viewing things through different lenses, we may ultimately perceive our own routine cultural practices with fresh insights. To become mindful intercultural communicators, we have to develop fresh visions, new ways of listening to others, and a soulful alertness.

References

[1] BENNETT J M, BENNETT M J. (2004). Developing intercultural sensitivity: An integrative approach to global and domestic diversity [C]. In D. Landis, J. M. Bennett, & M. J. Bennett, (Eds.), Handbook of intercultural training (3rd ed.). Thousand Oaks, CA: Sage.

[2] BRISLIN R W, and CUSHNER, K., et al. (1986). Intercultural Interactions: A Practical Guide [C]. Beverly Hills, London: Sage Publications.

[3] CHEN G. M., STAROSTA W. J. (1996). Intercultural communication competence: A synthesis [C]. In B. R. Burleson (Ed.), Communication Yearbook.

[4] CHEN G. M., STAROSTA W J. (1997). A review of the concept of intercultural sensitivity [J]. Human Communication.

[5] CHEN G. M., STAROSTA W J. (1998). Foundations of intercultural communication [D]. Boston, MA: Allyn & Bacon.

[6] COHEN R. (1991). Negotiating Across Cultures: Communication Obstacles in International Diplomacy [M]. Washington, D. C.: U. S. Institute of Peace.

[7] GUDYKUNST W. B., KIM Y. Y. (2003). Communicating with Strangers: An Approach to Intercultural Communication [M] (4th ed.). New York: McGraw – Hill, Inc.

[8] GUDYKUNST W. B. (ed.) (2003). Cross – Cultural and Intercultural Communication [M]. Sage Publications, Inc.

[9] HORWITZ E. K. (2001). Language Anxiety and Achievement [J]. Annual Review of Applied Linguistics, Vol. 21.

[10] KIM Y. Y. (1991). Intercultural Communication Competence. In Ting – Toomey,S. and Samovar L A,Porter R E,McDaniel E R. Communication Between Cultures[M]. 6th ed. Beijing:Peking University Press,2007.

[11]TING – TOOMEY S. 1999. Communicating Across Cultures[M]. New York:The Guilford Press,1999.

[12]窦卫霖. 跨文化交际基础[M]. 北京:对外经济贸易大学出版社,2007.

[13]贾玉新. 跨文化交际学[M]. 上海:上海外语教学出版社,1997.

[14]姚君伟,张向阳,张伊娜. 跨文化语境下的文化教学[M]. 徐州:中国矿业大学出版社,2002.

[15]张红玲. 跨文化外语教学[M]. 上海:上海外语教育出版社,2007.

提高大学生跨文化交际能力的策略

杨 静[*]

(首都经济贸易大学,北京,100022)

摘 要:随着全球化趋势的发展,《大学英语课程教学要求》(2007)提出"提高大学生的综合文化素养,以适应我国社会发展和国际交流的需要"。因此,提高大学生的跨文化交际能力变得更加紧迫。笔者通过多年的教学和教学实验的研究,探索出了一些提高大学生跨文化交际能力的策略。

关键词:策略;大学生;跨文化交际者;跨文化交际能力

---

[*] [作者简介]杨静(1974—),女,河北人,首都经济贸易大学外国语学院教师,研究方向为大学英语教学、跨文化交流。

对[自然]与 NATURE 的认知语言学探析

贾冬梅*

(首都经济贸易大学 北京 100070)

摘 要:[自然]的语义网络从原型意义[天然]出发,在概念借代[自然代自然界],概念隐喻[自然的关系是因果关系]以及[自然的状态是不受人力干预的状态]作用下拓展。NATURE 的语义网络从原型意义[力]出发,在概念借代[自然力代自然界],概念隐喻[事物的本质是 NATURE]以及[类型是 NATURE]的作用下拓展而成。[自然]与 NATURE 都可以指自然界,差异在于[自然]激活认知模式[状态],NATURE 与状态无关;[自然]强调来自人的物理力量和心理力量均为零,NATURE 强调力触发万事万物。基本层次认知模式为语言使用者理解词汇概念提供最基础的知识框架。

关键词:自然;NATURE;认知模式;语义网络;概念隐喻

引言

[自然]是中国传统哲学思想的重要概念之一,承载着中国人对自身、外部世界以及两者之间的关系的认知。无独有偶,英语中的概念 NATURE 也具有丰富的哲学内涵。本研究在认知语言学理论框架下对[自然]与 NATURE 的现代语义网络进行对比研究,尝试解答以下三个问题:

第一,现代汉语中的[自然]和现代英语中的 NATURE 各自遵循怎样的语义拓展路径,形成怎样的语义网络?

第二,[自然]和 NATURE 的语义网络有何异同,反映出现代汉语使用者与现代英语使用者对自然的认知有何异同?

第三:认知语义学的词汇概念与认知模式理论(Theory of Lexical Concepts and Cognitive Models,LCCM)(Evans,2009,2010,2013,2015)可以怎样改进?

---

* [作者简介]贾冬梅(1971—),女,首都经济贸易大学外国语学院教师,副教授,研究方向为英语教学、普通语言学、认知语言学。

在本研究中,[自然]和 NATURE 表示二者为概念和认知模式,"自然"和"nature"表示二者为词语。

一、文献综述

笔者以"nature"为主题词检索 EBSCOHost 数据库中 1998—2020 年对这一主题的英文研究,发现在这段时间内的相关研究主要涉及教育、自然保护、哲学、农业、伦理学和文学等领域,没有以 nature 为对象的语言学研究。

笔者以"自然"为关键词在"中国知网"检索国内学者 1998—2020 年所做研究,结果显示国内学者所做相关研究涉及语言文字、哲学、美学、文学、宗教、中医、生物、建筑及环境等 40 多个学科,其中外国语言文字研究有 38 项,中国语言文字研究有 35 项。在这 73 项研究中,有的就某部文学作品分析其作者的自然观,有的分析中外某一哲学思想中的"自然",而对"自然"所做的语言学研究屈指可数。其中,王敏(2006)从语义、语用及句法角度对比"自然"和"当然",认为"自然"的"自由发展、不经人力干预"用法为副词,不是连词和形容词,"自然"和"当然"的句法衔接功能基本一致,都含有"肯定、必然性"语气,但"自然"更强调动作与结果的顺承关系。龙娟(2006)认为可以用认知语义学的隐喻观来阐述自然与女性的关系,二者间的隐喻关系反映出人类对自然的统治与男性对女性的统治如出一辙。刘金波(2011)认为"自然"起初是短语结构,东汉时词汇化为形容词并开始语法化,六朝时虚化为状态副词,清朝时出现语气副词用法,在现代汉语里成为连词,这一语法化过程由语法位置的需要和语用推理促成。符蓉和胡东平(2014)从翻译角度对《道德经》中五次出现的"自然"一词进行研究,发现"自然"一般被处理为名词、形容词或者副词,被翻译为"the Self-so""Nature""which is naturally so"或"which is natural"。符蓉和胡东平(2014)认为这些翻译比较忠实地译出了老子的自然概念。叶树勋(2020)通过对"自"和"然"分别做语文探讨,对"自然"这个词的形成和意义演化进行分析,希望通过语文分析加深对这个概念的哲学认识。叶树勋认为,"自然"首先是形容词,基本义是表示事物由其本性而自发活动的状况,指向活动主体的本原性和自发性,其他义项与此义项有关联。

在前述研究中,王敏(2006)和刘金波(2011)只关注"自然"的语法功能。龙娟(2006)虽然采用认知语言学视角,但未对自然和女性之间的隐喻关系做明确的阐释。符蓉和胡东平(2014)提出在汉语典籍英译过程中应注意忠实伦理,但未对"自然"和"Nature"的异同进行剖析以说明译文的忠实度会对读者认知这两个概念产生怎样的影响。而叶树勋(2020)虽然提及"自然"的基本义是其他义项的基础,但是没有把将义项关联起来的因素纳入考虑。本研究对语料进行认知语义学分析,试图呈现现代汉语中的[自然]和现代英语中的 NATURE 的语义网络,并对它们背后的认知机制进行对比。

二、理论框架

本研究在认知语言学辐射型范畴理论(radial categories)(Lakoff,1987;Brugman & Lakoff,1988;Evans & Green,2006)和词汇概念与认知模式理论框架下进行。

认知语言学认为,每个词语都代表着一个概念范畴,是进入这个范畴的"门",拉开这扇"门",我们可以看到范畴成员就是词语的各个义项,这些义项既相互区别又互相关联,表现出原型效应,形成有系统的辐射型结构,这类范畴因此被称为辐射型范畴(Lakoff,1987;Brugman & Lakoff,1988)。辐射型范畴也是语义网络的表征,具有规约性,长期存在于语言使用者的语义记忆中(Evans,2006:332)。语义网络的拓展由概念隐喻和意象图式转换等认知机制驱动(Lakoff,1987;Brugman & Lakoff,1988),其间认知模式的作用同样不容小觑(Evans,2009,2010,2013,2015)。

认知模式是有条理的多模态知识体系,这套体系植根于人类大脑的模态与感知系统中,起源于由大脑处理过的各种体验,包括感觉—运动体验、本体体验和主观体验等(Evans,2015)。在使用语言的过程中,当一系列认知模式被一个词汇概念重新激活时,意义的建构随即开始;也就是说,意义建构既包括语言表征,也包括存在于概念系统中的非语言表征,两者在建构意义的过程中功能不同,缺一不可。作为语言表征的词汇概念为知识提供编码,作为概念表征的认知模式是模拟知识(analogue knowledge)的集合,词汇概念是通往认知模式的思维通道。例如:

1. a. <u>France</u> is a country of outstanding natural beauty.
   法国是个自然环境极其优美的国家。
   b. <u>France</u> is one of the leading nations in the European Union.
   法国是欧盟的主要国家之一。
   c. <u>France</u> beat New Zealand in the 2007 Rugby world cup.
   法国队在2007年橄榄球世界杯上击败了新西兰队。
   d. <u>France</u> voted against the EU constitution in the 2005 referendum.
   (Evans,2015)
   在2005年的公投中,法国投票人投票反对欧盟宪法。

在 1a 和 1b 中"France"都取其字面意义"法国",在 1c 和 1d 中为引申意义,分别是"法国队"和"法国选民"。这类多义现象产生的原因是在词汇概念 FRANCE 所关联的认知模式集内,非语言知识结构的不同部分在言语活动中被激活(Evans,2015),如图 1 所示。

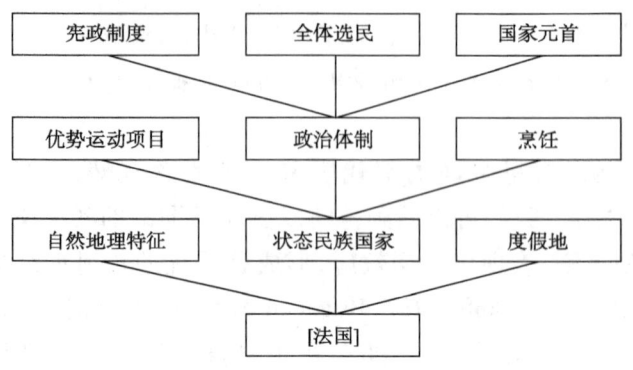

图 1　FRANCE 激活的部分认知模式

据伊文思(Evans,2015)的研究,[FRANCE]在 1a 中激活认知模式集内与本国自然地理特征相关的部分,在 1b 中激活与法国作为一个民族国家相关的部分,在 1c 中激活与国家级优势体育项目相关的部分,在 1d 中激活国家的政治体制中与公民的政治权利相关的部分——选民。在这个认知模式集中,[自然地理特征]和[民族国家]等是基本认知模式(primary cognitive model);[优势运动项目]和[政治体制]等是[民族国家]的二级认知模式(secondary cognitive model);[政治体制]同时又是[宪政制度]和[选民]等的基本认知模式,反过来[宪政制度]和[选民]等是[政治体制]的二级认知模式。在这一体系中,语言使用者对词汇概念与基本认知模式的关联的解读是字面的,对词汇概念与二级认知模式的关联的解读通常是比喻的(figurative)。换言之,词汇概念和认知模式理论认为概念借代映射和概念隐喻映射通常发生在词汇概念与二级认知模式的关联上。概念隐喻能够提供一条稳定的链接,使一个认知模式的概念内容的某些方面得以输入到另一个认知模式内,并成为其永久性知识表征的一部分(Evans,2009)。

2. Christmas is approaching (us).

圣诞节即将到来。

伊文思(2009)指出,在例 2 中 CHRISTMAS 和 APPROACH 为一系列认知模式提供了思维通道如图 2、图 3 所示。

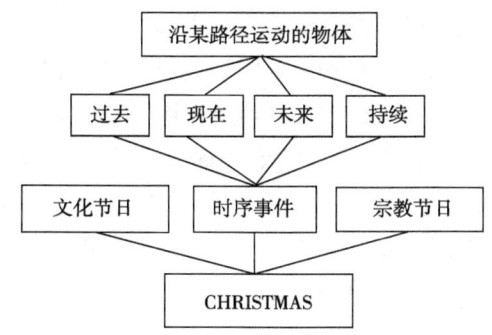

图 2 CHRISTMAS 激活的部分认知模式

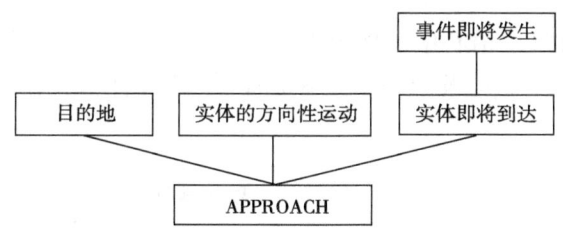

图 3 APPROACH 激活的部分认知模式

图 2 中,CHRISTMAS 为[文化节日]、[宗教节日]和[时序事件]等基本认知模式提供了思维通道,从[时序事件]又延伸出[过去]、[现在]、[未来]和[持续]等二级认知模式,这些二级认知模式同时又是[沿某路径运动的物体]的基本认知模式。CHRISTMAS 与[沿某路径运动的物体]之间的关联为隐喻关联,用虚线表示。在图 3 中,APPROACH 为[目的地]、[实体的方向性运动]和[实体即将到达]等基本认知模式提供了思维通道,[实体即将到达]为二级认知模式[事件即将发生]提供思维通道。将这两套认知模式体系整合在一起,概念隐喻[时间是(沿一条路径)运动的物体](TIME IS OBJECTS IN MOTION (ALONG A PATH))(cf. lakoff,1993)一目了然。

三、研究方法

本研究的汉语语料取自北京大学中国语言学研究中心语料库(CCL)现代汉语部分,英语语料取自英国国家语料库(BNC)。CCL 语料库中含有"自然"的现代汉语例句共计 85 496 条;BNC 中含有"nature"的语料共计 17 276 条。本研究从中各随机提取 1 000 条1 作为最终样本进行定性和定量分析。

本研究参考格鲁普(Group,2007)的隐喻识别程序(metaphor identification procedure)和查特瑞斯-布莱克(Charteris - Black,2014)的批评隐喻分析法(critical metaphor analysis)分析语料。语料分析的第一步是借助《汉语大词典》和OED完整地了解"自然"和"nature"的意义,第二步是确定"自然"和"nature"在例句所设置的语境中的意义,第三步是比较"自然"和"nature"的语境意义与其本源意义。如果语境意义与本源意义属于同一认知模式,但二者间存在整体—部分关系或者部分—部分关系,那么这个语境意义是借代意义;如果语境意义与本源意义不属于同一个认知模式,那么这个意义就是隐喻的。

四、研究发现

(一)[自然]

[自然]在现代汉语语料中表现出五种意思:"天然""自然界""当然""不经人力干预而自由发展""不勉强,不拘束,不呆板"。这五种含义在语料样本中的频率和所占比例见表1。

表1 [自然]的义项及其频率

义项	频率	比例(%)
天然	358	35.8
自然界	273	27.3
当然	255	25.5
不经人力干预而自由发展	60	6.0
不勉强,不拘束,不呆板	54	5.4%

语料反映出在现代汉语中"自然"作"天然"解时可做形容词或副词,指某种现象本来如此,完全没有掺入人为因素。例如:

3. 那么桃花峪则有它独具天趣的自然美。
4. 人与自然界应该是朋友。
5. 近年,日本成衣市场倾向自然化,以天然材料如棉、麻等制成的成衣特别受欢迎。
6. 洪水曾冲垮当时阿尔泰山脉西伯利亚一段湖泊和河流沿岸由冰块自然形成的堤坝。

"自然"在例3至例6中是形容词。例3中的"自然美"指天然的、不经人工雕琢的美;例4中的"自然界"指不依赖人的意识的客观存在;例5中的"自然化"指去除人工因素的趋势;在例6中,"自然"是副词,指现象的形成是非人力的。

"自然"在现代汉语中可以作名词,指自然界,与人类社会相对。

7. 这种哲学把人文科学和自然科学都放在恰当的位置上。

8. 提倡"顺应自然,保护自然,与大自然为友"已越来越成为全人类的共识。

例 7 中的"自然科学"以自然界的各种存在为研究对象,是关于自然界的科学。在例 8 中,"自然"和"大自然"都指人所依赖的外部世界。

语料显示"自然"在现代汉语中有"当然"之意,可做副词或形容词,表示对某一现象的确认或者推断。

9. 碰到这样一个大喜事,他们自然是乐开了花。

10. 他委婉地说出觉民的心事(自然他不会说到觉民和琴的事情上面去)……

11. 城市空间区位结构和社会结构的形成是竞争和选择的自然结果。

12. 她向他隐瞒自己的身份及历史近二十年,他有怨恨也很自然。

13. 生活自然不很容易,她却应付过去了。

"自然"在例 9 和例 10 中是副词,在例 11 和例 12 中是形容词。"自然"在这四个例句中都蕴含着因果关系,原因可以是显现的(如例 9、例 11 和例 12),也可以是隐含的(如例 10),引发的结果可预测、可理解。在例 13 中,"自然"一方面隐含着因果关系,即出于某种众所周知的原因生活不容易,一方面构成转折,表示尽管存在这种问题,但是结果还不错。

"自然"在语料中还表现出"不经人力干预而自由发展"之意,可做副词或形容词。

14. 你所顾虑的问题也会自然而然地解决。

15. 在"家庭中的自然劳动分工"问题上,……

在例 14 中,"自然"是副词,指听由某个事件自由发展,不需采取人为措施。在例 15 中,"自然"是形容词,指某种现象是自发形成的,非人力刻意而为。与作"天然"义解时不同,"自然"此类用法所指的事件或现象都与人的活动相关。

在语料中"自然"也有"不勉强、不拘束、不呆板"的意思,做形容词、副词或者名词。

16. 节目朴素自然、紧贴现实的风格内容,获得了评委们的普遍认同。

17. 王安忆自然而真诚地一一作答。

18. ……从而自然地导出了科学社会学的方法论。

19. 生活中我所遇的纯真与自然太少了。

在例 16 中是形容词,指节目不矫揉造作。在例 17 和例 18 中"自然"都是副词,分别指人的行为举止不勉强不拘束不呆板、导出方法论的过程和手段不牵强。"自然"在例19中是名词,指不做作的人或者事。本研究认为例16至例19所描述的自然的状态是由没有受到外力影响所致,而外力可能来自自己,也可能来自他人。

基于上述分析,[自然]在现代汉语使用者的思维中能够为一系列认知模式提供思维通道,如图4所示。

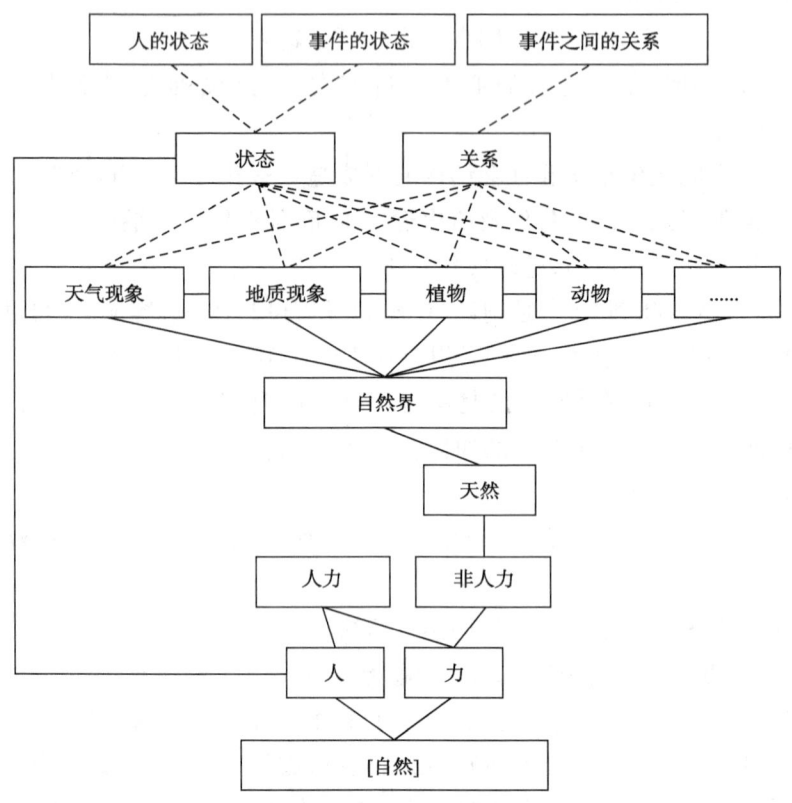

图4 [自然]激活的部分认知模式

[自然]在现代汉语使用者的思维中首先激活基本认知模式[人]与[力],继而激活[力]的二级认知模式[人力]与[非人力],其中[非人力]构成认知模式[天然]的基础,而[天然]是[自然界]的基本认知模式。[自然界]的二级认知模式[植物]、[动物]、[天气现象]以及[地质现象]等相互关联,为认知模式[状态]和[关系]提供思维通道。人与其他存在和现象的状态以及这些存在和现象之间的关系都随之与词汇概念[自然]关联在一起。

根据以上分析,本研究认为,[自然]在现代汉语里的原型意义为[天然]。[自然]的语义网络如图5所示。

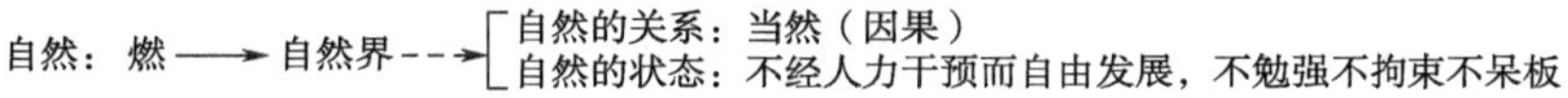

自然：燃 ——→ 自然界 --→ [自然的关系：当然（因果）
　　　　　　　　　　　　　　自然的状态：不经人力干预而自由发展,不勉强不拘束不呆板

图5　[自然]在现代汉语中的语义网络

图5中从原型到[自然界]的拓展是借代关联,即概念借代[自然代自然界],其背后是借代关系[范畴特征代范畴](Radden & Kövecses,1999),用实线箭头标识。从原型到[自然的关系]和[自然的状态]之间的拓展是基于概念借代的概念隐喻拓展,可表述为概念隐喻[自然的关系是因果关系]以及[自然的状态是不受人力干预的状态],图中用虚线箭头标识。

（二）NATURE

NATURE在本研究使用的英语语料中表现出六种意思:"事物的性质、本质""自然界"、"生命体的本性"、"类型"、"自然力"以及"人体的先天功能"。NATURE的所有意义在英语语料样本中的频率和占比见表2。"nature"在所有语料中都是名词。

表2　NATURE的义项及其频率

义项	频率	比例(%)
事物的性质、本质	571	57.1%
自然界	228	22.8%
生命体的本性	91	9.1%
类型	64	6.4%
自然力	43	4.3%
人体功能	3	0.3%

"nature"在大量语料中表现为事物的性质、本质之意。例如:

20. ... and they regarded intelligence as a refined material substance with a fiery nature.

……并且他们把智慧看成一种具有火的性质的精炼物质。

21. Some other cellular event was involved, but its nature remained obscure and unexplained for another 30 years.

还涉及其他某种细胞活动,但其性质晦涩,又过了三十年仍无法解释。

22. Second, some responses are specifically social in nature and create opportunities

for adult caretakers to interpret the infant's behaviors as …

其次,一些回应在本质上就是社会性的,为成年看护人创造了将婴儿的行为解释为……的机会。

23. ARPS being the larger organization has the personnel resources and by its very nature tends to be pro – active rather than reactive.

作为较大的组织,ARPS 拥有人力资源,并在本质上倾向于主动而不是被动。

24. … when political upheavals in Zaire disrupted cobalt supplies, highlight the crucial nature of the strategic metals.

……当扎伊尔的政治动荡破坏了钴的供应时,战略金属的关键性得以显现。

例20 至例24 中的"nature"都指事物的本质,比如例20 中的人类智慧(intelligence),例21 中的细胞活动(cellular event),例22 中的婴儿的回应(responses),例23 中的组织机构(ARPS)和例24 中的具有战略意义的金属(strategic metals)。

25. I have no doubt that every mystery of nature has a scientific explanation that may, one day, be expressed in terms of …

我毫不怀疑,自然界的每一个奥秘都有其科学解释,总有一天可以用……来表述。

26. He retired in 1898 and devoted the rest of his life to nature study and wildlife photography.

他于1898 年退休,余生致力于自然研究与野生动植物摄影。

27. But er Nottingham's er city that's proud of its nature it's not generally realized that there's about a hundred nature reserves…

不过(嗯)诺丁汉是(嗯)这样一座城市,它以自然环境为荣,但人们普遍没有意识到它有大约一百个自然保护区……

在例25、26 和27 中,"nature"都指自然界,只不过例27 中第一个"nature"的内涵较之第二个更为狭窄,指诺丁汉当地的自然环境。

"nature"也可以指人和其他动物的天性、本性。

28. His refusal to compromise and his deeply suspicious nature was spoiling the pleasure of actually being part of the group.

他拒绝妥协以及疑心太重的天性正在毁掉他作为小组一分子的快感。

29. He is a man who is by nature a Windsor, but who has tried hard to be a Mountbatten.

他骨子里是个温莎人,却非要当蒙巴顿人。

30. It's true that you can't blame an animal for its nature, but it's also true that they do a lot of harm.

诚然您无法责怪动物的天性,可的确它们造成了不少破坏。

"nature"在例 28 和 29 中指人的天性,在例 30 中指动物的天性。

语料中还可见"nature"指"类型"。

31. Coleman met several newsmen of a less trusting nature.

柯尔曼碰到了几位不那么轻信别人的记者。

32. Few modern examples, even those of a routine nature, would be as bad.

很少有现代示例,即便是那些惯例性的,会和这个一样糟。

33. Should a department be shut down? Decisions of this nature often have long-term consequences.

应该关闭一个部门吗?这类决定通常会造成长期影响。

从例 31、例 32 和例 33 可以看出"nature"指类型的用法与其指事物的本质以及生命体的本性的用法相关,性质相同的事物可归为一类。

"nature"还有自然力之意。

34. ... an attractive unspoiled shore unaffected by its growing holiday business. But nature has decreed otherwise.

……一处尚未被破坏的迷人海岸,它还没有受到与日俱增的假日业务的影响。但是自然力已另有决定。

在例 34 中,"nature"都指一种在物质世界中运行着的具有独立形式的存在,这一存在能够创造和调节,是许多现象发生的直接动因。

"nature"在本研究使用的少量英语语料中指人体功能。

35. ... unable even to answer the calls of nature on her own, so that she had to be lifted like a child…

甚至无法独立回应自然的召唤,她必须由别人把她像孩子一样地抬起来。

在例 35 中"nature"指人体的排泄需求。

通过上述分析,本研究认为在现代英语使用者的思维中 NATURE 能够至少为几种认知模式提供思维通道,如图 6 所示。

图 6 告诉我们,在现代英语使用者的思维中,NATURE 首先打开进入基本认知模式[人]和[力]的通道。随后,[人]激活二级认知模式[先天]和[后天],[人]和[力]共同激活二级认知模式[人力]和[非人力]。接下来,[先天]激活认知模式[人体功能],[人体功能]和[人力]共同激活认知模式[人性];[非人力]引出认

知模式[自然力],[自然力]激活认知模式[自然界],[自然界]引发出[动物]与[植物]等认知模式,继而引出[兽性]与[物性]等。在上述认知模式的基础上,认知模式[存在与现象的本质]和[类型]被相继触发。

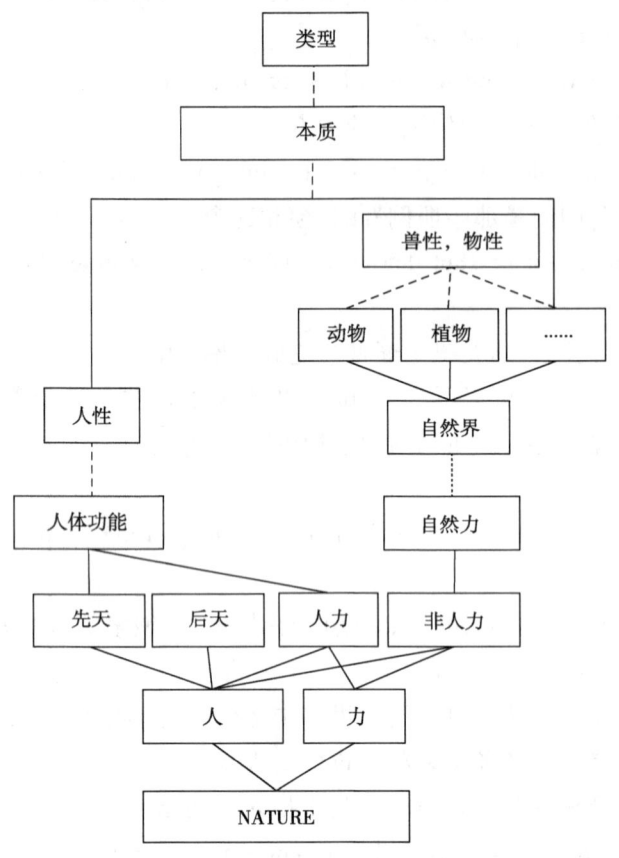

图6　NATURE激活的部分认知模式

现代英语中的NATURE所激活的认知模式集表现出两条拓展线索,一条与人相关,一条与自然界相关,这两条线索起自人对于人体的先天功能和力量以及对于一种似乎掌控着物质世界的力量的认识。据此,本研究认为NATURE的原型意义是[力],其语义网络如图7所示。

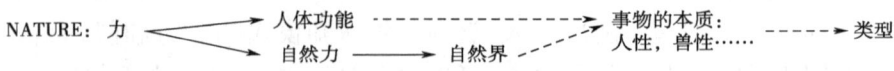

图7　NATURE在现代英语中的语义网络

在 NATURE 的语义网络中,从原型到[自然界]的拓展为借代拓展,即[自然力代自然界],其背后是借代原则[事件代地点](Radden & Kövecses,1999)。从原型到[事物的本质]的拓展为隐喻拓展,其背后是概念隐喻[事物的本质是 NATURE],随后进一步拓展为[类型是 NATURE]。

结语

现代汉语中的[自然]与现代英语中的 NATURE 异大于同。它们的相同之处仅在于都可以指自然界,不同之处可从以下三个方面阐述:

第一,按照传统语法的词类划分,"自然"可做名词、形容词和副词,而"nature"只能做名词。按照认知语法(Languacker,1986)的划分,"自然"既属于事体(THING)类,也属于关系(RELATION)类,而"nature"只属于事体类。这一方面可以在语言层面解释为什么"nature"不能像"自然"一样可以指示状态,另一方面可以在思维层面为认知模式[状态]和[关系]在[自然]所开启的认知模式集内的存在提供支持。

第二,作为事体的[自然]指自然界和人在没有外力影响时所表现出的情状,作为关系的[自然]指事件之间的因果关系。作为事体的 NATURE 除了指人体的先天功能和自然力外,还指自然界、事物的本质及其类型。[自然]强调来自人的物理和心理力量均为零,其语义网络蕴含着现代汉语使用者对人与自然界的关系、对人的主观能动性对自然界的影响的思考。NATURE 强调力是万事万物的根源,其语义网络反映出现代英语使用者对事物本质的好奇与探究。[自然]和 NATURE 的差异归根结底是中国人整体思维方式与西方人分析逻辑思维方式之间的差异。

第三,在本研究中,[自然]的原型意义[天然]是其频率最高的义项,而 NATURE 频率最高的义项[事物的本质]靠近其语义链终端,不是原型意义。在基于语料库的认知语言学研究中,范畴原型和频率最高的成员不重合是常态(Shortall,2007;Gilquin,2008;Nordquist,2009;Arppe et al.,2010)。以吉尔昆(Gilquin,2008)为例,吉尔昆将突显度和频率这两个指标分割开来测试它们对确定"give"的原型所起的作用,发现原型效应作为认知现象等同于突显度而非频率。频率虽然可为某种语言表达或者语言结构的规约性提供支持,但语料与认知真实性之间的关联尚待验证(Arppe et al.,2010)。

本研究还发现词汇概念与认知模式理论关于词汇概念与其激活的基本认知模式之间的关系的论述过于绝对。伊文思(Evans,2015)提出,语言使用者对词汇概念与其激活的基本认知模式之间的关联进行字面解读,对词汇概念与二级认知模式的关联通常做比喻解读。在本研究中,[自然]的原型"天然"在其认知模式体系发展到第三个层级时才出现,其概念借代和隐喻拓展发生在第四以及更高的层级上(见图4)。因此更贴切的说法是基本层次认知模式的作用是为语言使用者理解词汇概念提供最基础的知识框架,字面层次的解读不一定总是发生在基本认知模式层级。

限于篇幅,本研究未对[自然]和 NATURE 展开历时对比研究,也未对"natural"和"naturally"进行分析。不过,以上遗憾正是本课题进一步发展的契机。本研究对英语和对外汉语教学都有一定参考价值。在世界的各种语言和文化中,类似[自然]和 NATURE 的蕴藏着丰富哲学内涵的词汇如繁星般熠熠生辉,它们为我们深入了解相关文化提供了通道。

注意:BNC 自备随机提取功能。由于 CCL 没有随机提取功能,本研究首先提取全部带有"自然"的语料,再使用许家金博士与熊文新博士设计的软件 Concordance Randomizer 从中随机提取 1 000 条。

参考书目

[1] ARPPE A, GILQUIN G, GLYNN D et al. Cognitive corpus linguistics: Five points of debate on current theory and methodology[J]. Corpora, 2010, 5(1):1 - 27.

[2] BRUGMAN C, LAKOFF G. Cognitive topology and lexical networks[G]// SMALL S, COTTRELL G, TANNENHAUS M. Lexical ambiguity resolution. San Mateo: Morgan Kaufman, 1988:477 - 507.

[3] CHARTERIS - BLACK J. Analysing Political Speeches: Rhetoric, Discourse and Metaphor[M]. Basingstoke: Palgrave Macmillan, 2014.

[4] EVANS V. Lexical concepts, cognitive models and meaning - construction [J]. Cognitive Linguistics, 2006, 17(4):491 - 534.

[5] EVANS V. Metaphor, lexical concepts, and figurative meaning construction [J]. Cognitive Semiotics 2009, 5:73 - 107. DOI:10.1515/cogsem.2009.5.12.73.

[6] EVANS V. Figurative language understanding in LCCM Theory[J]. Cognitive Linguistics, 2010, 21(4):601 - 662.

[7] EVANS V. Language and Time: a Cognitive Linguistics Approach [M]. Cambridge: Cambridge University Press, 2013.

[8] EVANS V. A unified account of polysemy within LCCM theory[J]. Lingua, 2015, 157:100 - 123.

[9] EVANS V, Green M. Cognitive Linguistics: an Introduction[M]. Edinburgh: Edinburgh University Press,2006.

[10] GILQUIN G. What you think ain't what you get:highly polysemous verbs in mind and language[G]//LAPAIRE J - R,DESAGULIER G,GUIGNARD J - B. Du fait grammatical au fait cognitif. From gram to mind:Grammar as cognition (Volume 2). Pessac:Presses Universitaires de Bordeaux,2008:235 - 255.

[11] GROUP P. MIP:A method for identifying metaphorically used words in discourse[J]. Metaphor and Symbol,2007,22(1):1 - 39.

[12] LAKOFF G. Women,Fire,and Dangerous Things:What Categories Reveal about the Mind[M]. Chicago:University of Chicago Press,1987.

[13] LAKOFF G. The contemporary theory of metaphor[G]//ORTONY A. Metaphor and thought. New York:Cambridge University Press,1993:202 - 251.

[14] LANGACKER R. An introduction to cognitive grammar[J]. Cognitive Science,1986,10:1 - 40.

[15] NORDQUIST D. Investigating elicited data from a usage - based perspective [J]. Corpus Linguistics and Linguistic Theory,2009,5(1):105 - 30.

[16] RADDEN G,KÖVECSES Z. Toward a theory of metonymy[G]//PANTHER K,RADDEN G. Metonymy in language and thought. Philadelphia:John Benjamins Publishing Company,1999:17 - 59.

[17] 符蓉,胡东平.《道德经》英译的忠实伦理研究:以"自然"一词的翻译为例[J]. 湖南科技学院学报,2014,35(6):177 - 178,182.

[18] 刘金波. 自然的词汇化和语法化[J]. 绥化学院学报,2011,31(1):128 - 130.

[19] 龙娟. 认知语义学视阈下的自然与女性之隐喻[J]. 湖南科技大学学报(社会科学版),2006,9(3):102 - 106.

[20] 王敏."当然"和"自然"的异同考察[D]. 广州:暨南大学,2006.

[21] 叶树勋. 从"自""然"到"自然":语文学视野下"自然"意义和特性的来源探寻[J]. 人文杂志,2020(2):15 - 36.

Ways to Cultivate Cultural Awareness in Intercultural Communication

Suo Xuxiang

(Capital University of Economics and Business, Beijing 100070, China)

Abstract: On the basis of reviewing the history of intercultural communication in China and the current situation of intercultural communication, this article sorts out several main concepts in Intercultural communication and expounds the cultivation strategies and approaches of cross – cultural awareness and discusses the necessity of cross – cultural interpretation of the "the Belt and Road". In the era of information technology innovation and globalization, cultural exchange is the hub of cross – border development, correctly conveying the "the Belt and Road" in cross – culture to countries and regions along the line so that they can further realize the importance of culture in international exchange.

Key words: cross – culture; cultural awareness; the Belt and Road; intercultural communication; globalization

1. Introduction

The word "culture" in English originates from Latin culture and its earliest basic meaning is "farming, planting and crops". With the development of social civilization and the deepening of human recognition, the extension and connotation of the word culture has been continuously extended. According to the statistics of Encyclopedia Britannica, there are as many as ten kinds of definitions of culture in publications from all over the world. The connotation of culture is extremely rich. Although it has been concerned by many disciplines, its connotation and extension is not clear. Since the last century, many philosophers, anthropologists, historians and linguists have been trying to give a satisfactory definition of culture from the perspective of their respective disciplines. However, due to their different perspectives, the definition of culture is also different.

People generally divide the concept of "culture" into broad and narrow categories. In a broad sense, culture refers to the sum of material and spiritual wealth created by human beings in the process of social and historical development. It includes three aspects: material culture, institutional culture and psychological culture. In a narrow sense, culture refers to people's social customs and habits, ways of life, mutual relations, etc. Culture is a complex synthesis. Cross – culture refers to having a full and correct understanding of customs, customs and cultural phenomena that are different or in conflict with the national culture, accepting and adapting them in an inclusive manner. In communication, participants not only rely on their own codes, habits, concepts and behaviors, but also experience and understand other's codes, habits, concepts and behaviors. Cross – culture also means that the culture crosses the boundaries of different countries and nationalities, crosses the cultural difference among different nationalities, countries and groups, and develops the interaction between people who experience cultural attribution through crossing the system. First of all, Cross – culture is a question of axiology and ontology, and understanding between cultures is naturally a question of axiology and ontology. Cross – cultural understanding is not the subject's understanding of the object, but the understanding between subjects, not subjectivity, but intersubjectivity. If we regard different cultures as objects of knowledge, it means that the subject can dispose of the object at will and the object becomes the object to be studied, watched, disposed of and enslaved. It means inequality. This was the attitude adopted by the colonists towards the indigenous culture during the colonial period. Cross – cultural understanding should regard different cultures as equal subjects to themselves. Moreover, this understanding does not pursue the identity of subject and object, but is premised on the recognition of differences. That is to say, such understanding does not have an absolutely correct answer and can be understood differently, just as we read and understand a novel. Cross – cultural understanding is the understanding between different cultures. The coexistence of difference and identity makes it possible to understand between different cultures. Cross – cultural understanding is the unity of cultural differences and commonalities.

2. The Importance of Cross – cultural Awareness in Intercultural Communication

Culture is the core of the nation and also an important bond and adhesive for all social groups of the nation. Cultural autonomy is the autonomy power of groups with common cultural awareness in maintaining and inheriting culture. The vast majority of ethnic issues are related to cultural autonomy to a large extentin ancient and modern times, both at home or abroad. The relationship between culture and politics is a paradox, on the one hand, culture and politics are inseparable. Politics and culture must be separated in order to eliminate the conflict brought about by nationalism. With the information network sweeping the world today, the economic and political globalization is accompanied by the collision and blend of multiculturalism. If one nation's culture cannot draw lessons from others and absorb the cultures of other nations, it will be difficult to develop and even gradually shrink. However, the blending of cultures is by no means a culture that erodes and melts other cultures by virtue of its now strong economy, thus to establish a global single culture. That is to say, economic globalization should not and will not lead to the disappearance of national cultural characteristics. On the contrary, cultural integration will further promote cultural diversity, because cultural exchange and development should be based on national equality and cultural autonomy. Cultural blind obedience will inevitably lead to the loss of the national core and the disappearance of the culture with national characteristics. Cultural imperialism will lead to the rise of political hegemonism and the unification of social economy, which runs in opposite direction to economic globalization.

In the process of economic globalization, culture has both the tendency of seeking common ground and the requirement of reserving differences. It is unrealistic to fail to see the requirements for preserving differences and the efforts and effects under such requirements. Without communication and collision between different cultures, human culture will surely stagnate, lose the possibility of further development, and eventually go to a dead end. Human beings have always longed for peace, feared war and pursued peace and development. This idea has long been rooted in the hearts of people all over the world. We strongly support all policies and measures conducive to peace and development, and we strongly oppose and prevent those undermine peaceful development. How to make the world achieve real peace and make the world develop together is a question that every country and even every citizen is thinking about. The maintenance and establishment of world peace not only depends on more and more international organizations, but also requires the active participation of every country to formulate corresponding policies to maintain world peace and development. The strategic deployment of "Belt and Road Initiative" is just a product of this trend, conforming to the people's will and the times. The "Belt and Road Initiative" aims to promote economic and cultural exchanges and interaction between China and the countries along the Silk Road. On the one hand, it strongly advocates "telling Chinese stories" and actively promotes the soft power of national culture and cultural output. On the other hand, we should try our best to learn from the advanced cultural concepts of other nations, while inheriting and promoting Chinese civilization, we should inject new elements and vitality into it so that it can show its unique oriental wisdom and characteristics along the "the Belt and Road Initiative" and even on the world stage, and promote the international influence of Chinese culture.

3. The Role and Influence of Cross – cultural Awareness on "Belt and Road Initiative"

3.1　Cultural Implication of "theBelt and Road Initiative"

"The Belt and Road Initiative" and "Ancient Silk Road" have profound historical origins. The latter is the historical logical starting point of the former, both of which contain political and economic implications. A scientific understanding of "the Belt and Road Initiative" cannot be separated from a deep excavation of "Ancient Silk Road", and only in this way can the deep connotation of "the Belt and Road Initiative" be thoroughly understood. Opening up is the most basic spirit of the ancient Silk Road and the core idea of our construction of "the Belt and Road Initiative". The strategic layout of "the Belt and Road Initiative" is an open strategy, open to all countries, economies, international organizations and non – governmental organizations, with no closed circle or exclusivity. The strategic layout is not only open but also inclusive, which is different from other strategies. The strategic layout does not set any threshold, and all countries and regions willing to participate are builders and beneficiaries. Its cooperation methods are also diverse. It does not set uniform standards and rules, nor does it touch existing regional cooperation mechanisms, aiming to achieve a good interface with various mechanisms in an inclusive manner. The strategic layout does not only serve China, but also requires global participation and common construction, and therefore is mutually beneficial and win – win. Based on the complementary advantages of all participants, we should realize the sharing of interests and common development.

To ensure the sustainable development of "the Belt and Road Initiative" layout, co – operation is the foundation. Just like the ancient Silk Road, it is based entirely on the exchange of private business trips, which itself is jointly built and benefited. Although the initiative was put forward by China, its essence is that all participants discuss and build together. No matter what aspect of interconnection, we need to discuss, participate and build together. That is why we call it " interest community", "development community" and "destiny community".

The full name of "the Belt and Boad", is "Silk Road Economic Belt" and "21st Century Maritime Silk Road". It is abbreviated as "B & R" (formerly "One Belt, One Road" and abbreviated as "OBOR"). On September 7, 2013, Chinese President Xi Jinping, speaking at Kazakhstan's Nazarbayev University, proposed that the Silk Road Economic Belt could be built together with innovative cooperation models in order to make the economies of various countries more closely linked, all nations work together more deeply and have more space for further development. On October 3, 2013, President Xi Jinping said in a speech to the Indonesian parliament that China is willing to strengthen maritime cooperation with ASEAN countries, develop a good maritime partnership and jointly build the "21st Century Maritime Silk Road". On May 21, 2014, Xi Jinping pointed out in his keynote speech at the Asian Summit that China will work with other countries to accelerate the construction of "Silk Road Economic Belt" and "Maritime Silk Road in the 21st Century" and participate more deeply in the regional cooperation process to promote mutual benefit between Asian countries. From the perspective of cultural psychology, culture to a large extent will affect people's understanding, interpretation and response to the external environment or phenomenon, and then regulate or influence their behaviors.

Cognitive science believes that cultural values not only regulate people's behaviors, but also affect the cognitive process and information processing methods through cognitive factors such as perception, attention and memory. The study found that westerners often get semantic information by category, while orientals prefer to use context and similarity. At the same time, culture, as the soul and life of a nation, is symbiotic with the nation itself carrying its culture and blends with its economy, science and technology and other fields. Therefore, exchanges and cooperation in any field between countries or regions contain cultural elements without exception. Obviously, cultural differences and symbiosis exist at the same time. Symbiosis makes communication and cooperation possible and is the basis for bridging differences. Differences also promote the motivation of further communication and exchange, and learn fromeach other in the mutual collision. Human civilization has the value of communication and cooperation because of its diversity, and the power of communication and mutual learning because of its tolerance. Diversity brings communication, communication breeds integration, and integration produces progress. The strategic concept of "the Belt and Road" follows the ancient Silk Road, not only a commercial development road, but also a cultural exchange road.

Therefore, when constructing the cultural exchange mechanism in "the Belt and Road Initiative", we should transform the "heterogeneity" of different national cultures into national characteristics with a multi-perspective and further sublimate and expand the "homogeneity" so that the achievements of civilizations with different forms and styles can be inherited and carried forward through the development platform which is the enrichment and development of the cultural heritage of the countries along the line.

3.2　Significance of Cross-cultural Awareness Research under the Strategic Background of the "Belt and Road"

As China's top-level national strategy, "theBelt and Road" connects the two great ideas of "China Dream" and "World Dream" and carries the great historical mission of the great rejuvenation of the motherland and the prosperity and development of the world. "The Belt and Road Initiative" layout must be known, understood and recognized by the world. Only in this way can the role of the "the Belt and Road Initiative" layout be truly played, be demonstrated, and the grand idea of the "the Belt and Road Initiative" layout be realized. There are many countries along the "the Belt and Road" line, and there are many differences in culture, belief and thinking mode, which requires us to attach importance to the cross-cultural interpretation of the "the Belt and Road Initiative". We should not only let the world know, but also to let the world accurately understand the principles, concepts and connotations of the "the Belt and Road Initiative" layout. We must carefully think about how to interpret the strategic thought of " the Belt and Road Initiative" across cultures. Only by communicating with the countries along the line with diversified and accurate scientific communication methods can we provide a realistic basis for the implementation, long – term development and eventual successful realization of the strategy. In such a historical period, China has put forward the strategic layout of "the Belt and Road Initiative" with great courage and sense of world responsibility. "the Belt and Road Initiative" has received great attention from home and abroad since it was put forward, especially from relevant stakeholders. Most of the countries along the "the Belt and Road" line are undeveloped countries, and their desire for economic development is obvious. However, due to the incomplete understanding of "the Belt and Road", there are still many doubts, so they hold a conservative attitude towards the promotion of the construction. On the one hand, all countries hope to take advantages of China's development to promote their own rapid economic growth, on the other hand, the strategic layout itself involves policy communication, facility connection, trade and financial support, all of which require the active participation and in – depth cooperation of all countries, which makes some countries question the essential purpose of "the Belt and Road Initiative".

In addition, since China is the initiator, the proposal and implementation of "theBelt and Road Initiative" will greatly enhance China's economic strength and international status, and the relationship between China and other countries will also change accordingly. Each related country will consider it carefully according to its own situation. For example, the US – Japan alliance is highly concerned about the strategy and is vigilant, neither participating nor monitoring at all times. However, some developed European countries such as Britain and Germany have maintained an active attitude towards the "the Belt and Road Initiative". Of course, there are also some countries like India that have a selective support attitude towards the construction and actively participate in important projects such as Asian Infrastructure Investment Bank, while their attitude towards other activities is not clear. They are both welcome and cautious.

We all know that the relationship between countries determines the attitude towards "theBelt and Road Initiative". Benefit is an eternal topic. As the initiator of "the Belt and Road Initiative", we certainly hope that the world will actively participate in the construction of "the Belt and Road Initiative", but the relationship between countries is not stable and lasting, but fluctuating. We should strengthen the cross – cultural interpretation of "the Belt and Road Initiative". Although it is impossible for all countries to agree, we should take advantage of cross - cultural interpretation to understand each other and deepen communication with each other. We should not only grasp the attitude of all countries towards " the Belt and Road Initiative" at all times, adjust relevant policies and implementation strategies in time to ensure the steady progress of the strategy, but also incorporate more neutral countries into the construction of the "the Belt and Road Initiative".

4. Ways to Cultivate Cross - cultural Awareness

4.1 Break down language barriers and build a favorable communication platform

At present, the coverage of non - common language majoring in China's universities is not high, and the high - level non - common language talentsare insufficient, which affects the further improvement of China's cross - cultural communication. There are many countries and nationalities along the "the Belt and Road" line, covering a wide variety of languages. In order to break the barriers of reality and achieve the effect as soon as possible, we should pay more attention to the cultivation of non - common language talents, international language research and international Chinese communication education, and start from these three aspects to improve national language ability and pave the way for the landing of "the Belt and Road Initiative".

The popularity of Chinese in the countries along the line is very insufficient and the distribution is also poor. This situation is not only a matter of concern, but a fact that must be faced. Since the 21st century, Chinese has been used more and more widely in the world. More and more people are learning and using Chinese, and the value of Chinese learning has attracted more and more attention from all over the world. The proposal of the strategy has provided a new opportunity for Chinese to move towards the world. Accelerating Chinese teaching in countries along the line is of great significance to the cross - cultural interpretation of "Belt and Road Initiative".

First of all, according to the distribution of the countries along the line, the overall goal of international Chinese teaching is set so that more and more people along the line can contact Chinese, learn Chinese, use Chinese, and expand the base of Chinese learners as the overall goal of Chinese teaching. Only in this way can the internationalization of Chinese be gradually improved, from a large base to a high quality, so that it can achieve a change in the concept of learning Chinese. We should simplify the complexity and design Chinese teaching content in a targeted way in combination with the needs of the people along the line and cultural characteristics. At present, the international teaching of Chinese is mainly in Confucius Institutes and Confucius Classrooms, and the teaching staff are mostly Chinese volunteers. To truly achieve high quality and high efficiency in cross – cultural interpretation of the "Belt and Road", a Chinese language teaching team with local Chinese teachers must be established, which is also the only way and important symbol to develop Chinese teaching and promote the internationalization of Chinese. The establishment of such a Chinese localization teacher will provide immeasurable resources for the cross – cultural interpretation of "Belt and Road Initiative". They can not only be engaged in Chinese teaching, promote Chinese, but also contribute to the formulation and implementation of local Chinese teaching. Therefore, we should try our best to strengthen communication with the governments of the countries along the line, incorporate Chinese teaching into the education systems of the countries along the line, and ensure the status of Chinese teaching from the institutional point of view, fundamentally guarantee the internationalization of Chinese teaching and deepen the internationalization of Chinese teaching, so that Chinese teaching can truly achieve sustainable development. Language is the carrier of culture, and good language level must be based on deep cultural background. A person's cultural quality shapes his personality image in cross – cultural communication to a certain extent, affects his position in international communication, and further relates to the dignity of the country and the people. Deep understanding and mastery of Chinese traditional culture will not only help maintain personal self – confidence and dignity in cross – cultural communication, but also promote the essence of Chinese culture, tell good Chinese stories to the world and spread good Chinese voices. In the process of building a "the Belt and Road" talent tank, we should also give priority to training "cross – cultural talents" who are proficient in Chinese and foreign cultures from the perspective of cultural integration, that is, to train "foreign experts" who understand the language, culture and history of other countries, while also assisting the countries concerned to train more "Chinese experts". This requires us to appropriately and timely add some contents of Chinese traditional culture, such as lectures on Chinese traditional culture and appreciation of contemporary culture, in the process of training foreign language talents.

The strategy is a long-term great undertaking that needs us to develop continuously. Its profound and grand scientific connotation is advancing with the times. It is essential to explain the "the Belt and Road" thought for its implementation. It is a global strategy initiated by our country. Only we can explain the true meaning of "the Belt and Road Initiative" and only Chinese can truly explain the rich connotation of the strategy. Therefore, it is imperative to accelerate the internationalization of Chinese. Only when we have a clear goal and put Chinese teaching into practice can we provide a steady stream of fresh blood for the advancement of the construction of "the Belt and Road Initiative".

4.2 Balance multiculturalism and religious differences and adhere to the policy of multi-integration

In the external communication, culture has special charm and can greatly promote the realization of the effect of the external communication, because culture can assimilate, transform and integrate multiculturalism in the external communication and realize the integration of multiculturalism. On the basis of the cultural integration, the two or more parties have a stronger sense of identity with each other. In the political, economic and cultural cooperation, they will reduce friction and twist their respective forces into a rope, and the cooperation will be more carefree and effective.

Breaking the cultural myth in many countries and regions along the line and getting out of the dilemma of cross-cultural interpretation caused by cultural diversity and complexity is the premise of improving the effect of cross-cultural interpretation. "Cross-cultural interpretation of the strategic layout of "the belt and road Initiative" must break away from the shackles of culture and religion, and we should use culture and religion to quietly spread the profound connotation and core meaning of "the Belt and Road" strategic thinking. The existence of cultural centralism makes every country and every nation have a deep-rooted sense of superiority to their own culture, which makes people identify with the cultural instinct they know well, and will subconsciously belittle and exclude things from other cultures. This exclusivity is especially prominent when it is threatened by external threats or when it is already strong, such as Vietnam's attitude towards China and the U.S. attitude towards China. According to a poll conducted by Zero Point Group in 18 countries along the line, Vietnamese people show overall goodwill towards China, appreciation of Chinese culture, recognition of China's road, confidence in China's development prospects, and goodwill towards Chinese manufacturing and Chinese brands. They also show great attention to Chinese leaders and confidence in their correct handling of domestic and international affairs. Americans always show suspicious attitude to the strategy. The construction of "the Belt and Road" advocates that different nationalities and cultures should "communicate with each other" rather than "communicate with each other but hate each other". We should tear down more walls and build fewer walls, and use dialogue as the "golden rule" so that we can all be neighbors. Therefore, when interpreting the strategic layout of "the Belt and Road Initiative" across cultures, we should emphasize the principle of "sharing, co – construction and sharing" of "the Belt and Road" as a win – win path to promote the common development and prosperity of all countries along the line. At the same time, " the Belt and Road Initiative" is not a simple linear economy, but brings common values, not limited to "a certain area" and "a certain road", but is radioactive and brings values not only in economic aspects, but also in political, economic and cultural aspects, which is a strategy benefiting the whole world.

4.3 Strengthen and improve the two – way interactivecommunication between countries along the " the Belt and Road" line

The scientific dissemination of "Belt and Road" thought can't be separated from the positive guidance of public opinion and media. People along the line need to strengthen the cross – cultural interpretation of the media. At the same time, a good platform for interactive communication of public opinion is essential for people along the line. In the process of "the Belt and Road Initiative" one – way indoctrination communication should not be relied on, but feedback information should be obtained in time to understand the ideological trends of the people along the line. Their goodwill, recognition and support for "the Belt and Road Initiative" will have a great impact on the advancement of the strategy. However, at present, there is still a lack of professional interactive communication platform for "the Belt and Road Initiative" in China. We cannot understand the real feelings of the people along the route for the construction of "the Belt and Road Initiative" in a timely and accurate manner. We can only obtain relevant information through public opinion surveys conducted by some institutions, but by the survey method we cannot get feedback information quickly and timely. Moreover, such surveys are passive, not the spontaneous expression of the real thoughts of the people along the route, but also have certain limitations. Therefore, we should set up an effective public opinion communication platform as soon as possible, establish a long-term system, grasp the public opinion on the construction in a timely manner from the initiative itself to the implementation process, fully grasp the genuine aspirations of the people along the route, fully consider the public opinions and suggestions along the route, and promote the construction of "the Belt and Road Initiative" to truly benefit the countries along the route and all mankind. The construction of international discourse right needs solid theoretical support so as to enhance the persuasiveness of cross-cultural interpretation of "the Belt and Road Initiative".

The strategy is beneficial to the whole world. However, it is made from the perspective of our country, which is difficult to gain the recognition and understanding of foreign audiences in interpretation and resulted in frequent opposition and questioning from other countries. In order to really explain the leading power of the strategy worldwide, we must start from the vital benefit of other countries, actively think about it, and find out the root causes of different opinions and questioning voices in various countries. Only in this way can we grasp the initiative in discourse and deal with possible problems. It is important to make full use of international platforms to promote "the Belt and Road Initiative". At present, *Lianhe Zaobao* is the most similar position and viewpoint in the reports on "the Belt and Road Initiative" and "AIIB" to the Chinese media. The most important reason is that many of the voices in *Lianhe Zaobao* are from Chinese scholars and media, and their views and standpoints are naturally similar to those of China. In other international media, the reports related to "the Belt and Road Initiative" are mostly from foreigners, and their reports are completely different from China's position and viewpoints. This will easily lead to the transfer of the strategy discourse right, which will be held by the international community. Therefore, we should expand the scope and intensity of spreading information about "the Belt and Road Initiative" in the international media so that Chinese scholars and media people can participate in international public opinion. Finally, improve the content and ways of interpretation of "the Belt and Road Initiative" by Chinese state media, shape credibility and win more international audiences.

In an era when new media is in vogue, we should break through the traditional propaganda ideas and let "the Belt and Road Initiative" not only speak out to China, but also start from countries along the line, explain and spread the strategy in a "indigenous" way, and let the seeds of the strategic thinking spread to all parts of the world, so that participating countries can become the new force of international voice, thus to strengthen the international voice of China's strategy. We should strengthen the construction of the discourse system by transforming the traditional foreign discourse system and taking "integrating China and foreign countries" as the core, actively explore new categories, new concepts and new expressions to adapt to China's foreign communication discourse in the new era.

5. Conclusion

After demonstrating the necessity of cross-cultural interpretation of "the Belt and Road Initiative", this paper analyzes the current situation of national languages and cultures along the line and the internal mechanism of cross-cultural interpretation itself, demonstrates various dilemmas of thoughts in the process of cross-cultural interpretation, and puts forward some feasible measures according to the dilemmas found. On the whole, this paper focuses on the current cross-cultural interpretation of the strategic layout of "the Belt and Road Initiative" and the practical difficulties encountered in cross-cultural interpretation, and makes a series of preliminary explorations, connecting with the objective reality, and puts forward some effective measures, hoping to pave the way for cross-cultural interpretation of "the Belt and Road Initiative" construction, clear some obstacles and help it out of the practical difficulties. Cross-cultural interpretation of "the Belt and Road Initiative" has both opportunities and obstacles. Only by continuously strengthening the research on issues related to "the Belt and Road Initiative", building a discourse system for interpreting the strategy, training translators, and building a platform for cross-cultural communication of Chinese publishing media, can the doubts and concerns of the international community be alleviated, China's development be objectively viewed, and the strategic thought, which carries the world's political, economic and cultural heritage, be fully and clearly interpreted through the construction of the cross-cultural communication platform.

Countries should adhere to the principle of co-construction and sharing and strengthen coordination and cooperation. We should do a good job of connecting people's hearts and minds with feelings, and enhance people's sense of identity and support for the construction of "the Belt and Road Initiative" in various countries. We should combine the cause of empathy with practical cooperation of all parties more closely to enhance the universality of empathy projects. We should uphold the principle of inclusiveness and openness and advocate the awareness of cultural inclusion. The connection between people is the most basic, solid and lasting connection. I hope all parties will adhere to the people – oriented principles under the guidance of the spirit of the Silk Road, deepen the mutual learning of civilizations, build bridges between people , and pave the Silk Road for the soul.

To sum up, in the "theBelt and Road Initiative", the countries along the line have large population, complex language, great differences in ideology, cultural background and value system, and have many difficulties in communication. Increasing dialogue and integration among different religions and civilizations is one of the important measures that we can take friendly with many countries along the line. It is urgent for us to change those deep – rooted "stereotypes" and promote the vigorous development among regions. In the era of information technology innovation and globalization, cultural exchange is the hub of cross – border development, correctly conveying the "the Belt and Road Initiative" in cross – culture to countries and regions along the line so that they can further realize the importance of culture in international exchange. If we can fully analyze the communication obstacles encountered in "the Belt and Road Initiative" from a cross – cultural perspective, the countries along the line will be able to better drive the world's cross – cultural awareness, that is, talents will be able to change their horizons in the face of complex, changeable and new cultural communication scenes, accelerate the pace of Chinese culture's adaptation to the times in an open and equal manner, and go abroad to show their unique charm in the world's cultural pattern.

The construction of the "Belt and Road Initiative" layout will surely bring great achievements to China and realize its peaceful rise. It is not only the responsibility and mission of Chinese academic circles but also the responsibility of Chinese media companies to explain the "Belt and Road Initiative" to the outside world. The Initiative itself contains rich political and economic implications. We can start with the difficulties encountered by the main media of the cross – cultural dissemination and further discuss the necessity of the "the Belt and Road Initiative" layout to the outside world and the relevant countermeasures for cross – cultural dissemination in the light of its political and economic background.

References

[1] ZHANG LONGXI. Literary History Thought:A Comparative Study between China and the West[M]. Hong Kong:Sanlian Bookstore Co. ,Ltd. ,2012.

[2] GAN XIANFENG. History of China's Foreign News Dissemination[M]. Fuzhou:Fujian People's Publishing House,2004.

[3] CHEN RINONG. History of China's Foreign Communication[M]. Beijing:Foreign Languages press,2010.

[4] GUO KE. Introduction to International Communication[M]. Shanghai:Fudan University Press,2004.

[5] LI YINING,LIN YIFU,ZHENG YONGNIAN,et al. Read "the Belt and Road"[M]. Beijing:CITIC Press,2015.

跨文化交际中文化意识的培养策略和途径

索绪香*

摘 要:在回顾我国跨文化交际历史和跨文化交际现状的基础上,本研究梳理了跨文化交际中的主要概念,阐述了跨文化意识的培养策略和途径,论述了"一带一路"跨文化阐释的必要性。在信息技术创新和全球化时代,文化交流是跨境发展的纽带,将"一带一路"跨文化的内涵正确传达给沿线国家和地区,使其进一步认识到文化在国际交流中的重要性。

关键词:跨文化;文化意识;"一带一路";跨文化沟通;全球化

---

* [作者简介]索绪香(1973—),女,首都经济贸易大学外国语学院,博士、副教授,主要研究领域为翻译理论与实践、认知翻译学。

A Comparative Study of Diet Cultures between China and English – Speaking Countries: Taking Britain, the United States, Canada and Australia as Examples

Liu Yiran

(Capital University of Economics and Business, Beijing, 100070)

Abstract: From the perspective of intercultural communication, this article analyses the causes, specific manifestations and coping methods of dietary culture differences between China and English – speaking countries in terms of dietary ideas, food contents, dining styles and catering etiquettes, so that readers can increase the understanding of different cultures and promote the friendly exchanges between different cultures. The author has collected and studied a variety of literature documents so as to understand the causes of the differences between Chinese and western dietary cultures. This article will clarify the increasing convergence and the common development of the diet cultures between China and English – speaking countries. It will also help readers to understand the culture of the English – speaking countries, so as to better promote the friendly exchange of cultures and make a minor contribution to the integration of our culture and world culture.

Key words: intercultural communication, dining differences, cultural integration, common development

1. Introduction

A certain diet culture reflects characteristics of the nation where it is rooted. Therefore it is closely related to intercultural communication. Different dietary cultures also reflect the characteristics of cultures all over the world.

1.1 The research status on the diet culture in China

With the increasing frequency of cross – cultural communication in today's society, people's research on diet culture is also increasing. However, the researches on Chinese catering culture didn't start at home, but was initiated and studied by Japanese scholars. After Japanese scholars, it was studied by overseas Chinese scholars and some European and American Sinologists. From the late 1940s to the mid – 70s, there were few people studying diet culture in the Chinese mainland. But it was until 1970s that the study of Chinese food culture developed gradually.

1.2 Research motives

With the continuous development and progress of human society, people's lives have become increasingly open, and exchanges between different countries and regions, different nationalities and races have become increasingly frequent. This kind of communication is called intercultural communication (Huang, 2015). In order to achieve successful cross – cultural communication, it is necessary to understand each other's world view, way of thinking, value orientation, and even behavior and customs. Cross – cultural communication is complicated. This article analyzes the connotation of different ethnic cultures only from the perspective of dietary culture communication, and makes sure to have a restricted view to the deeper cultural differences in the history, culture, and national character of different countries, and find a way to better convey various kinds of information among different cultures, help them accept each other and understand each other, so as to achieve successful communication. The differences and influences of diet cultures are discussed from environment, social and historical aspects, so we can absorb the essence and discard the dregs, sum up a more nutritious, healthy and scientific diet to improve the quality of life of the Chinese people, and promote the integration of economy and culture from the perspective of diet communication under the environment of economic and cultural globalization.

1.3 Research Structure

This article can be divided into three parts. The first part introduces the whole work

A Comparative Study of Diet Cultures between China and English – Speaking Countries: Taking Britain, the United States, Canada and Australia as Examples

and reviews the literature. The second part summarizes different dietary ideas, food contents, dining styles and catering etiquettes in China and English – speaking countries, and then analyzes causes, specific manifestations of different dietary cultures and mutual influences of different diet cultures. The last part concludes the study and prospects the future research. This study hopes to help readers increase their understanding of different cultures and promote the friendly exchanges between different cultures.

Because of different cultural backgrounds, different economic developments and different geographical environments, there are great diet differences between China and English – speaking countries in terms of dietary ideas, food contents, dining styles and catering etiquettes. For example, Chinese people believe rice and flour mainly provide them strength and energy, while English – speaking countries regard meat as the most important part of their food construction. When eating, Chinese people use chopsticks, and they usually cook several big dishes, and share them together. People in English – speaking countries use knives and forks, they prefer divide a big dish into several pieces and put them into small plates, then distribute to everyone before eating. What's more, Chinese people enjoy dinning together. They will seize any chance to get together with family or some friends and have a warmly and hilarious dinner party. People in English – speaking countries prefer eating quietly and orderly. From the perspective of intercultural communication, this paper will analyze the causes, specific manifestations and coping methods of dietary culture differences between China and English – speaking countries like Britain, the United States, Canada and Australia.

1.4 Theoretical Framework

In this article, I mainly used a comparative study to explore the Chinese food culture and the diet culture of English – speaking countries. Through my comparative research, I discovered that due to historical, geographical, social, religious and other reasons, Chinese food culture and English – speaking countries are distinct. In this article, I mainly discuss about geographical reasons, national characteristic reasons and religious reasons. By studying these differences and under the environment of cultural globalization and economic globalization of today's society, I also discovered the convergence of the two dietary cultures. This helps deepen the understanding of cultural exchanges and integration between China and English – speaking countries.

1.5 Literature review

Muqun Wang (1995) discussed the diet habits of Australian people. Wang thinks that influenced by the factor of immigration, the Australian diet is similar to that of the British, but the food calories are much higher. As a result, more and more Australian people have begun to pursue low calorie healthy foods. This research helped my present study by building a good foundation for the research.

Panpan Wang (2010) gave three principles of Canadian dietary etiquette through examples. It shows that although a multi – national country, Canada has formed a distinctive diet culture in its historical evolution. It can be seen that the diet culture of Canada is similar to the diet culture of China.

Junhu Yang (2014) researched the geographical, climate and other reasons that have caused the differences between Chinese diet culture and Western diet culture. He also discussed different cooking styles, dietary structures, cuisine styles and even religious differences to explore the distinctions of Chinese and Western diet culture and their reasons. Although this article compares the Chinese and Western dietary cultures in general terms and lacks a more detailed analysis and description, it does point out the right direction for my research.

Jinghong Sun and Haoyun Deng (2016) made a series of comparisons on the diet cultural differences between Chinese and English. According to their findings, the differences are mainly decided by geographical environments, historical influences, social circumstances, cultures and religions. Different environments create different cooking and eating habits.

Luxi Liang (2016) mainly introduced the Chinese diet culture and Western diet culture. Then she made a comparison between Chinese diet culture and Western diet culture through diet content, dining tools, types of dining and so on. From this article, it is easy to learn that Chinese diet culture is different from most of the western countries. This study enlightens me on how to make the present comparative study.

Xuetai Wang (2006) analyzed the changes in the diet of Chinese society and vividly described the eating habits of different classes of people in Chinese society in his book, pointing out the development prospects of China's diet. This work deepens my present understanding of Chinese food culture.

A Comparative Study of Diet Cultures between China and English - Speaking Countries: Taking Britain, the United States, Canada and Australia as Examples

These studies motivated me thinking about the diet differences between China and English - speaking countries in cross - cultural communication. After studying these documents, I found out that the Chinese diet culture and English - speaking countries' diet cultures have their differences, but they also have similarities. The food culture of China and English - speaking countries is now in a transitional stage of mutual influence.

2. Diet Cultural Differences of China and English - speaking Countries

Diet cultures between China and English - speaking countries are different in terms of diet ideas, food contents, dinning styles and catering etiquettes. This part sums up those differences and Looks for their similarities.

2.1 Different diet ideas

Eating food is the most basic activity of human beings. It is not only a phenomenon of human activities, but also a reflection of consciousness or concepts. People in different countries, regions and nationalities also have great differences in diet ideas.

2.1.1 Diet ideas of Chinese people

There is a proverb saying that "hunger breeds discontentment". From the beginning of Chinese civilization, Chinese people started to believe that food is the basic need of human (Wang, 2006). Since our nation has been at a low level of productivity for thousands of years, people are always hungry, so there is a unique dietary culture that places eating more important than everything. As a result, people in different areas of the country have invented all kinds of cuisines, and each kind of cuisine has its own characteristic. People focus on the organic integration and unification of color and scent of food. They pay a lot of attentions to the taste of food and if the dishes have satisfied their sense of taste, visual and smell, but ignore the reasons why the food is delicious and whether all kinds of nutrients are well matched (Wang, 2006). This shows that Chinese people put taste in the first place of their diet ideas. Great Chinese cooks believe that the spirit of Chinese culinary art is the unified and harmonious combination of different materials (Wang, 2006). Chinese people often mix many kinds of materials together in cooking one dish, which makes them almost lost their own natural taste, but produces a new and complete delicacy. For example, there is a kind of traditional Beijing cuisine made from eggs, chicken soup, lean minced meat and some water chestnuts. All together into the wok these ingredients can make a dish of delicacy without any disharmonious taste.

In addition to pursuing the delicious food, the Chinese people also pay attention to the physical and mental pleasure and satisfaction brought by food (Chen,2011). This makes the Chinese diet full of imagination and creativity and tends to be artistic. Its greatest feature is randomness. Each dish can be developed and changed on the basis of the original to adapt to different requirements of regions, seasons, objects, roles, and grades.

Chinese cuisine's pursuit of taste and sense of enjoyment are also consistent with Chinese traditional philosophy (Xie,2015). The distinctive features of traditional Chinese philosophy are macroscopic, intuitive, vague and unpredictable. The method of making Chinese cuisines is to grasp the sense of proportion, the overall coordination and the degree of heating. These are also the subtlety of Chinese cuisine, reflecting the vagueness of traditional philosophy.

Nowadays, because of the improving of living quality of Chinese people and the tendency of globalization, more and more Chinese people are being aware of the importance of eating healthy, and are starting to keep a balance between delicacies and nutrition.

2.1.2 Diet ideas of people in English – speaking countries

People in English – speaking countries have a more rational dietary idea. They emphasize science and nutrition, and pay attention to the energy, protein, and vitamins contained in foods, rather than the color, fragrance, taste, and shape of food (Huai,2010). That's why people from the United States, Britain and even Canada eat steaks with similar simple flavor but also satisfy the nutrients obtained from them. Some schools also provide dietitians for primary and middle school students to ensure a balanced nutrition for teenagers.

The pursuit of science and nutrition of food is consistent with their traditional philosophy (Huai,2010). The distinctive feature of their traditional philosophy is metaphysics, which is mechanical and rigid in methodology. Under the influence of this philosophy, people in English – speaking countries have a mechanistic understanding of life, believing that the only usage of food is to fill their bellies. For example, their main staple food is basically bread or oatmeal. Steaks are always taste the same. Even some kinds of garnish are placed separately to the steak. The flavors of different kinds of food are distinctive and not related to each other.

2.2 Different food contents

The study of food contents is to understand what people eat. The differences of diet contents are influenced by the cultural backgrounds of different nationalities, and they also reflect some national characteristics of different countries.

2.2.1　Food contents in China

China is a major agricultural country. For centuries, it has maintained a diet that mainly includes rice and flour, supplemented by vegetables and meat. Also being influenced by Buddhism, traditional diet content of Chinese people is mainly vegetarian food (Wang,2015). According to the survey of Western botanists, the Chinese eat more than 600 kinds of vegetables. In fact, vegetarianism dominates the normal structure of Chinese food contents. Vegetarian food in Chinese cuisine is essential for all meals. In our daily diet, most of the beans and soy products occupy a certain important position. Compared with the western diet, Chinese people consume relatively less meat, while the intake of legume protein is relatively more.

Chinese people also are used to eating warm and cooked food. They think warm and cooked foods are more flavorful than cold foods. Their preference has a lot to do with the advancement of Chinese civilization and the advancement of cooking technology.

The formation of Chinese people's food contents is closely related to the traditional culture. Chinese civilization is dominated by agricultural civilization. People hate to relocate indiscreetly, and they always stick to their duties.

2.2.2　Food contents in English – speaking countries

People in English – speaking countries mainly eat meat, and they obtain nutrients by ingesting animal protein and fat. The dishes are mostly made from beef, chicken, lamb, pork and fish (Liang,2016). These kinds of dietary habits are related to Western nomadic and maritime cultures. In the traditional nomadic life, people mostly rely on fishing, hunting and breeding, supplemented by gathering fruits and planting vegetables, so meat has occupied the main position of people's diet. The main structure of their food contents is like a triangle. At the bottom of the triangle there are bread, potatoes, corns, fruits and vegetables; the third level includes fish and other kinds of seafood, the second level includes poultry, egg and dairy products; the top of this food triangle is beef, pork, lamb and other kinds of meat.

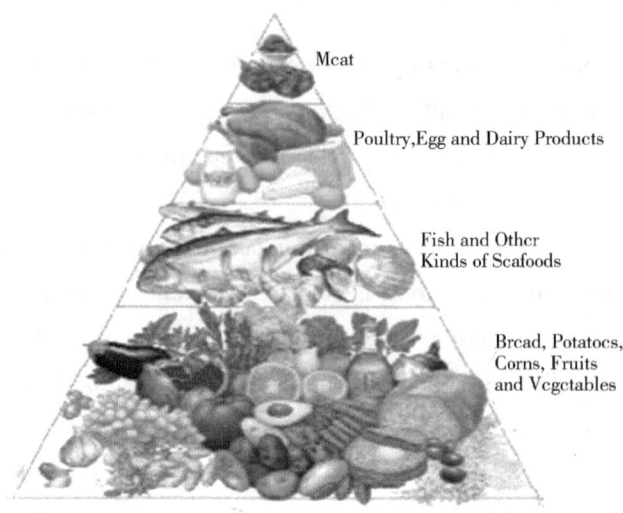

Image: the main food structure of English – speaking countries

In addition, people also enjoy eating cold food and raw food. The formation of this kind of eating habit is mainly related to the traditional culture, too. Both cooking methods and kitchenware products are not as abundant as those in China (Wang,2015).

2.3 Different dining styles

Chinese people and people in English – speaking countries use different kinds of tableware. Chinese people are used to use chopsticks, spoons and eating bowls. Eating utensils are like artworks to them. They use wares in variety of shapes, colors and sizes to match with different dishes. People in English – speaking countries are used to use knives and forks. Although there are different types of tableware for different dining occasions, western food is not as exquisite as Chinese food on matching utensils, and tableware is very simple in category.

The types of staple food are different for Chinese people and people in English – speaking countries. Rice and flour are the main staple food ingredients in China (Wang, 2015). Because of the traditional agricultural structure, geographical conditions and climate, there are variety types of grain and vegetable. As a result, in daily life, people have formed a diet habit mainly based on plant materials and supplemented by animal materials. In contrast, rice and flour often play supporting roles in the diet of people in English – speaking countries. The developed animal husbandry in English – speaking countries has created people's eating habit, but the status of flour products is still of vital position. People prefer having cereal and bread for breakfast. Pasta, pizza, pie, and other kinds of food made of flour are also very popular.

Chinese and people in English – speaking countries have different dinning times. Chinese people take only three meals a day without any other snacks, so they value the three meals a lot. They usually have breakfast at seven or eight o'clock, lunch at noon and dinner at around seven. For thousands of years, Chinese people value their dinner very much. After a day of hard work, the whole family would sit around the table, and share the most important meal of the day. However, except breakfast, lunch and dinner, people in English – speaking countries are also used to have some meals between two regular meals, such as brunch and afternoon tea. Brunch time is about ten o'clock in the morning, and the afternoon tea time is around five o'clock in the afternoon. They also treasure the importance of the dinner, and it usually is the most abundant meal of the day. For this reason, there are often some kinds of liquor served on the table.

During a dinner party, people enjoy a cheerful mood. It is very special that they would make toasts to each other and help themselves or others to food with their own chopsticks. They like sitting around a big round table, which means reunion and satisfactory. Chinese people are used to take food from the same plate. This way of dining obviously has the shortcomings of "not being hygienic", yet it conforms to the universal mentality of our nation's "happy reunion" and is a reflection of the "harmony" thinking in Chinese philosophy (Du, 2015). People are used to sitting around a big table and talking cheerfully while eating. This form of dining has not changed much, but with the continuous integration of Chinese and Western cultures, there are many young people like to eat buffet, and some new dining forms like buffet weddings or meeting meals also have appeared in China.

2.4 Different catering etiquettes

Regional differences and traditional cultural differences between China and English – speaking countries determine the differences in table manners (Li, 2016). The following will discuss about table manners in China and English – speaking countries from several aspects, so as to inherit and develop food cultures of China and English – speaking countries.

2.4.1 Catering etiquettes in China

The "harmony" in Chinese traditional philosophy and the agricultural civilization made Chinese people formed a "group consciousness", that is, the individual will obeys the collective will (Wang,2016). So people like to get together and eat together, which enhances their feelings and creates a harmonious dining atmosphere.

Seating: While eating, the Chinese generally like to use the round table, a symbol of "harmony" (Wang,2016). The most important guest will be set to seat by the best position of the table, and the rest of the guests will be set to seat around him/her. Normally, the hosts or hostesses will seat at the left side of the table and leave the right side of the table for their guests. In ancient China, most of the women were not allowed to seat around the table and join in the feast as men did. Nowadays, most of the Chinese families still remain the principle of respect for seniority. They obey the rule even at home.

Atmosphere: In China, people prefer a noisy and delightful environment when having a feast. They would talk and make toasts frequently, as well as smoke and drink. If the atmosphere is quiet and stressful, the hosts or hostesses will see this as an impolite situation to the guests, while the guests will also look down at the banquet skills of the host family. But people in China also have deeply influenced by the thought of Confucius (Wu,2013). He once said to his students that, "One should not speak when eating and sleeping". However, this rule is cruel for Chinese people. They can't imagine people in a world full of delicacy and wine feast but muffled and dumb. So when several family members (the father, the mother and the children) are having a meal together, they try to eat as quiet as possible in order to stay healthy and respect the teachings of the ancients.

Serving order: Usually when having a great dinner party, the cold dishes will be served firstly. Then the food will be served in the order of wine, main dishes, soup and fruit or dessert. In a casual situation, the order won't be that strict. Dishes will be served casually.

Dress: the Chinese are more casual, wearing T – shirts, jackets and so on. It's just a big occasion to wear something good and elegant.

2.4.2 Catering etiquettes in English – speaking countries

The philosophical thoughts of Western human metaphysics and the nomadic and maritime civilizations have led to the formation of "personal consciousness" of English –

speaking people (Wu, 2013). They are individual - centered, they respect individual rights, and they never interfere with the privacy of others. Influenced by these thoughts, people prefer separating meals into small pieces and serve to everyone before eating.

Seating: When having a dinner party with people sitting around a table, the host will sit at the side which is closer to the kitchen in order to serve foods and drinks. The guests will general sit at positions designated by the host family. Usually the person who seats nearest to the host or the hostess is the most important guest. A gentleman will take a look at the lady on the right before he sits down. If she is not yet seated, he will help her adjust her chair of the best position and invite her to sit down.

Atmosphere: When eating, people prefer eating quietly and orderly. They just eat what they have in their plates and are not allowed to make any unsuitable noise like sneeze, cough, hiccups, or pick teeth. People behave gracefully, chew slowly, and drink soup silently. In order to keep the silence but relaxed atmosphere of the dinner, people only talk to those who are sitting next to them.

Serving order: The first course is appetizers. This kind of dish is very flavorful, its taste is mainly salty and acidic, and it has less quantity and higher quality. Next the soup will be served. The soup is generally divided into four categories: broth, cream soup, vegetable soup and cold soup. The third course is mostly fish, also known as side dishes. Meat and poultry dishes are the fourth course. Desserts are served after the main course, followed by drinks such as coffee or tea.

Dress: When having a dinner party, people will dress more formally and elegantly. However, at some casual situations, it's not necessary to wear fancy dresses. So people pay less attention to what they wear. In English - speaking countries, people like going out for picnics or barbecues at weekends, when they choose to wear clothes not easily to get dirty and broken.

2.4.3 Comparison of different dining etiquettes

Chopsticks and knives and forks are outstanding representatives of differences between Chinese and English - speaking countries' table manners.

First is the difference in the tableware. Chopsticks are the models of Chinese tableware. They appeared in China at least 3 000 years ago (Du, 2015). There are some legends about how did chopsticks appeared. Some contemporary scholars believe that chopsticks originated from bamboo. There were many woods in the North of China, but a lot of bamboos in the west of the country. So the ancestors used what they had and made bamboos into chopsticks. The knife and fork that appeared after chopsticks are representative of Western cutlery. Cutlery originated from the habits of ancient nomadic people in Europe (Du,2015). They would use a knife to carry grilled meat. Around the 15th century, two toothed forks appeared, and in the 18th century four toothed forks appeared.

Second is the difference in national characters. The chopsticks are consistent with the traditional Chinese agricultural civilization and the ancient Chinese "harmony" thought, and are also coordinated with the system in which the Chinese sit around the table (Du,2015). The fork is consistent with the Western tradition of nomadic civilization and Western values of respect for individuality, and thus became the most distinguished representative of tableware in a meal – based system. At the same time, the use of knives and forks formed the habit of Westerners to solve problems independently. It also matches their aggressive, risky characters.

The third difference is time schedules. People in different countries have different concept of time, which leads them to have very different time in dealing with the same event. For example, there is a big difference between Chinese and people in English – speaking countries in their grasp of the time for dinner. According to the concept of human time proposed by the famous American anthropologist Edward Hall (as cited in Wang,2015,p. 57), the Chinese view of time is "diversified". People do not have the habit of scheduling. People in English – speaking countries, by contrast, have the concept of a "singleness" of time. They must strictly abide by the schedule when doing anything. Under the influence of this conception of time, the Western people's feast was extremely consistent with the owner's mind. However, if you are late, don't be later than 10 minutes. Otherwise, you won't respect the owner.

3. Causes, Specific Manifestations and Mutual Influences of Different Diet Cultures

Food and drinks are an eternal topic throughout the development of human history. Culture is the general term for the lifestyle that people gather in long – term life. Food and culture are closely related. Different ethnic groups have created a variety of different dietary cultures because of the distinct living areas, climate, environment and customs. There are many reasons for the differences in dietary culture between China and

A Comparative Study of Diet Cultures between China and English – Speaking Countries: Taking Britain, the United States, Canada and Australia as Examples

English – speaking countries. This part mainly studies the geographical reasons, national characteristic reasons, religious reasons and some other typical influences from special changing periods and immigrants.

3.1 Causes of Different Diet Cultures

3.1.1 Geographical reasons

China is located in East Asia, in the monsoon climate zone in the eastern part of the Eurasian continent. The weather and geography guarantees the lushness of the crops. The Chinese foods were also meat – based during the primitive period, and people also hunted for a living (Du,2015). However, as the population continues to increase, hunting could no longer meet people's needs. As a result, Chinese people have also developed diet structures dominated by plant foods. At the dinner table of a Chinese family, despite the wide variety of meat, rice ornoodle and other plant foods still play a major role.

Most English – speaking countries are located in temperate maritime climate zones and are natural pastures (Du,2015). Due to the regulation of the North Atlantic current and the year – round westerly blowing, the main agricultural types of the UK include the cultivation of forage crops and pasture, and dairy farming. Canada is located near the northern part of North America, with the Pacific Ocean in the west and the Atlantic Ocean in the east. Due to the location, Canadian people eat special kinds of food like maple syrup and all kinds of seafood.

3.1.2 National characteristic reasons

China's traditional agricultural civilization and monsoonal geographical characteristics have enabled the Chinese to form a plant – like national character, which is consistent with the implicit and harmonious nature of traditional Chinese thought (Tang,2017). People put more emphasis on "harmony with peace", "harmony between human and nature", they like to live and work in peace. This national character makes Chinese people gracious and gentle with food. This national character is also very consistent with Chinese people's use of chopsticks as their main tableware. The elegance of using chopsticks is a concrete manifestation of Chinese people's national character.

Being deeply influenced by their ancestors, traditional hunting, maritime civilization and temperate maritime climate characteristics make people from English – speaking countries form a meat – like national character, which in turn embodies their persistent pursuit and willingness to take risks. Under the influence of this national character, they are used to using knife forks on the table, which reflects the strong sense of conquest of them.

3.1.3 Religious reasons

People in English – speaking countries generally believe in Christianity. They are deeply influenced by Christian doctrine of justification by faith (Liu,2010). In addition, they are socially democratic, open, advocating respect for women, and greatly enhancing their social status. Therefore, there is a habit of "equality between men and women, priority for women" at Western banquets (Liu,2010).

In the teachings advocated by Confucianism, Taoism, and Buddhism in China, women have no social status. The traditional Chinese women have always been in the education of "Feminine Virtue", losing all their rights. Under the influence of this traditional ideology, women were not allowed to sit in Chinese banquets for a long time. Until the founding of New China, the status of women could be improved. It is precisely because of this that women can be seen more and more in banquets.

3.2 Manifestations

Different countries, regions and nationalities are bound to experience the process from exclusion to integration because of their cultural traditions, and diet as a cultural phenomenon is no exception.

Nearly 2 000 years ago, China not only introduced silk to the West through the Silk Road, but also introduced tea, porcelain and spices to the Western food culture. Since then, wearing Chinese silk, drinking Chinese tea with Chinese porcelain, and eating Chinese cuisine has become a symbol of Western National enjoyment (Wang, 2006). In modern times, the emergence of Chinese overseas immigrants made Chinese cuisine culture brought to all parts of the world by overseas Chinese. They set up Chinese restaurants abroad, spread Chinese food culture, and made great contributions to the Chinese diet entering the world food hall.

As early as Emperor Wu Di of the Han Dynasty, when Zhang Qian visited Western Regions, he brought back Western foods such as zucchini, watermelon, tomato, pepper, sweet potato, carrot, pepper, and wolfberry. After the Tang Dynasty and the Yuan Dynasty, Western foods were mass – produced. Into China, missionaries like Marco Polo made significant contributions to the introduction of Western diets into China.

3.3 Mutual influences

Through the study I found that in the context of economic globalization, cultural glo-

A Comparative Study of Diet Cultures between China and English – Speaking Countries: Taking Britain, the United States, Canada and Australia as Examples

balization and the information age, the food culture of China and that of English – speaking countries are quietly interacting and promoting. As mentioned earlier, more and more Chinese today have recognized the importance of a healthy diet through the communications and studies with food cultures of other countries, and have begun to pay more attention to the nutrition of foods than the taste of foods ingredient. For example, they realized that fried foods contain a lot of trans – fatty acids. The over – heated oils are not good for preserving the nutrients in vegetables. Therefore, people are beginning to advocate the way of cooking while maintaining the original deliciousness of Chinese food. Now, the habits of eating raw vegetables, boiled chicken and other cooking methods have begun to be accepted slowly. In addition, more Chinese are also beginning to pay attention to table manners and other issues like diet health. The combination of Chinese cuisines and cuisines of English – speaking countries is gaining popularity. They found that in some specific dining occasions, it is very appropriate and polite to use some of the Western dining etiquettes. For example, a person will pay attention to his/her dress before he/she goes to a dinner party, he/she will pay attention to civilized use of tableware at the time of eating, and he/she would also politely thank the host and the hostess after dinner, then leave cheerfully. After that, he/she would even call back or write back to the host family and would invite them to have another party for appreciation. This is not a disrespectful behavior of our own country, but of respect for ourselves and others as a manifestation of the blending of cultures.

In recent years, the cultural confidence of Chinese people has been increasing day by day (Chen, 2015). The development of e – commerce has also made Chinese culture even more powerful. Affected by these factors, people in English – speaking countries are increasingly interested in China. Especially in terms of diet, more and more foreigners can often enjoy Chinese food without having to go out to enjoy the delicious Chinese cuisines. In ancient countries such as Britain, where there are few immigrants from China, people are also surprised by the country's economic development and applauded for the profound Chinese dietary culture. In countries such as the United States, Canada, and Australia, where Asians live, Chinese food is more glutinous for them. It can be seen that more and more people from English – speaking countries are also gradually attracted by Chinese food, and come to China to travel, take their favorite souvenirs and recipes back with them.

4. Conclusion and Prospects of the Research

Diet culture is a major part of human culture. It is also an important part of non-verbal communication in cross-cultural communication. The difference of Chinese and English-speaking countries' diet culture is one of the many phenomena of cross-cultural communication between China and English-speaking countries. Therefore, in the context of cross-cultural communication, it is of great significance to study the two kinds of diet culture. There are huge diet differences between China and English-speaking countries from history to reality and from reasons to performance. The root of this difference is the different values of Chinese people and people in English-speaking countries.

As a comparative study of dietary cultures in Chinese and English-speaking countries in cross-cultural communication, we can take a stand at the international level to see the differences of the two dietary cultures. We should use dialectical thinking to analyze problems, actively embrace other kinds of food culture, then study and learn different social etiquette norms so as to grasp the cultural characteristics of the Chinese nation in comparison. In addition, we can also strengthen our resilience to cross-cultural communication. Through the comparative study of diet cultures between China and English-speaking countries, we can effectively avoid communication errors.

Through this study, the author believes that the Chinese food culture and English-speaking countries' food cultures have their own differences and similarities. The food cultures in China and in English-speaking countries are now coming at a stage of interaction and transformation. The cultural blending between China and these countries can also be demonstrated from this perspective. The differences between Chinese food culture and English-speaking countries' food cultures are obvious, but they also have their own advantages and disadvantages. Studying these differences and commonalities will give us a better understanding of different dietary cultures. Now more and more Chinese are beginning to pay attention to nutrition, health and scientific cooking. With the acceleration of economic globalization and information flow, different food cultures will continue to blend in the collision and complement each other in the collision. They will develop together in exchanges and enrich the world culture together. Different national cultures and different geographical features have created completely different dietary backgrounds. However, in essence, the meaning of "eating" does not change due to these differences. It emphasizes variety, balanced nutrition, rationalization and health has become China and Western English food science consensus. With the development of economic globalization, the exchange of food culture is also present in our daily life. Due to the continuous exchange of Eastern and Western cultures, the Chinese food culture will also have new features in the collision with the cultures of other countries. On the one hand, it will be more conducive to the Chinese food culture to draw upon others in the exchange and collision, and constantly improve development; on the other hand, it will promote the wide spread and development of the Chinese food culture in the world. Only when we correctly grasp the advantages and disadvantages of different dietary cultures in cultural exchange and collision, can we correctly grasp these differences to improve our life and make various dietary cultures complementary and compatible.

The limitations of this study mainly lie in the following aspects. Firstly, some of the wordings and sentences are not quite rigorous, the written English skills need to be improved. Secondly, a lot of efforts have been put into the research on the dietary culture of some countries by means of a large number of documents, whereas field study might have given more support to the conclusion.

In summary, more detailed and extensive studies of the dietary cultures of different countiries will be done in the future. So does field visits to these countries while using a wealth of information and research methods to acquire more innovative, forward - looking findings.

References

[1] ANATOMY. Image:The Main Structure of American Food[B/OL][2012 - 10 - 20]. http://i7. hexunimg. cn/2012 - 10 - 20/147011153. jpg.

[2] CHEN L. A comparative study of Chinese and western diet culture[J]. China Food Safety Magazine, 2015(30):57 - 58.

[3] CHEN Y. A comparative study of Chinese and western diet from a cross - cultural perspective[J]. Literatures, 2011(3):220 - 225.

[4] DU L. Discussion on the characteristics and causes of the cultural exchange between Chinese and western food culture in ancient time[J]. Forum on Chinese Culture, 2015(5):178 - 180.

[5] FANG J R. Differences of dietetic Culture between China and America[J]. English on Campus,2017(21):223.

[6] HUAI B Z. An analysis of the jnfluence of dietary culture on English eating idioms in English speaking countries[J]. Journal of Shandong Institute of Commerce and Technology,2010.

[7] HUANG Y Y. The Chinese and western diet culture from the perspective of intercultural communication[J]. Intelligence,2015(14):265-266.

[8] JIANG Y F. A review of American culture[J]. College English,2006(1):140-143.

[9] LI C L. A guide to Australian culture[M]. Shanghai, Xian, Beijing, Guangzhou:World Book Inc,2004.

[10] LI D J. A brief study on American diet culture[J]. Overseas English,2014(2):246-248,252.

[11] LI X M. Cultural differences from the Chinese and western diet culture [J]. Kao Shi Zhou Kan,2016(66):14.

[12] LIANG L X. On the differences between Chinese and western food culture[J]. English Journal for Middle School Students,2016(18):127-128.

[13] SUN J H, DENG H Y. Analysis of the causes of Chinese and English dietary differences[J]. Heilongjiang Science and Technology Information,2016(2):145.

[14] SUN T Q. A comparative study of Chinese and American dietary culture [J]. Journal of Qiqihar University:Philosophy & Social Science Edition,2009(1):113-115.

[15] TANG R. Study on the differences of Chinese and American dietary culture from the perspective of intercultural communication[J]. Overseas English,2017(2):165-166.

[16] WANG M Q. Food culture in Australia[J]. The Knowledge of English,1995(9):7-8.

[17] WANG P P. Canadian cuisine[J]. Meat Research,2010(8):1.

[18] WANG P P. Australian cuisine[J]. Meat Research.2010(11):1.

[19] WANG Q Y. An exploring on cultural differences between China and western countries from the view of diet[J]. Kao Shi Zhou Kan,2015(89):16,47.

[20] WANG X. A comparative study of Chinese and western dietetic culture from the perspective of cross-cultural communication[J]. Journal of Hunan Industry Polytechnic,2015:57-59.

[21] WANG X M. A guide to Canadian culture[M]. Shanghai, Xian, Beijing, Guangzhou: World Book Inc,2004.

[22]WANG X M,LI C L. A guide to British culture[M]. Beijing:People's University Publication House,2015.

[23]WANG X M,LI,C L. A guide to American culture[M]. Beijing:People's University Publication House,20156.

[24]WANG X T. The history of Chinese diet culture[M]. Guangxi:Guangxi Normal University Press,2006.

[25]WANG Z Y,ZHANG W J. A glimpse of British culture[J]. The Knowledge of Language,2007(7):8-9.

[26]WU F S. On the differences between Chinese and western diet culture [J]. Kao Shi Zhou Kan,2013(75):13-14.

中国和英语国家饮食文化比较研究：以英、美、加拿大和澳大利亚为例

刘伊然*

（首都经济贸易大学 北京 100070）

摘 要：本研究从跨文化交际的角度，从成因、具体表现形式及应对方法三个主要方面对中国及西方英语国家在饮食观念、饮食内容、饮食习惯及饮食礼仪上进行了比较分析，期待从饮食文化方面增加对不同文化的理解，并促进不同文化之间的友好交流。通过比较研究、文献翻阅、影音资料研究及实际考察等研究方式，作者收集了各方面的资源并编纂成文，以期了解中西饮食文化差异的形成原因，阐明随着跨文化交际日益频繁，中西饮食文化将日益融合、共同发展的趋势，为我国与世界文化的交融做出微小的贡献。

关键词：跨文化交际；饮食差异；文化融合；共同进步

---

* [作者简介]刘伊然(1995—)，女，北京人，研究方向为跨文化研究。

浅谈中英颜色词的文化差异

王立华*

(首都经济贸易大学 北京 100026)

摘 要:中英颜色词是互通的,具有丰富的文化内涵和延伸意义,也体现了民族特色和文化特征。但是色彩词在不同的国度和不同文化中有不同的意义,涉及文化、传统习俗、政治、宗教信仰。不了解颜色词的引申义,会在和不同国家的人士交流时造成误解。本研究探讨中英颜色词的意义及在不同文化中的不同引申义,以期避免交流上的障碍,促进文化交流。

关键词:颜色词;跨文化交际;文化差异

引言

世界民族表达色彩的词不同,分类也不一样。但是英语和汉语对基本的颜色词的分类差别不是很大,所以表达颜色的词汇大致相通。但是由于受民族心理、风俗传统、宗教文化以及地域风貌的限制,各种颜色词对不同国家和民族而言,在视觉和心理上引起的联想和象征意义不尽相同,所以我们要注意其中的差异,避免与不同国家和民族的人们交往时产生尴尬。

下面简要列举主要的颜色词在中西文化中的差异内涵和象征意义。

一、白色(white)

在东西方文化中,白色都代表纯洁,有权贵之气。

美国总统生活和办公的地方叫白宫(White House),成为总统权力和美国政府的代名词。无独有偶,英国法庭和政府机关都集中于一条宽阔的街道叫作白厅(White Hall),南北走向,位于特拉法尔加广场与议会大厦之间。英美政府的官方报告叫作白皮书(white book);后来白皮书成为各国政府,包括中国政府,发表关于政治和外交问题的文件。

---

* [作者简介]王立华(1971—),女,首都经济贸易大学教师,研究方向为翻译、大学英语教学。

白色是纯洁的化身,西方传说中的天使的翅膀,现实中较为传统的婚纱礼服和美丽的百合花都是白色的。

坐办公室的,不从事体力劳动的人,被称为白领(white collar),就连谎言(lie),前面加上白色(white),也成为"善意的谎言"(white lie)。按照中国传统,在葬礼上人们穿白色衣服,婚礼上穿红色衣服。但是现在有不少年轻人也穿白色的婚纱,学习西方的传统文化。

20世纪中国有两个品牌的产品——"白象"(White Elephant)电池和"白翎"(White Feather)金笔投放欧美市场,产品包装精美,质量顶尖,却都严重滞销,原因就在于我们不懂欧美文化,"White Elephant"和"White Feather"在欧美和在中国有不同的含义。在泰国(古称暹罗),人们认为白象是神圣之物,只有王室才能饲养,一般作为国礼赠送。当国王不喜欢哪位大臣、贵族时,就"赏赐"给他一头白象,大臣诚惶诚恐地接受,不得使唤它干活,也不敢买卖、转让,更不敢杀死,只好精心侍候,成了一大负担和累赘。因此,白象成为了昂贵而没用的东西,这样的电池出现在欧美市场,必然滞销。"White Feather"来源于斗鸡比赛,斗败的公鸡落荒而逃,往往垂下翅膀,露出翎毛下的白色杂毛,于是西方人用 show one's white feather 表示甘拜下风,临阵脱逃。送"白翎"(White Feather)金笔暗示着送人一根"白羽毛",是对人的极大侮辱和挑衅,所以没人会出钱给自己找不痛快。

二、黑色(black)

(一)表示死亡、不幸和悲哀

基督教的地狱和中国的地狱都是没有光亮的地方,而且都是那些做了坏事的人去的地方,因此,在中西文化中黑色都与死亡联系在一起。例如,于14世纪广泛传播的淋巴腺鼠疫就被称作"the black death",汉语中被叫做黑死病。

由于死亡是一件令人很伤心的事情,所以黑色也经常和不幸、悲哀联系在一起。如"in a black mood"指情绪低落,"a black dog"指一个伤心的人,"The future looks black."指前途暗淡,令人伤心。无论在中国还是在西方,人们去参加葬礼时都习惯穿黑色的衣服。这既体现了人们悲伤的心情,同时也显示了对死者的尊重。

再如英语中的"Black Friday",其中"Friday"对基督教教徒来说,是指复活节前的星期五,是耶稣的受难日。因此,在西方国家"Black Friday"即指大灾大难、凶险不祥的日子。这具有典型的西方宗教传统的色彩。

(二)表示庄重、尊严

以上讨论的是黑色的消极含义,黑色除了有消极的一面之外,还有积极的一面。黑色色泽较暗而显沉稳,因此,在英国文化中,黑色通常是"庄重、谦虚和严肃"的象征。黑色西装(black suit)和黑色礼服(black dress)历来是英国人最为崇尚的传统服装。在一些庄重的正式场合,达官贵人、商界巨贾等都喜欢身着黑色服装;法官也身披黑服,以体现法律的尊严。在中国,人们在一些庄重的正式场合通常也都身着黑色服装。

同样,在中国和现代欧美国家,人们去参加别人的葬礼时总是身穿黑色的衣服,系黑色领带,戴黑色帽子、黑色围巾或黑色面纱。他们认为黑色使人显得严肃,借以表达对死者的悼念和尊敬。因此,在节日期间穿黑色衣服被认为是不礼貌和不吉祥的行为。

三、红色(red)

中国人崇尚红色,它可以体现人们在精神和物质上的追求。例如,人们把促成他人美好姻缘的人称为"红娘",传统婚礼中,新娘裹红挂彩,新郎胸前戴大红花,洞房内贴一对大红喜字(红双喜),这时的红色是对美满爱情的期望;每逢传统佳节,家家都要挂大红灯笼、贴"福"字,来烘托幸福、喜庆的气氛;人的际遇好被称为"走红",生意兴旺叫"红火",得到上司宠信的人叫"红人",分到合伙经营的利润叫"分红",表示运气好、旗开得胜叫"开门红",这些时候的红色是吉祥、幸运的化身。

在西方,红色也有喜庆、欢乐的象征意义,但是带有喧闹的意味。在西方国家,人们把圣诞节和其他节日称为"喜庆的日子"(red-letter day),圣诞节时圣诞老人戴红帽子,着红装。美国人用红色表示高温和激情,"red carpet"表示"隆重的欢迎"。

然而,红色在英语中,更多是含贬义,表示残酷、狂热、灾祸、血腥等意思,是血与火的颜色,象征激进、暴力、危险。如"red flag"(用作危险信号的红旗),"the red rules of tooth and claw"(残杀与暴力统治)。它还象征着放荡、淫秽,如"red light district"(红灯区)。同时,红色在英语中,还有负债、赤字和亏钱的意思。红色在表达情感时,喻指"恼怒,生气和害羞"时,英汉都有此意。如汉语的"脸红脖子粗,面红耳赤"表示生气、恼怒,脸红表示"害羞",而在英语中,"see red,like a red rag to the bull"等表示愤怒、恼火。

四、绿色(green)

绿色是生命最旺盛时期的颜色,人类在自然界生存之初,就是从采野果、食树叶开始的。人类掌握了农业生产技术后,以农作物为代表的绿色植物更成了为人类提供安全、和平、富足的物质基础。在英美国家,绿色是备受人们喜欢的颜色。许多地方都用绿色来修饰,甚至连美元都是绿色的。所以"green"用来表示"金钱"和"财富",并用来比喻"有活力,有希望,幸福快乐"。例如,"green power"表示"金钱的力量","Green old age"表示"老当益壮"。在许多大饭店厨师戴的是绿帽子,在美国的一些大学,学生毕业庆典的长袍和帽子都是绿色的。在汉语中,绿色同样代表着生命,象征着生机、春天、希望、和平等。王安石的名句"春风又绿江南岸"就是典型的例子。在汉英两种语言中,绿色均有和平、友善、环保、生命、希望和生机的象征意义。

绿色在东西方的含义又不是完全一一对应的。英语 green 的引申义比汉语的要多,常常用来表示没有经验,比如:Green Hand(生手),as green as grass(少不更事),Do you see any green in my eyes?(你以为我幼稚可欺吗?)此外英语的绿色还表示嫉妒的情绪,如:green - eyed(嫉妒的,眼红的)。汉语中的绿色有不太好的引申义,如:"绿帽子"。但是,英语中的"绿帽子"(have a green bonnet)则是生意失败、债台高筑的意思。

结语

颜色词的本义和引申义很多,限于篇幅,只解析白、黑、红、绿这四种基本颜色。学会颜色的本义和引申义,可以使我们在和不同国家和文化人士的交往中,了解不同颜色的文化背景,避免冒犯他人,从而做到有效沟通;在和不同文化背景的人士沟通时,弘扬我们灿烂的中华文化。

参考文献

[1]杨玮玮."黑"和"Black"中英跨文化交际[J].科技创新导报,2011(14).

[2]张玉春.汉英颜色词"黄色"和"YELLOW"象征意义分析[J].考试周刊,2013(64).

[3]李青.颜色词在中西方的差异[J/OL].中国学术期刊网卷宗,2015(10).

[4]吕红梅.如何处理英汉互译中颜色词的不对应现象[J].新课程.教师,2013(3).

[5]戴炜栋,何兆熊.新编简明英语语言学教程[M].上海:上海外语教育出版社,2002.

[6]林纪诚.语言与文化综论[M].上海:上海外语教育出版社,1999.

读书会驱动的翻译专业硕士自主学习模式探索*

李双燕**

(首都经济贸易大学 北京 100070)

摘　要:高校读书会是一种以学生为中心的自主学习方式,对于人才培养的重要价值逐渐凸显。本研究结合首都经济贸易大学翻译专业硕士读书会的开展经验,探讨读书会的实施背景、整体规划、主要特色与初步成果等,以期逐步建立"学院—教师—学生"翻译学习共同体,拓展学生自主学习能力,培养社会所需的高层次、应用型、专业性语言服务人才,推动翻译硕士专业内涵式发展。

关键词:翻译硕士;读书会;自主学习;学习共同体;内涵式发展

引言

《礼》曰:"独学而无友,则孤陋而寡闻。"学习过程中与朋友共同切磋,集思广益,取长补短,是一种有效的学习方式。我国一直有以文会友的传统,比如竹林七贤、竟陵八友等是我国早期读书会的典型代表(赵俊玲,2015)。现代意义上的读书会起源于瑞典,被称作"study circle(学习圈)",是指一群朋友根据事先确定的题目或议题,共同进行学习的组织。欧美国家大力推广读书会活动,例如《英国国家公共图书馆的读书会发展计划》将读书会的发展提升为国家政策(Reading Agency,2015)。而教育领域主要关注读书会与学习效能的关系,比如帕罗特(Parrott,2011)探讨如何将读书会和大学课堂教学结合起来,促进深度学习(deep learning)等。

在当前我国推行全民阅读的时代,高校读书会逐渐得到关注,相关探索也逐步兴起,主要包括对高校图书馆开展的各类读书活动的推介(张亚军、孟昭和,2004;刘宝明,2014)、读书会推广策略(张希侠,2015;万春珍,2016)、港台地区高校读书

---

* [基金项目]:本研究为2019年度首经贸教学改革立项重点项目"首都经济贸易大学研究生公共英语能力评测体系建设与应用研究"(02491954211139)和北京市教育委员会2020年度社,科计划资助项目"译者技术传播能力的构成与培养研究"(SM202010038001)的部分成果。

** [作者简介]:李双燕(1982—),女,河北邯郸人,首都经济贸易大学讲师,硕士生导师,研究方向为翻译理论与实践、技术传播等。

会推广经验(曹桂平,2014;向剑勤,2016)等。这些成果为本研究提供了重要参考。除宏观层面的研究外,还有针对特定学科或专业读书会的研究,比如辛婷婷(2013)、陈蔓琪、祖艳凤(2016)、张媛军(2016)等通过调研,证明读书会可有效提升英语专业学生的阅读、思辨、解决问题等能力。

然而,针对翻译硕士专业(Master of Translation and Interpreting,MTI)开展读书会的探索还比较少,尚未充分认识到读书会对 MTI 学生成长的重要性。本研究在分析当前 MTI 教育目标与主要问题的基础上,结合首都经济贸易大学外国语学院 MTI 读书会的实施情况,分析读书会的实施背景、整体规划、实施特色及效果等,以期集合各方优势,建设"学院—教师—学生"翻译学习共同体,创造良好的自主学习生态圈,促进 MTI 专业内涵式发展。

一、MTI 读书会的实施背景

党的十九大明确提出"加快一流大学和一流学科建设,实现高等教育内涵式发展"。内涵式发展就是强调事物"质"的发展,以事物内部因素作为动力和资源,如要素优化、结构协调、资源配置等,强调质量与效益的提高。高校内涵式发展强调以人为本,核心在于促进和实现人的全面自由发展,传承学术传统,凸显学科特色,形成专业品牌。在具体教学活动中,需要创新教学形式,强化实践育人,改变简单地以知识传授为目的传统教学范式,探索以学生为中心的启发式、合作式、参与式和研讨式学习方式,使学生能够深度参与、有效体验教学过程,培养自主学习和创新思考的能力。这为探索翻译硕士专业教育指明了方向。

我国翻译硕士专业学位自 2007 年设立以来,已经走过 10 余年的发展历程。截至 2020 年 4 月,全国设立 MTI 学位点的高校已达 259 所。翻译硕士的培养目标是:培养德、智、体全面发展,能适应经济全球化及提高国家国际竞争力的需要,适应国家经济、文化、社会建设需要的高层次、应用型、专业性口笔译人才。然而,目前翻译人才的培养和供给状况与社会对高端翻译人才的需求还有很大的差距。MTI 招生表面一片繁荣景象,但逐渐暴露出来的问题已经相当严峻。何刚强(2016)分析了 MTI 教学面临的重重忧患,认为若不及时应对,培养出来的学生将是"庸译五短,不成一技"。这里的"五短"为:汉语水平低、外文功底浅、杂学知识寡、文化视野窄,以及想象能力弱。其结果是当下大量 MTI 毕业生并没有缓解高水平翻译人才匮乏的严峻局面,而学生也面临就业困难。

刘敬国、陶友兰(2011)认为,造成这些问题的关键原因是翻译教学模式不能适应培养高级翻译人才的要求,呼吁 MTI 教学应突破以教师为中心的知识传递型翻译教学模式,转向以学习者为中心的新型教学模式,并提出了三种有效操作模式,包括读书报告会、翻译研讨班和以项目为基础的训练等。杜欣欣(2010)在总结对上外高翻短期参访后的收获时,重点提到谢天振教授非常重视学生讨论会,亲自组织硕博士学生和教师齐聚一堂,定期交流读书心得和研究进展,相互分享,开展辩论,这是推进学生思考的绝佳平台,也是提升学生研究素养的不二法门。石曼(2017)调研上海5所高校MTI发展现状时提道,针对MTI学生双语基础薄弱的问题,参访教师提议开展读书会或研讨会加以弥补,但并未探讨如何具体开展。因而,有必要进一步探索MTI读书会的实施方案,培养学生自主学习能力,弥补课堂教学的不足,缓解当前的困难状况。

二、MTI读书会的实施规划

读书会的顺利开展需要提前进行整体规划,国外在读书会运营和管理方面进行了深入研究。比如雅各布森(Jacobsohn)的《读书会手册》(1998:10)对读书会的运营提供了详细的指导,包括读书会成员的选择、讨论技巧、建议书单、团体动力等多个方面的知识。奥斯本(Osborne)出版的《读书会指南》(2002:7)探讨如何运营读书会,如何选择图书等。据此,我们对MTI读书会的预期目标、学习内容、活动时间、参加人员、考核要求、奖励措施以及管理平台等进行全盘考量,学习内容遵循学生的认知发展规律,尽量与课堂教学安排相匹配,课上课下双线并行,互为补充。在此基础上制订具体可行的实施方案,采取一系列监督措施,确保方案落实到位。因而,我们采取"以终为始(Begin with the end in mind)"的管理理念(Covey,2013),即在启动读书会之初,拟定目标,明确告知学生整个读书会的具体安排,让学生对读书会有一个清晰的整体认知,认清它的重要性和具体要求,从而更有针对性地做好各个阶段的读书规划。

鉴于我校的MTI为两年制,第一学年结束时进行开题答辩,第二学年以实习和论文写作为主,因而读书会主要在MTI研一期间开展,分为4个阶段,每个阶段在阅读目标、内容、考核方式等方面各有侧重。详见表1。

表1 首都经济贸易大学MTI读书会日程表(2019—2020)

阶段	阅读目标	阅读内容	考核要求	时间	备注
1	了解翻译理论 夯实双语基础	中西翻译理论书籍(书单) 中英文经典背诵(书单)	撰写读书报告 检查经典背诵 小组探讨分享 (记录研讨日志)	2019年5月至9月	2019年9月中旬举行读书会,教师分组指导并评分

续表

阶段	阅读目标	阅读内容	考核要求	时间	备注
2	深化翻译理论 发展自我特长 夯实双语基础	翻译理论书籍（自选） 专业领域翻译书籍（自选） 中英文经典泛读（自选）	探讨自选书目（至少1本） 小组探讨分享（记录研讨日志）	2019年9月至12月	2019年12月中旬举行报告会，教师分组指导并评分
3	了解语言服务行业概貌 丰富翻译实践经验	观看译直播等学术讲座 自选材料进行翻译实践	撰写观看报告 分享翻译心得 小组探讨分享（记录研讨日志）	2019年12月至2020年3月	2020年3月中旬举行读书会，受疫情影响，本次以提交学术报告为主，教师评阅
4	学习翻译理论与实践结合途径与相关研究 确定自我毕业论文选题	学习《MTI毕业论文写作方法》 阅读MTI优秀学位论文 探讨学位论文选题构想	每个小组以PPT形式展示优秀毕业论文学习心得 每位同学以PPT形式谈谈自己的选题构想 小组探讨分享（记录研讨日志）	2020年3月至2020年6月	2020年6月中旬举行读书会，受疫情影响，本次采用在线形式研讨，教师分组指导并评分

纵向来看，这4个阶段的目标和任务逐步递进，从语言巩固、理论学习到行业概貌、翻译实践再到论文研读和选题研究，步步为营。横向来看，每个阶段都遵循自主阅读—撰写读书报告—小组研讨—记录要点的操作程序，每个阶段都为下一阶段奠定基础，环环相扣，循环往复，成为学生自主学习的重要组成部分。

下面将重点分析读书会的目标及其在内容、组织形式、评价机制等方面的特色。

三、MTI读书会的实施特色

我院MTI读书会以学生为中心，以学院为依托，以教师为辅助，以社会为导向，形成了四维一体的翻译学习共同体，在阅读目标、内容题材、时间安排、评价机制、管理机制等方面积极探索，初步形成校本特色。

(一)四维一体式目标内容

与 MTI 的人才培养目标相契合,读书会承载着多重目标,并落实到具体的阅读内容上来,回答"为什么读"和"读什么"的问题。刘敬国、陶友兰(2011)认为,MTI 读书会的主要目的是解决学生的三种知识或能力:语言能力(包括英语能力和汉语能力)、文化意识和百科知识。除此之外,我院读书会还增加了翻译实战与鉴赏、科研素养等维度的考量,具体目标如下:

1. 提升双语能力与人文素养。MTI 归根结底是一个语言类专业,语言功底的修炼需要贯彻始终。然而,目前 MTI 学生,包括英语专业学生,整体的中文和英文基础都较为薄弱,这一点可以从学生平时的翻译作业或翻译实践报告中体现出来。其原因在于多年来的应试教育,使学生疲于应对各种测试,忽略了阅读中英文经典,甚至出现了阅读危机,快餐式阅读、浅阅读等现象大量存在。通过读书会,引导学生阅读中外经典著作,如英语散文、小说、中国典籍《大学》,掌握地道的中外文表达方式,提升双语驾驭能力;更为重要的是还可以滋养心智,汲取古今中外智慧,提高阅读品味,打开人生格局。

2. 拓展专业领域知识。高端翻译人才不仅要有扎实的双语基本功,还需要有丰富的学科知识。因而,MTI 入学考试设有"百科知识"这一科目,涉及文化、历史、科技、医疗、军事等诸多方面,然而仅仅通过这一门考试还远远不够,还需要不断阅读,积累各领域知识。历年的考试暴露出许多考生知识薄弱的问题,对我国优秀典籍和前沿科技发展不甚了解。除了经典著作,学生也可以阅读《经济学人》等外刊杂志,还可以根据个人本科专业背景或未来职业规划等阅读相关书籍,如有的学生选择法律翻译方面的文本,有的学生倾向阅读金融、专利、机械、物理方面的书籍。

3. 提升翻译实践与鉴赏能力。MTI 是面向实践的,需要进行大量的翻译实践。MTI 教指委对取得学位资格的要求为:完成最低翻译量,笔译不少于 15 万字,口译不少于 400 小时。要成为优秀的译员,一方面需要增加翻译量,另一方面需要具备翻译鉴赏能力,尤其是在当下人工智能时代,机器翻译质量日益提高,在某些垂直领域甚至超过了人工翻译,这对译员是极大的挑战,更需要译员在平时练习中,对照优秀译文寻找差距,发挥主动创造性,提高翻译能力。此外,学生还需要密切关注行业发展和市场需求,不仅要满足现有市场需求,还要预见和应对新的市场需求。这一点可以通过阅读语言服务行业报告,参加翻译职业交流大会、观看相关讲座等来弥补。总之,要尽早做好学习和职业规划。

4. 训练科学研究能力。翻译能力的提升除了依靠大量的翻译实践外,还需要理论的指引,"理论具有预测、认识、解释、批判、方法论和指导实践等六大功能"

(杨自俭,2006:37)。MTI 学生整体上在理论应用方面显得力不从心,这一点最为明显地表现在学位选题与论文撰写方面。因而,一方面需要引导学生研读中外翻译理论,比如《中国译学理论史稿》、《会议口译》、《口译:技巧与实践》(Interpretation:Techniques and Exercises)等;另一方面,需要将理论与实践结合,学习如何应用理论对翻译过程中遇到的问题或现象进行预测、解释、分析等,从而将个体经验转变为群体智慧,实现知识共享、传承与创新,推动翻译行业发展。

可见,读书报告会既有语言人文和知识目标,又有理论与实践目标;其所涵盖的内容已经超越了传统读书会的范围,不仅包含经典阅读,还包含行业实践与课题研究。四个阶段各有侧重,前两个阶段以双语能力与翻译理论素养为主,后两个阶段以口笔译实践练习与论文研讨为主。各阶段的目标和内容并非割裂,而是相互联系、一脉相承的:双语基本功、百科知识的不断积累能够促进翻译实践;关注行业动态,大量翻译实践为课题研究提供基础,同时,理论研究又能指导实践,促进知识创新。这四维目标及其内容如图 1 所示。

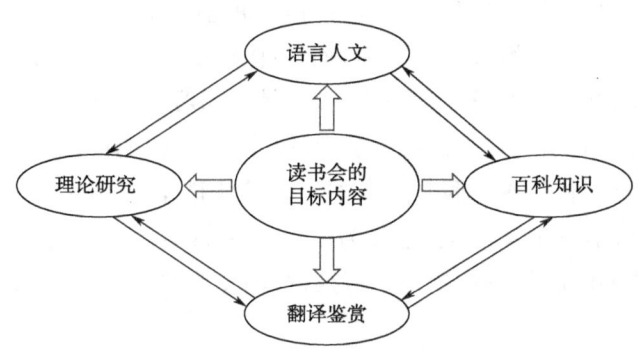

图 1　MTI 读书会目标与内容

(二)自上而下式组织模式

读书会是一种学生自主学习模式,然而自主知识体系的建构不是漫无目的的,而需要较强的规划力、执行力和监督力。读书报告会有多种规划推行机制,有学校图书馆推动开展的全校读书活动,如深圳大学图书馆"荔鸣读书会";有师生自发成立的读书会,如上外高翻的硕博士读书会;有导师自发组织的师门读书会;还有学生自发组织的读书会。在各类形式中,学生自发组织的读书会多因学生自我约束力不强和学业繁忙,无疾而终。我院最开始实行读书报告会时,以学生自主组织为主,教师监督为辅,因监督力度不够,出现过部分学生应付了事的情况。后改为学院主管部门负责,MTI 教育中心组织,导师及任课教师共同指导,学生分组研讨的形式,读书会的开展才日益规范。

为提高读书会活动的管理效率,采用线上和线下并行的管理模式。线上利用"课堂派"建立读书会管理平台,便于发布通知、上传资料、接收作业、进行查重、统计数据、评分反馈等,教师能够实时获取学生作业、留言等信息,简化了沟通流程,提高了管理效率。线下主要采取小组研讨的形式,邀请 MTI 导师、任课教师参与,每组安排一两名教师,面对面互动交流,进行个性化辅导。教师不仅进行辅导,还会根据学生表现进行综合评分,评分结果会累计纳入学生评优评奖等活动,由学院主管部门统一核定,凸显了读书会的重要性,因此学生对读书会更加重视,参与的积极性更高。

(三)把握先机式时间管理

考虑到我校 MTI 学制为两年,学习时间较短,为充分利用时间,读书会活动从新生录取后开始实施,一般从 5 月开始,而不是等到入学后才开始,这样等于将学习时间延长了近 4 个月。更为重要的是,时间上的提前也使学生很快转换角色,明确研究生阶段的学习目标和任务,方向感和归属感更加强烈,也由于在这个时间段,大部分学生完成了本科阶段的学习,研究生阶段学习尚未开始,基本上没有外在的学习任务,能够更好地投入到阅读上来,是读书习惯养成的绝好时机。

读书会活动目前主要安排在第一学年,第一、三阶段的活动时间安排在新学期之初,督促学生充分利用寒暑假时间自主阅读,第四阶段安排在开题答辩前一个月左右,以研读优秀学位论文为主,主要为学生开题做准备。时间与事件上的契合,有利于学生将读书活动与学业进度并行推进,内化为自主学习行为,从而确保了读书活动的效果。

(四)多元全程式评价机制

评估方式对于学习效果具有重要的检验、指引与反拨作用。就读书会而言,学生自发组织的读书会之所以往往无疾而终,也跟缺乏有效的评估方式有关。我院采取过程性评估方式,将四个阶段读书会的成绩累计纳入学年评优活动。不同阶段的评估方式有所不同,大体上包括背诵或复述中英文经典,撰写读书报告、学术讲座报告,鉴赏译文,研讨优秀学位论文,阐述个人选题等,并明确要求学生汇报时制作 PPT,活动结束后撰写总结日志。根据每个阶段的不同特点,采取个人或小组 PPT 汇报的形式,制定评分细则,请辅导教师对学生读书报告及现场汇报的表现进行打分,据此评选优秀报告,公开展示,并择优集结成册,编订出版。

更为重要的是,这 4 次读书会的分数会累计进行班级排名,评选一、二、三等及优秀读书奖,作为学年奖学金等活动的评选依据,并举行隆重的颁奖仪式,颁发获奖证书,同时还会给予一定的物质奖励,比如奖励《英汉大词典》等书籍,并邀请获奖者发言,分享读书经验。这对新生来说具有很好的榜样引领作用,激励新生发奋读书,积极准备每次读书会,形成读书研讨的良好学风。

四、MTI 读书会的实施效果

截至 2020 年,我院已连续举办 4 年读书会,在学院师生的共同努力下,读书会日益完善,效果逐渐凸显。在与指导教师和学生的交流中发现,绝大部分师生对这一活动持肯定态度。指导教师高度评价学生的认真准备和出色表现,肯定了学生奋发进取的学习精神。学生则认为通过读书交流,不仅了解了很多经典作品,课下要广泛阅读,还从同伴身上看到了自身不足之处,鞭策自己不断努力。另外,学生还特意强调了教师的指导作用。教师启发式的提问、高屋建瓴的总结等,能激发学生对问题进行多元化、辩证式分析思考,提升了学生的鉴赏能力和思辨能力。这种思辨不仅包括与他人辩论,更包括自我内心针对某一问题的是非辩论和论证推理,以及对真理永无止境的探寻,有助于构建新的知识体系。可见,读书会的价值不仅在于引导学生"学什么",更在于"怎么学"。或者说,读书会不仅有助于学生提升人文素养,巩固双语基础,了解专业领域知识,还能指引学生自学、自研、自治方法。正如法国哲学家、科学家笛卡尔所说,最有价值的知识是关于方法的知识,这正是读书会的深层价值所在。

更为重要的是,通过这种方式,逐步建立起"翻译学习共同体"(learning community for translation)。学生提升翻译综合能力,不仅需要教师在课堂传授技巧,还需要学生自己课余多加揣摩,同时需要同伴之间的正向影响,当然,学院主管部门应提供组织保障,营造良好的学习氛围。各方都为了共同的学习目标、学习任务等凝聚在一起,从而形成"学院—教师—学生"这样一个翻译学习共同体。在这个共同体中,学生既是学习者,也是知识的主动建构者,在发现问题、分析问题、解决问题的过程中形成自主探索的能力,继而培养终身学习的能力。而教师则是组织者、辅导者,由"知识的传递者"变为"知识的促进者",同时也是学习者,在指导学生的同时也了解到学生的所思、所想、所需,因材施教,更具针对性地开展教学。这一共同体有助于增进师生、生生之间的了解,提升学习者的参与感、归属感、价值感以及从同伴身上获得的尊重感,有利于维持学生持续、认真地参与读书活动。

结语

我院读书会活动虽然在活动的规划与实施管理等方面积累了一些经验,取得了初步成效,但在未来还有待进一步完善,比如增加活动频次,拓展阅读的深度与宽度,丰富组织形式,增配师资指导。除校内导师外,还可以邀请校外导师参与,更好地把握社会对人才的需求等。而读书会除了可以作为日常教学的一种补充学习形式,还可以作为课堂教学的内在有机组成部分,纳入具体课程的教学活动中来。教师通过设计学习任务,提供多种学习资源,制定多元评估机制等,鼓励学生自主探索、协作学习、共享知识,逐步突破以教师为主导的传统教学模式,赋能课堂,赋权学生,真正实现翻转课堂,促进翻译硕士专业的内涵式发展。

参考文献

[1] COVEY S R. The 7 Habits of Highly Effective People[M]. New York:Simon & Schuster,2013.

[2] JACOBSOHN R W. The Reading Group Handbook[M]. New York:Hyperion Books,1998:10.

[3] OSBORNE S. Essential Guide for Reading Groups[M]. London:Bloomsbury Publishing PLC,2002.

[4] PARROTT H, ELIZABETH C. Using structured reading groups to facilitate deep learning[J]. TeachingSociology,2011,39(4):354-370.

[5] READING Agency. A national public library development program for Reading groups[EB/OL]. [2015-05-30]. http://readingagency.org.uk/about/Programme_for_reading_groups.pdf.

[6] 曹桂平. 台湾地区高校读书会的推广与运作[J]. 图书情报工作,2014(23):102-109.

[7] 陈蔓琪,祖艳凤. "读书会"对英语专业学生阅读能力发展影响研究[J]. 教育教学论坛,2016(45):135-137.

[8] 杜欣欣. 上外高翻短期参访有感[J]. 东方翻译,2010(4):92-95.

[9] 何刚强. "四重忧患"伴"三关失守":我国翻译专业研究生教育何去何从?[J]. 上海翻译,2016(2):1-5.

[10] 刘宝明. 思扬读书会:天津财经大学图书馆经验分享[J]. 图书馆杂志,2014(4):100-102.

[11] 刘敬国,陶友兰. 突破传统,自主学习:建立以学习者为中心的MTI笔译能力培养模式[J]. 东方翻译,2011(5):18-22.

[12] 石曼. MTI专业硕士培养机制及培养现状改革:基于上海市五所高校的

调研[D]. 上海:华东政法大学,2017.

[13]万春珍. 国内高校读书会发展策略研究[J]. 新世纪图书馆,2016(7):72-74.

[14]向剑勤. 读书会的演进及其功能探析[J]. 图书情报工作,2016(3):38-76.

[15]辛婷婷. 读书会对于英语专业研究生学术能力发展影响的探索性研究[D]. 长沙:湖南大学,2013.

[16]杨自俭. 关于翻译教学几个个问题[J]. 上海翻译,2006(3):36-40.

[17]余政峰. 读书会的团体动力因素之研究[D]. 嘉义:国立中正大学,1999.

[18]张希侠. 高校图书馆组织开展读书会活动的策略探析[J]. 内蒙古科技与经济,2015(11):160-161.

[19]张亚军,孟昭和. 对大学图书馆读书会的实践与认识:以贵州大学图书馆为例[J]. 贵图学刊,2004(2):12-14.

[20]张媛军. 一项关于英语读书会对独立学院学生学习能力发展影响的实证研究[J]. 2016(3):37-38.

[21]赵俊玲. 国内外读书会研究现状及展望[J]. 图书情报研究,2015,8(3):15-21.

译者——翻译行为主体研究简述

陈媛媛*

(首都经济贸易大学 北京 100070)

摘　要：本研究以翻译理论的发展脉络为考察依据,探讨了翻译研究不同阶段的译者研究状况,总结出译者研究经历了传统翻译研究阶段以及语言学翻译研究中的"隐身的译者",到文化转向翻译研究中的"译者现身",再到当今社会学视阈下的"作为社会行动者的译者"的身份递进。翻译研究中社会学相关理论的引入,为译者研究带来了更广阔的视野。最后,本研究引用了布迪厄的社会实践理论中的概念,尝试探讨了译者与社会之间的相互建构关系。

关键词：译者；翻译研究；布迪厄

引言

传统翻译研究主要有两种路径——翻译活动的内部研究和外部研究,即关于文本与翻译标准等问题,或是探讨文本外制约翻译活动的现实因素。译者作为翻译行动的承担者,是进行内外部翻译研究的最佳切入点。翻译活动回归社会历史文化语境,译者即是这一活动的社会行动者,因此有必要对译者进行聚焦,梳理译者研究在翻译研究不同历史阶段的状况。

一、"隐身的译者"：传统翻译研究、语言学派翻译研究中的译者

在20世纪50年代以前,即罗曼·雅各布逊(Roman Jakobson)的"On Linguistic Aspect of Translation"一文发表之前,翻译研究仍处于传统翻译学阶段,亦即"前科学"时期。这一时期的翻译研究者多停留在感性经验描述阶段,翻译论述多为点评式的随想或体会。这一传统阶段的翻译研究是以原文本为中心的。他们关注的焦点主要是"怎么译"的问题,或是对"直译"还是"意译"、"忠实"还是"自由"、"内

---

*　[作者简介]陈媛媛(1982—),女,河南洛阳人,首都经济贸易大学外国语学院讲师,博士,研究方向为翻译研究等。

容"还是"形式"等问题进行争论。在翻译研究的这一阶段,对译者的研究是缺失的。因为如果关注翻译的创造性,或是译者的主体性,就意味着要偏离原作,那就是误译、滥译。

从20世纪50年代起,形式主义语言学成为翻译研究的理论导向。翻译研究者开始借助结构理论、转换生成理论、功能理论、话语理论等现代语言学中的理论,对翻译问题展开科学、系统的研究。在翻译研究的语言学派看来,翻译就是找出不同语言在不同层次上的对等关系,译者只需掌握语言转换的法则,就可以实现译作与原作的对等。如此一来,翻译过程中便不需要译者发挥任何主观性,译者的主体性不再显现,译者成了"隐身人"。对译者主体性的研究自然也就没有任何基础与需求了。翻译研究的"语言学派"关注的是文本本身,是语言的结构与形式之间的对应。译者在其中是"隐身"的。但是,随着翻译研究中"文化转向"的兴起,翻译研究开始从关注文本本身延伸到文本外的文化环境,研究视野不断拓展。

二、"译者现身":文化转向下的译者研究

兴起于20世纪七八十年代,形成于90年代的翻译研究的文化转向(Bassnett and Lefevere,1990)中,翻译研究不再文本至上,转而开始关注翻译活动所处的译入语语境等因素。在翻译研究的文化转向影响下,吉迪恩·图里(Gideon Toury)等人开始关注翻译的社会操纵性,力图揭示翻译活动背后的意识形态因素,由此,翻译被视为特定社会的一种操纵工具;弗米尔(Vermeer)、莱斯(Reiss)、诺德(Nord)等人将翻译看作一项为实现特定目的的复杂活动;曼塔瑞(Manttari)、尼兰贾娜(Niranjana)等认为翻译是社会语境下的跨文化交流活动,强调译者、原文本作者、读者等在此过程中的作用,以及翻译活动的社会意义;罗宾逊(Robinson)等人强调译者的作用,质疑传统翻译研究中以原文本为中心的认识。在文化学派的翻译研究者看来,文化不再是静止地保存传统与认同的载体,而是不断变化的动态过程。译者以及翻译过程中的其他参与者都被置于特定的文化动态之中考察,翻译也对文化的构建做出了贡献。当翻译开始转为面向译入语文化时,翻译主体研究必然成为译学研究的重要课题,译者也因而逐渐"显身",成为翻译研究所关注的焦点问题。翻译主体被"发现",译者研究的渐次展开,是翻译研究逐渐深入的结果。潘文国曾指出,近年来,"翻译研究的趋势经历了从原文转向译文,从规定性转向描写性,译文地位从'低于原文'经过'等于原文'一直到'比原文更重要',译者的地位从低于作者到被认为在翻译活动中起决定作用等一系列转变"。

自从翻译研究的文化转向以来,译者的研究主要集中在以霍姆斯为代表的翻译研究学派、佐哈尔的多元系统论、图里的描述翻译研究、女性主义翻译理论、后殖民主义翻译理论的研究中。在霍姆斯提出的描写翻译研究中以翻译过程为导向的研究维度之下,他肯定了译者主观选择的权利,从而还原了译者的主动性和能动性。佐哈尔的多元系统论把社会历史文化因素引入翻译研究中,指出译者在面对译入语的文学与文化系统时,会基于自身对它的认知和判断,有意识地选择不同的翻译策略,译者的主体性从而得到了关注。图里认为,翻译是一种受社会文化规范(norms)制约的活动,翻译过程实际上是译者不断选择规范的过程。这一论述彰显了译者的选择性与主体性。翻译研究的文化转向风潮在20世纪90年代初达到最盛,翻译研究从此进入全面的文化研究领域。在后现代主义理论的指引下,女性主义有了消除男性中心主义、实现男女平等的理论基础。女性主义翻译理论则是在上述理论基础之上,将女性主义与翻译活动结合在一起。女性主义翻译理论的论点主要是,消除翻译研究中对女性的歧视;解构原文本,瓦解男性中心主义;颠覆原文与译文的主仆关系;强调译者的主体性与创造性等。译者在女性主义翻译理论中拥有很大的自由度,积极参与意义的建构,从而获得了与原作者同等的地位。后殖民主义的翻译理论认为,殖民者通过文化传播等方式,通过翻译实现文化霸权,塑造殖民话语。翻译因而变成传统殖民统治结束后的一种新型殖民工具。后殖民主义的最终目的即是消除这种殖民话语,解构殖民主义。由此,翻译成为后殖民主义的主要武器,即通过翻译抵制文化霸权,重塑文化身份。在后殖民主义的文化权力和话语关系这一核心论题中,译者进入权力的中心,为殖民者文化身份的重新塑造发挥着积极的作用,译者的主体性地位得到凸显。

在译者主体研究方面,国内外研究内容主要包括译者主体性、主体间性、译者创造性等。在《语篇与译者》(Hatim & Basil,1990)一书中,哈蒂姆(Hatim)和罗勒(Basil)指出,语言学的新发展,如语境因素、话语研究等,有助于重新确立译者在跨文化交际过程中的核心与纽带地位。他们认为译者需要双语工作能力,以及一个双文化视角,以便在原文作者和译文读者的文化交流过程中起到连接纽带作用。鲁宾孙(Robinson)在他的《译者登场》一书中,将翻译研究历程当中诸多关于译者的主体性思想进行了较为全面的阐释,多角度,多层面地对译者进行了综合性研究,开启了"重视译者因素"的研究潮流,使译者的主体性逐渐得到相应的重视。维努蒂(Venuti)在他的名著《译者的隐身》一书中,从解构主义的哲学观出发,批判了归化翻译的各种弊端,并认为译者"隐身"乃至文化地位的边缘化,正是由于归化翻译造成的。因而,维努蒂从文学文化和政治的高度,大力倡导异化或阻抗式的翻译,以保留原文的语言和文化差异。鲁宾逊的《谁翻译?》一书谈论的正是译者主体性的问题。他指出译者是感性的个体,而不是理性的工具。强调译者是真实存在的群体化的个体,以及他们真实存在的价值、创造性工作的意义。在《翻译中的评价:译者决策关键之处》一书中,"Munday 运用评价理论,对译者决策过程中的评价性语言加以描述和阐释,从而建构了译者主体性研究的新途径"。

国内关于译者研究的论述,多见于许钧(2003)、查明建(2003)、穆雷(2003)、屠国元、朱献珑(2003,2009)、杨武能(1987,1993,2003)、袁莉(1996,2003)、谢天振(1992,2008,2012)、胡庚申(2004,2014)等学者的研究论述。如许钧 2003 年在《中国翻译》上发表了一篇名为《'创造性叛逆'和翻译主体性的确立》的文章,同年在《外语教学与研究》上发表了一篇名为《翻译的主体间性与视界融合》的文章。他在这两篇文章中,分别就译者的主体意识和翻译的主体性这两个概念进行了厘清与界定,凸显了译者在翻译活动中的中心地位,并对主体间性的问题展开了讨论,认为"积极、互动的主体间性能使作者、译者和读者三者之间的和谐共存成为可能"。查明建的研究主要探讨了译者边缘化地位的历史由来,并从"翻译过程、译者的译入语文化意识和读者意识、译作与原作和译入语文学的互文关系、译者与原作者和读者的主体间性关系四个方面,分析译者主体性的内涵及其表现"的问题。屠国元等人主要从阐释学的角度,呼吁人们提高对译者主体性问题的重视。杨武能是我国较早开始关注译者定位问题的学者。他从阐释学的角度出发,说明作者、译者、读者都参与了创作与解读的全过程,并认为文学翻译的中心和主体应该是从事翻译活动的译者,呼吁学界重视翻译家的研究,尊重译者的劳动与作品。谢天振则提出了"文学翻译的创造性叛逆"等命题,对翻译家的地位和主体性进行了重新认定。袁莉也是从诠释学的角度,提出了以译者为基点,与原作、译作和世界(包括译入语读者)构成的一个诠释循环图式,"译者是这个阐释循环的中心,也是唯一的主体性要素"。胡庚申在《中国翻译》上分别于 2004 年和 2014 年发表了题为《从'译者主体'到'译者中心'》《从'译者中心'到'译者责任'》的两篇文章。在文中,胡庚申对"译者中心"的定位、取向、界定进行了阐释,并提出译者担任着翻译过程中的主导角色,因而需要承担翻译伦理所规定的"译者责任"。

从目前有关译者的研究概述中可以看出,译者研究多从文化研究的视角出发,不再把翻译视为单纯的文本活动,而是将其置于历史文化的大语境下进行考察。译者在这一过程中的作用凸显出来,他们不再是"隐形人",而是积极发挥主观能动性的社会人。

三、"作为社会行动者的译者":社会学转向下的译者研究

从上述文化转向影响下的翻译研究就可以看出,翻译活动不仅关涉文化的因

素,而是同时有着文化与社会两个层面的含义。文化层面强调的是结构的概念,其核心的因素包括权力、控制、宗教、经济等;而社会层面关注的是翻译活动中的各种参与者,这些参与者将文化结构内化在自身的活动之中,并根据其文化结构影响下的价值观念和意识形态进行活动。但是,翻译的社会因素却长期为研究者所忽视。而单纯强调文化层面的翻译研究,似乎不足以系统化地解释翻译活动的社会特性。因此,文化和社会本就不应该被割裂开来。正如内德哈特(Neidhardt)在 *My Translation* 中所述:"Culture creates social structures and is shaped by existing ones."(1986:15)翻译显然在这种构建过程中起到了重要的作用。把文化和社会研究联系起来,将有助于翻译研究超越这种二元对立,更有效地分析考察翻译问题。因此,迈考拉·沃夫(Michaela Wolf)在 *Constructing a Sociology of Translation* 一书中具体写道:"文化实践和社会实践,以及各自的理论和方法论概念,本就不可相互割裂"(2007a:6)。而当翻译被强调为一种社会实践时,翻译研究自然就导向了"关于社会翻译学的研究"。

早在1972年,詹姆斯·霍姆斯(James Holmes)就在他的翻译学科的奠基之作"The Name and Nature of Translation Studies"中提出了"翻译社会学"这一名称。霍姆斯在这篇文章中为翻译研究勾勒了一个学科框架。他把翻译研究分为两个主要部分:纯翻译学和应用翻译学。其中,纯翻译学有两个主要目标,即描述翻译学和理论翻译学。描述翻译学,描述经验世界中与翻译和翻译作品有关的现象。描述翻译学可以有多个研究导向,其中包括产品为导向、功能为导向、过程为导向的描述翻译学。在以功能为导向的描述翻译学中,翻译研究的对象是翻译在目的语社会文化情境下的功能,关注的是语境,而非文本。霍姆斯在论述该部分构想时写道:"对这一部分加大研究力度,可将其发展成'翻译社会学'(translation sociology),也许还可以称之为'社会翻译学',这样的名称也许不太恰当,但是准确的。因为在翻译学和社会学中,它都是合法的领域。"

20世纪90年代,翻译研究兴起了引入社会学理论和方法的新风气。其中,法国社会学家皮埃尔·布迪厄(Pierre Bourdieu)的文化行为理论、德国社会学家尼克拉斯·卢曼(Niklas Luhmann)的社会系统理论、法国贝尔纳·拉伊尔(Bernard Lahire)的个人社会学理论以及布鲁诺·拉图尔(Bruno Latour)的行动者网络理论(Actor - Network Theory, ANT)等对于翻译社会学研究影响深远。最早提出将布迪厄的社会学理论引入翻译研究的学者之一是让-马克·古安维克(Jean - Marc Gouanvic)。古安维克指出,布迪厄并没有把翻译视为一个独立的场域(field),因为在布迪厄看来,翻译文本如同本土文学一样,遵从同样的客观逻辑。丹尼尔·西梅奥尼(Daniel Simeoni)在"The Pivotal Status of the Translator's Habitus"(1998)的文章中,引用了布迪厄的"惯习"(habitus)概念,探讨译者对已获得惯习的依赖性问题。尹戈莱芮(Moira Inghilleri)在布迪厄的"场域"和"惯习"概念的基础上,讨论了译者的从属地位的问题。塞拉莎菲(Sela-Sheffy)(2005)也引用了布迪厄的惯习概念,批判性地继承了西梅奥尼对于"惯习"与"规范"相关性问题的讨论。迈考拉·沃夫(Michaela Wolf)(2005)则审慎地探讨了重构翻译场域的可能性问题,并试图借用霍米·巴巴(Homi Bhabha)的"第三空间"(Third Space)概念原理扩展布迪厄的场域概念。杰拉德·帕克斯(Gerald Parks)于1998年发表了一篇题为"Towards a Sociology of Translation"的论文。帕克斯在文中尝试利用社会学方法把翻译视为一种社会互动形式,从而研究译者在文化转换过程中所起的作用。此外,他还将译入语文化视为一个权力场域,认为译本必须进入译入语文化的场域之中。目前国内对于翻译社会学的讨论,大部分还处于对社会翻译学的界定,或是对翻译学所借鉴的社会学概念进行理解与融合的阶段。许钧认为,翻译是基于人类交流的需要而产生的,因而具有社会性。王洪涛在他的《构建'社会翻译学':名与实的辨析》(2011)一文中,主要从"名"的层面论证了翻译社会学存在的意义,同时从本体论的角度阐述了翻译社会学的研究方法。在《文化资本与翻译的话语权力》(2003)一文中,杨柳运用布迪厄的文化生产场的理论,论述了文化资本的占有与翻译话语权力的相互关系。李红满的《布迪厄与翻译社会学的理论建构》(2007)对西方翻译学术界如何借鉴布迪厄的社会学概念与理论模型构建翻译社会学的子学科进行了系统的论述。王悦晨的《从社会学角度看翻译现象:布迪厄社会学理论关键词解读》(2011)一文对于翻译社会学的基本概念进行了梳理和解读。同时,还有研究者使用布迪厄的社会学理论和概念,对中国翻译研究中具体问题展开探讨。如山东大学鄢佳的博士论文《布尔迪厄社会学视角下的译者葛浩文翻译惯习研究》(2013),利用布迪厄理论中的"场域"和"惯习"概念,对译者葛浩文的译本选择、翻译思想的形成、不同时期翻译特色的变化,以及影响译者翻译活动的社会因素进行了深入的考察。邵璐在《布迪厄社会学维度的中国近代翻译史研究》(2013)一文中,详细论述了布迪厄社会学理论中的一个核心概念"场域",并将其运用到中国近代翻译史的考察之中,对翻译文化与社会实践进行了探讨。葛佳彬的硕士论文《布迪厄社会学视角下《红高粱家族》英译研究》(2014)则利用布迪厄的"场域""资本""惯习"三个核心概念,对《红高粱家族》的英译本如何在美国获得青睐的原因进行了探究。

自此,包括"社会系统""场域""惯习""资本"等概念纷纷被引入到翻译研究之中,这一趋势则被丹尼丝·默克勒(Denise Merkle)称为翻译研究的"社会学转向"。迈考拉·沃夫(Michaela Wolf)将翻译社会学研究的方法论框架大致分为以下几个方面:翻译行为参与者的社会学研究、翻译过程的社会学研究、翻译作品作为文化产品的社会学研究。翻译活动参与者的社会学研究路径从不同的角度强调参与者的角色。例如,巴雷·迪克罗克(Barret-Ducrocq)(1992)曾讨论过译者在建构统一的欧洲中所起的作用。科妮莉亚·劳伯(Cornelia Lauber)(1996)做过一项研究,试图通过译者的性别、职业以及与原文本相关的问题重构法国译者群体的身份特征。翻译过程的社会学研究中,描述性翻译研究为其提供了广阔的发展空间。例如,克莱姆·罗宾斯(Clem Robyns)在"Towards a Sociosemiotics of Translation"(1992)一文中强调了对历史文化因素和通过翻译而发生的认同形成过程的考量,并认为源语文本和译入语文本都是一种内嵌在社会话语中的结构。翻译作品作为文化产品的社会学研究路径不是一种单一的研究方法。对翻译作品的研究不仅需要强调参与翻译产品的生产和接受的行为者,而且还要考虑他们在各自权力关系中的所起到的塑造者作用。除此以外,还要关注翻译作品作为文化产品在国际的传播。按照此种研究方法,对译本的研究要着重关注翻译作品对社会认同、形象、社会角色、意识形态等因素的建构。而翻译行为参与者、翻译过程、作为文化产品的翻译作品之间是一个相互影响的过程。其中,译者研究作为一个社会人或者行动者在理解翻译过程选择、翻译活动意义和影响方面有着十分重要的地位。丹尼尔·西梅奥尼(Daniel Semeoni)曾指出:"译者的特性是社会文化史汇聚到译者个人身上、经过复杂演化形成的结果。"迈考拉·沃夫也强调了译者在将翻译活动作为社会行动的研究中的重要地位,"把译者认定为某一社会建构的主体和客体,有助于将翻译作为一种社会活动来研究"。

那么,译者作为社会行动者(agent)与所处的社会文化环境或社会结构(structure)之间是一种什么样的关系,又会对翻译作品这一文化产品产生什么样的影响?主观能动性与社会结构这两者之间的关系也是社会科学探索已久的问题。社会科学中的结构—功能主义强调社会对个人的制约性。以涂尔干为代表的法国年鉴学派强调社会事实的研究,认为社会支配着个人的行为,而不能促进其创造力和能动性。相反,社会科学界中弗雷德里克·巴特(Fredrik Barth)的互动理论以及曼彻斯特学派的理论等人却强调个体能动性的重要性。巴特认为,人可以通过自身的行动、生成、维系、改变社会。曼彻斯特学派认为,现实生活中充满矛盾,社会是通过对这些对立和矛盾的吸纳而达到平衡的。人们的实践和行动应该是关注的焦点,而非社会结构。对于行动者具有能动性与社会结构固化这一冲突关系在布迪厄的实践理论中被消解。布迪厄超越二元对立的具体方法是将结构主义与建构主义两种途径综合起来。布迪厄提出了"惯习""场域""资本"等一系列概念。他认为,人们在社会实践的过程中,会将社会规律内化在自己的行为中。同时又经过自己的实践活动,对这些社会规律产生影响,即对社会关系进行再生产。惯习是一种社会化了的主观性,是个体与社会的统一体。布迪厄认为语言是一套具有象征性权力的符号系统,能够"维持或推翻社会秩序",可以参与社会结构的建构。因而,我们可以说翻译活动参与了社会建构,同时亦受到社会结构的影响。

结语

总之,布迪厄的思想和概念从译者角度出发,为研究翻译问题提供理论分析工具,阐释了译者与社会之间相互建构的关系及其对翻译作品这一文化成果的影响。同时,布迪厄实践理论是一个动态的过程,而不是一个静态的历史片段。

参考文献

[1] WOLF M. The Emergence of a Sociology of Translation: Constructing a Sociology of Translation[M]. Amsterdam: John Benjamins Publishing Company, 2007.

[2] PIERRE B. Language and Symbolic Power[M]. Trans. Gino Raymond and Matthew Adamson. Cambridge: Harvard University Press, 1999.

[3] 潘文国. 当代西方的翻译学研究:兼谈"翻译学"的学科性问题[J]. 中国翻译, 2002(1).

[4] 侯林平, 李燕妮. "评价理论"框架下译者主题性研究的新探索[J]. 中国翻译, 2013(4).

[5] 许钧. 翻译的主体间性与视界融合[J]. 外语教学与研究, 2003(7).

[6] 查明建, 田雨. 论译者的主体性[J]. 中国翻译, 2003(01).

[7] 袁莉. 文学翻译主体的诠释学研究构想[J]. 解放军外国语学院学报, 2003(3).

[8] 许钧. 翻译论[M]. 武汉:湖北教育出版社, 2003.

[9] 刘超祥. 浅述人类学理论对结构与能动性关系的讨论[J]. 贵州民族学院学报:哲学社会科学版, 2011(6).

[10] 刘统霞. 结构与能动性的关系流变探讨[J]. 山东社会科学, 2008(2).

[11] 李军平. 结构和能动性[J]. 牡丹江大学学报, 2010(11).

对外法语教学中的熟语教学探究

毕研婧　李思如　Aurore Durand**

（首都经济贸易大学　北京　100070）

摘　要：熟语是语言的重要组成单位，也是自然语言中普遍存在的语言现象，凝聚了一个民族文化的精华。本研究从语言学以及教学法的双重角度重新审视熟语特征，明确熟语教学在整个教学活动中的地位，探讨熟语在构成、结构、语义层面上的特征以及这些特征给外语学习者带来的学习困难，旨在为学习活动和熟语教学活动提供依据和支撑。

关键词：法语熟语；中文学习者；语义解读；困难

引言

在语言系统中有各种组合，除了临时性的自由组合，还有现成型的固定组合，即不同程度定型、定义的熟语。熟语远不是语言的一个偶然现象，熟语数量巨大，使用广泛，是自然语言的重要组成部分。巴黎第十大学的研究团队表明熟语所在的语料占比20%（Fiala et al.，1978）。语言学家塞内拉尔（Senellart，1998：120）在近百万词的英语语料库中发现，动词性熟语结构占比30%。另外，熟语因其具有丰富的历史文化内涵，最能反映一个民族文化的精华，而得到普遍的应用。熟语的普遍存在和广泛使用，也使其成为语言学习的关键点，能否根据语境准确理解及运用熟语往往反映出法语学习者的语言水平和文化水平的高低。正如当洛斯（Danlos）

---

*　［基金项目］本研究是2020年度"首都经济贸易大学校级教改项目（02492054210112）：“中外籍法语教师合作教学模式探究"的部分成果。

**　［作者简介］毕研婧（1985—　），首都经济贸易大学外国语学院讲师，博士，研究方向为法汉语言学。李思如（1997—　），首都经济贸易大学外国语学院研究生，研究方向为英语笔译。Aurore Durand（1996—　），首都经济贸易大学外国语学院外教，硕士，研究方向为对外法语教学。

所言,忽略语言的此类结构即忽略语言很重要的一部分(ignorer ces constructions revient à ignorer une bonne partie du langage),从而导致语言学习不完整。而熟语的学习和教学给学习者和教师都带了诸多困难。因此,对于法语学习和教学来说,对熟语的处理和认知都具有重要的学术研究价值。

从教学法的角度出发,熟语教学法(phraséodiadactique)由彼得·库恩(Peter Kuhn)于 1987 年命名,之后在格雷西亚诺(Gréciano)、冈萨雷斯(I. González Rey)等学者引领下发展壮大,熟语的学习越来越引起学界的重视。熟语学习也被欧洲语言共同参考框架纳入评估语言学习与能力的标准中。在 2018 年版的参考框架(North et Goodier,2018)中主张从 A1、A2 阶段即可教授日常固定表达类熟语(formule pragmatique),从 C1 阶段开始外语学习者应该理解一系列不同语级的熟语并根据不同语境合理使用熟语,熟语的学习和教学应该循序渐进地贯穿 A1 至 C2 的整个学习过程。

一、熟语的定义和特征

法语熟语(unité phraséologique)的定义和界定标准一直都是复杂和充满争议的,例如 expression figée(Gross,1996),séquence figée(Mejri,1997),phrasème(Gréciano,1997)等。本研究用熟语来代指语言中"两个或两个以上词构成的,在词汇、词法、句法层次上相对凝固,语义上具有一定程度的不透明性的整体表义语言单位"(毕研婧,2016)。我们把法语熟语分为惯用搭配词组(collocation)、固定短语(expression figée)、谚语类句子(parémie)、日常固定语(formule pragmatique)四个大类。

熟语的主要特征为:

第一,构成的多词性(polylexicalité),即熟语由多个词汇单位组成,并且"组成该熟语的词汇单位失去了自己运用和语义上的独立性"(毕研婧,2016)。

第二,结构的定型性,表现为构成成分聚合关系的固定性以及构成成分之间组合关系的固定性。

第三,语义的整体性,即熟语的表意是指整个熟语的意义,而非其各组成成分的意义和语法关系的简单结合,字面义也因此往往不是熟语义(张辉、季锋,2008);语义对具体说话者而言,可能具有透明性(transparence),也可能具有晦涩性(opacité)。

第四,表意双层性,即熟语的真正意思或比喻义(sens dénotatif)往往跟其字面意(sens littéral)相差甚远,这也给法语学习者造成了理解和使用的困难。

第五,熟语的凝固性是相对与词的自由组合而言的,并非绝对的,而是表现为一个连续体(continuum)(François & Mejri 2006:7;G. Gross 1996;Lamiroy 2006;张辉,2017)。一端为自由组合的词组,中间为有一定程度的凝固性又有一定程度能产性的熟语,右端为凝固性程度最高的熟语(毕研婧,2017)。

二、熟语的教学难点和教学方法

根据前面所描述的熟语的特征,我们发现相较于熟语结构的定型性,熟语语义的复杂性给学习者和教学者带来更多的困难。熟语惯用搭配词组,"指的是两个或若干个词的熟语性组合,在这种词组中,各个词受某种词汇约束的限制,但保留独立性及意义,从而使人得以看出该词组的意义"(梁守锵,1999)。该类熟语的凝固性程度较低,语义较透明。而熟语的日常固定语,更受到熟语外部因素即话语语境的制约。例如,Après vous!(您先请)这个礼貌用语用在给别人让路时,A vous souhaits!(祝您心想事成)通常被应用在某人打喷嚏之后。本研究聚焦于凝固性程度更高、语义更复杂、给学习者和教学者带来更大困难的固定短语以及谚语类句子。例如,donner sa langue au chat,字面解读为把舌头给了猫,实指某人放弃努力,放弃寻找解决方法。再如,prendre le traureau par les cornes,字面义为抓住公牛的角,意指迎难而上。该类熟语经过人们长期使用在法语中固定下来,给教学带来了更大的困难。

针对固定短语(expression figée),传统的熟语教学法有三种:一是词义法(approche sémasiologique)。该方法或基于熟语某组成部分的意义对熟语进行归类学习,或基于熟语的句法结构进行分类学习。例如,fier comme un coq(像雄鸡一样骄傲)和 passer du coq à l'ane(从鸡说到驴,意指突然改变话题)两条熟语都有共同的组成部分 coq(鸡);又如 poser un lapin(放鸽子)和 donner le feu vert(开绿灯)都是动宾短语。然而熟语的意义跟其字面意思往往相差甚远。这个方法侧重熟语结构,但忽略了熟语意义的双层性,因而受到不少学者的质疑。二是语义主题法(approche onomasiologique)。该方法根据熟语表达的主题而对其归类学习,例如avoir un coeur d'artichaut(花心),l'amour est aveugle(爱情是盲目的)是两条意思不相同但都跟爱情有关的熟语。此教学法不仅弥补了词义法忽略熟语内涵的缺陷,而且可以给学习者补充了相关主题文化背景知识,是第一种方法的进阶版。"在二语习得过程中,母语是一种不可忽略的学习基础"(陆效用,2002:15)。三是比较法(approche contrastive)。该方法主要针对以下三种情况。对于能在中文中找到对应结构的法语熟语,学习者可以利用母语"正迁移"(transfert positif),也就是将通过母语获得的对熟语的认识正向转移到法语熟语学习中,熟语学习过程也就变得相对容易。对于在母语中有对应结构但语义有差异的法语熟语而言,母语可能会产生"负迁移"(transfert négatif)或者"干扰"(interférence)。反之,在中文中完全没有对应结构的法语熟语学习就会相对困难。本研究采取第三种方式进行对比分析,在法语熟语教学中利用母语对外语学习的影响,充分发挥母语的正迁移作用,减少负迁移带来的影响,以更有效地促进法语熟语教学。

三、研究方法与实验结果分析

根据熟语语义特征,格拉茨伯格(Glucksberg)与卡恰利(Cacciari)(1991)将熟语按照功能分为四类:非组构性熟语,组构但语义晦涩的熟语,组构但透明的熟语以及准隐喻的熟语。格拉茨伯格(2001)分类强调熟语组成成分的字面义对熟语非字面义的贡献有着不同程度的差异,在考察熟语语义的加工时应区别对待这些不同类型的熟语(张辉,2017:14)。受该理论的启发,结合前面提到的第三种对比分析法,本研究选取50条法语常见法语熟语建立语料库,以本校法语专业大三25名学生作为研究对象。学生需在无工具辅助的情况下,分别标注每条熟语字面意思、比喻意思,以及其在中文中的对应表达。本研究旨在研究法语熟语学习以及法语熟语语义解读与学习者母语之间的关系,以便找到适合教授中国学生法语熟语的方法。我们根据法语熟语语义特点与中文熟语的对比关系,把熟语分为五种类型通过分析25名学生对这五种熟语的解读,我们得出以下结果,见表1:

表1 五种类型熟语的正确率和例句

类型	正确率(%)	例句
第一种	89.6	noir sur blanc 白纸黑字
第二种	67.7	pêcher en eaux troubles 浑水摸鱼
第三种	61.6	trouver chaussure à son pieds 找到适合的东西
第四种	42.8	couper les ponts 切断联系
第五种	32.4	tomber dans les pommes 晕倒,昏厥

第一种为字面义、比喻义皆跟中文已知熟语表达一致的法语熟语。此类熟语所占法语熟语比例较小。学习者很容易对该类熟语进行解读,这类熟语解读正确率也是最高的。例如,noir sur blanc(白纸黑字),意指有字面证据,清清楚楚,明明白白;se sentir comme un poisson dans l'eau(如鱼得水),比喻找到了适合自己发展的环境;donner le feu vert,字面义为开绿灯,与中文惯用语"开绿灯"都比喻给与别人方便。

第二种为字面表达不能在中文中找到完全对应的表达,但得益于其类似的语言结构和透明的语义,学生也比较容易对其进行正确的解读并可以在中文中找到比喻义相同或相似的中文熟语。例如,Il n'y a pas de fumée sans feu,字面义为没有火就不会有烟,对应中文熟语为无风不起浪,虽然两条熟语的字面表达不同,但其比喻义都为形容事出有因;chat échaudé craint l'eau froide,字面义为被烫的猫见到凉水也会害怕,对应中文为一朝被蛇咬十年怕井绳,两者都比喻在某件事情上吃过苦头,日后碰到类似的事就会害怕。

第三种为在中文中找不到对应的熟语表达,但语义透明的法语熟语。例如,trouver chaussure à son pied,字面意思为给他的脚找到合适的鞋,学习者通过这个隐喻很容易理解这个熟语的比喻义,即找到适合自己的伴侣或东西。虽然在中文中没有现成的熟语与之对应,但其隐喻使其语义仍具有透明性,学生对其解读的正确性也是较高的。

第四种为字面义可以在中文中找到对应表达,但比喻义实则不同的法语熟语。例如,couper les ponts,字面意思为切断桥梁,实指与某人完全切断联系,而中文类似熟语过河拆桥,则比喻达到目的后就把帮助过自己的人一脚踢开。再如,avoir le bras long,字面意思为有较长的胳膊,多数学生会联系到中文的"胳膊太长,管得太宽",而该法语熟语意指有影响力。

第五种为语义完全融合的法语熟语,一般学习者通过其字面意思无法推断其比喻义。例如,tomber dans les pommes,字面意思为摔倒在苹果里,实则指昏厥、晕倒。又如,manger les pissenlits par la racine,字面意思为从根部吃蒲公英,实则常以戏谑的方式表达过世、入土为安。此类语义透明度极低且有时候含有特定文化概念的熟语解读准确性最低,也是给学习者带来最多障碍的熟语。

四、对熟语教学的思考

根据以上分析,我们可以得知在法语熟语学习过程中,学习者往往依赖母语,把中文知识运用到法语熟语的解读中,当母语跟法语熟语在结构或语义上表现出共性时,就会提高学习者对熟语的学习效率;反之,当法语熟语表现为跟学习者母语不同的特性或者学习者无法从母语知识中获取对法语熟语的解读分析时,就会阻碍法语熟语的解读。

学习者对前三种类型熟语的解读很大程度上依赖于熟语的字面义,熟语是具有一定程度的可分析性的(analybilité)。第一种类型的熟语语义虽是非组构的(non-compositionnel),但得益于母语正迁移作用,学习者会很容易理解该类熟语的意思。对第三种类型的熟语,学习者可以根据其透明的隐喻推断(déduction)出熟语的意义。第二种类型的熟语介于两者之间,学习者在母语的正迁移和透明隐喻的帮助下较为容易理解。在分析前三类数据的过程中,我们发现学习者会因为没有正确掌握组成熟语的某一个词的词义,或者没有正确理解熟语的语法结构而导致熟语解读失误。因此,针对前三类熟语,我们建议熟语学习和教学应重视语言知识的积累,排除熟语字面义理解的障碍,从而更好地解读法语熟语。

第四种类型熟语的字面义与中文相关表达相似,因此母语在对熟语解读过程中可能会对学习者造成负迁移现象,从而起到一定的干扰作用。第五种类型的熟语处于字面义独立模式,即"熟语非字面义的激活与其字面义没有太大的关系,字面义和非字面义的激活是并行的"(张辉,2017:16)。这两类熟语语义一般是非组构的,不可分析的。这两类熟语往往给学习者带来更多学习障碍。针对此类熟语,我们建议在学习过程中注重收集、对比归类。同时,教学活动中通过溯源、增加文化背景知识以及丰富多样的练习来促进该类熟语的学习。

结语

熟语是语言系统中一种非常复杂的语言单位。其凝固性表现在词法、句法、语义等各个层面,其语义的整体性和双层性给法语熟语的学习带来了较大的障碍和困难。本研究仅针对大三法语专业的学生,从熟语语义特点以及学习者母语对熟语语义的影响着手,从广义的角度分析各种类型熟语的特点并提出针对各类熟语的学习和教学反思。熟语字面义与非字面义的加工解读过程是一个非常复杂的认知过程,加之汉语熟语系统有着明显差异,要求我们在今后的工作中扩大语料库和研究样本,并加强与之配套的具体课堂活动的开发。

参考文献

[1] BALDINGER K. Sémasiologie et Onomasiologie[J]. Revue de linguistique romane, N° 28, 1964.

[2] BI Y. Constructions figées en français et en chinois [D]. Thèse de doctorat, Université de Bourgogne.

[3] CACCIARI C. Gluckberg S. Understanding idiomatic expressions: The contribution of word meaning[C]//Simpson G B. Understanding Word and Sentence. Amsterdam, Netherlands: North – Holland, 1991.

[4] DOROTA S. Locutions en apprentissage de langue seconde [R]. Congrès Mondial de Linguistique Française – CMLF2018.

[5] FIALA P. , Habert B. , Lafon P. , et Pineira C. Des mots aux syntagmes. Figements et variation dans la Résolution du congrès de la CGT de 1978? [R]// Mots, n° 14, 1978: 47 – 88.

[6] GONZALEZ REY I. La didactique du français idiomatique[M]. Louvain – la – Neuve, EME, 2007.

[7] GRÉCIANO G. Signification et dénotation en Allemand. La sémantique des expressions idiomatiques[M]. Paris: Klincksieck, 1983.

[8] GROSS G. Les expressions figées en français. Noms composés et autres locutions[M]. Paris: Ophrys, 1996.

[9] HUDDLESTON D. , PULLUM K. The Cambridge Grammar of the English Language[Z]. Cambridge: UK Cambridge University Press, 2002.

[10] LAMIROY B. Le français de Belgique et les locutions verbales figées[J]. Revue belge de philologie et d'histoire, tome 84: 829 – 844.

[11] MEJRI S. Les expressions idiomatiques[M]. Paris: Edition Garnier, 2017.

[12] MEJRI S. Le figement lexical: descriptions linguistiques et structuration sémantique, série linguistique, vol. X[M]. Tunisie: Publications de la Faculté des lettres de la Manouba, 1997.

[13] NORTH B. , GOODIER T. Cadre européen de référence pour les langues: apprendre, enseigner, évaluer[Z]. Volume complémentaire avec les nouveaux descripteurs. Strasbourg: Conseil de l'Europe, 2018.

[14] SENNELLART J. Reconnaissance automatique des entrées du lexique – grammaire des phrases figées[C]. Lamiroy B. (dir.), Travaux de linguistique: Le lexique – grammaire, n° 37, 1998: 109 – 121.

[15] 毕研婧, 林海平. 对法语熟语属性的探讨[J]. 法语学习, 2016(06): 25 – 31.

[16] 梁守锵. 新编法语搭配词典[M]. 北京: 商务印书馆, 2013.

[17]陆效用. 试论母语对二语习得的正面影响[J]. 外语界,2002(04):11-15.

[18]孙维张. 汉语熟语学[M]. 长春:吉林教育出版社,1989.

[19]张辉,季锋. 对熟语语义结构解释模式的探讨[J]. 外语与外语教学,2008(09):11-15.

[20]张辉. 熟语表征与加工的神经认知研究[M]. 上海:上海外语教育出版社,2017.